To Marie-Claude

Other books by M. Cabanac:

Démonstration expérimentale de l'existence dans l'hypothalamus d'une sensibilité au froid. Grenoble, Allier, 1961

Introduction aux contrôles et aux régulations en biologie (with M. Russek). Québec, Presses de l'Université Laval, 1982. Spanish transl., 1983, 1991.

Human Selective Brain Cooling, Austin, R. G. Landes Co. (Springer), 1995. Japanese transl. 1997.

La quête du plaisir, Montréal, Éditions Liber, 1995.

La cinquième influence, ou La dialectique du plaisir. Québec, Presses de l'université Laval, 2003. English transl. iUniverse, 2010.

Le bonheur et les morales des grandes religions. Un regard scientifique (with M.-C. Bonniot-Cabanac). Québec, Presses de l'université Laval, 2007.

Place du comportement dans la physiologie. Paris, Publibook, 2010.

The Fifth Influence
The Dialectics of Pleasure

Michel Cabanac

Translated by Peter Frost, from:
LA CINQUIÈME INFLUENCE, ou LA DIALECTIQUE DU PLAISIR
Presses de l'Université Laval, Québec, 2003

iUniverse books may be ordered through booksellers or by contacting:

iUniverse
1663 Liberty Drive
Bloomington, IN 47403
www.iuniverse.com
1-800-Authors (1-800-288-4677)

Because of the dynamic nature of the Internet, any Web addresses or links contained in this
book may have changed since publication and may no longer be valid. The views expressed
in this work are solely those of the author and do not necessarily reflect the views of the
publisher, and the publisher hereby disclaims any responsibility for them.

ISBN: 978-1-4401-8836-7 (sc)
ISBN: 978-1-4401-8837-4 (ebook)

Printed in the United States of America

iUniverse rev. date: 05/11/2010

Contents

FOREWORDS TO THE ENGLISH EDITION

It gives me great pleasure to write this foreword for my old friend Michel Cabanac. What do I mean by this? I mean that I derived pleasure from being invited to write the foreward, and I now derive pleasure from writing it. Suppose Michel were to attach me to his physiological apparatus and discover that, when I say I experience pleasure, my physiological reactions are quite different from those of other people in the same situation. If I say that I feel pleasure, it would be difficult for a physiologist to contradict me. If I say that I believe that I am having pleasurable sensations, then the physiologist could contradict me, by saying "what you are experiencing is usually called x." In the first case I am reporting on a subjective state, and in the second case I am making a propositional statement. In the first case I cannot be contradicted by rational argument. In the second case it would be possible for the physiologist to convince me that my belief about pleasure was incorrect. As you can imagine, there could now follow all sorts of philosophical arguments about the nature of pleasure. The beauty of Michel Cabanac's book is that he makes it perfectly clear where he stands. Philosophically he is a realist in the sense that he believes that pleasure is a mental state that really exists in the brain in a material sense. It is a state of affairs in the brain that is (in principle) physically (or physiologically) identifiable. Moreover, he believes that pleasure plays a causal role in our behaviour, because the pleasure/displeasure axis is the common currency of our proximal decision making, our decisions about what to do next. The reasons that Michel Cabanac gives for his views on pleasure are good reasons, because they are supported by arguments about evidence, and not simply opinions based upon introspection. Indeed, the main pleasure that I gained from this book came from reading about the very elegant experiments that Michel and his colleagues have conducted over the years.

In this respect, I find it hard to believe that other people's experience will be different from mine.

David McFarland, Oxford

7

I completely agree with David McFarland, author of the Foreword to the French edition of this book, that reading it is a sheer pleasure. The book is finally within reach of the small minority of booklovers who can read English, but not French. This is a profound scientific work, written with such clarity, that it can be easily appreciated by the interested lay person as well as the specialist. And what human being is not interested in the subject of pleasure?

After all, this is a book about a fellow *Homo hedonicus,* who indefatigably labors in the pursuit of happiness, so closely connected to pleasure. Since we are also *Homo sapiens,* we *hedonicus* sometimes strive to understand how the relentless "springs of action" push us around. Almost everything one wants to know about pleasure can be found in this book.

This book is written by a brilliant theoretician and experimenter after about fifty years of intensive work on the subjects of the physiology, psychology, and philosophy of pleasure. Cabanac skillfully merges his original ideas with cutting edge scientific information that he presents in the context of a broad historic perspective. This allows the book to be used effectively as a college textbook.

Hedonism is one of the most fundamental trends in the explanation of human behavior. According to Berlyne, Utilitarians made hedonism into the more or less standard theory of motivation through most of 19th century. Subsequently, it was abandoned and tabooed for much of the 20th century by the social sciences. During this period, Michel Cabanac was one of the few scientists dedicated to the subject of hedonism, who did not follow this trend. He had the courage to trust his own scientific instincts and pursue his interests. In my view, he meets the definition of a visionary.

Thank you for this wonderful book! Good luck with your future scientific endeavors, Michel!

Alexander Ovsich, Boston

Preface

Gnothi seauton
Socrates, 470-399 BC

This book describes how human behavior is determined. It subscribes to the utilitarianism of Bentham, Stuart Mill, and several others since Aristotle. The only difference from my predecessors—in my mind a key one—is that my utilitarian conclusions are not based on intuition, which in turn is based on philosophical introspection. They're based on replicable experimental studies whose evidence is "shareable."

This utilitarianism runs counter to three presumptions:

- The presumption of the Stoics and their successors, who, in striving for an ideal of human perfection, lose what is best in human nature. To seek virtue is also to seek pleasure. The most rewarding behaviors, the ones that provide the greatest joys, are altruistic behaviors. Reread the Bible: "It is more blessed to give than to receive." [1]

- The presumption of reductionist pseudo-scientists who claim to explain everything by neural circuits and who deny the notion of emergence. As Victor Johnston has pointed out, the properties of a car emerge from the totality of its parts, and these properties cannot be predicted from those of each part. Similarly, thought emerges from the brain, and thought can be neither predicted nor explained through our knowledge of cellular mechanisms.

- The presumption of those who say: "What you're doing is obvious." Nothing is harder to study than the obvious. This attitude is humorously summed up by the psychologists Cosmides and Tooby (1995) and likewise by the physicist F. Hoyle (1994). For them, scientists, like all of us, respond to new ideas in three stages.

For Cosmides and Tooby:
1. "It's not true."
2. "Well, it may be true, but it's not important."
3. "It's true and it's important, but it's not new. We knew it all along."

---

[1] Acts 20: 35

For Hoyle:
1. "The idea makes no sense."
2. "Someone thought it up before you did."
3. "We've always believed it."

This humor belies a serious problem. The new idea is often later taken up and accepted without the original paper ever being cited. As J-F. Revel notes sardonically:

> "When one wishes to guess today ... which preceding authors have most inspired a new book, one need only read through the bibliography: they are the ones whose names are not listed" (Revel 1997).

This behavior is often encountered—and condemned—in the scientific community. It can come about quite innocently for two reasons. First, the volume of scientific literature has expanded, with dramatic growth during the late 20th century. Second, scientific activity itself has become ever more specialized and compartmentalized. The first reason is increasingly suspect. Today, you can easily find relevant material at any university library through a number of online services. Just click a key word and the references will pop up on your screen. Any self-respecting researcher, myself included, can and should do a thorough review of the literature.

But the second reason still holds true. Indeed, it is a truism to say that the modern scientific world has become a Tower of Babel. Alexis Carrel concluded *Man, the Unknown* with the conviction that it was still possible in 1935 to produce a Renaissance man, like Jean Pic de la Mirandole, who could accumulate all the knowledge of his time (Carrel 1935). Those days are long gone. The sciences have fallen victim to their own success. Knowledge has become too abundant to be contained in one brain. As a result, everyone is specializing, a true liberal education has become a seldom if not impossible thing, and the barbarism of Michel Henry (1987) is making headway. People speak only with others of their own science, be it mathematics, physics, biology, or psychology. And each science has become a bundle of mutually ignorant or even mutually antagonistic disciplines. And each discipline has in turn branched out into subdisciplines with often hermetically sealed boundaries. Molecular biologists, for example, know nothing about behavior—the field of ethologists. This book is about behavior and one might think that behavior occupies just one discipline. Alas, there have emerged subdisciplines such as eco-ethology, whose proponents show no interest in speaking with classical ethologists, who likewise cold-shoulder their colleagues in animal psychology.

Like many before me, I've encountered this problem when addressing specialists from related fields: once you're labeled as coming from another discipline, you're left to cry in the wilderness and your proposals go unnoticed or are dismissed. I saw my friend, Ted Hammel, a physiologist by background, run into no end of trouble gaining acceptance for his experimental findings on the physics of aqueous fluids. I myself left physiology for psychology. This research path has taken me across several disciplinary boundaries: Bernardian physiology, cellular electrophysiology, study of behavior and objective psychology, 'mentalist' psychology, and now the psychological subdiscipline of decision-making mechanisms.[2] I've learned how hard it is to convince those who consider you an uninformed outsider, since they hold the seats of authority in the subdiscipline you've moved into. Nonetheless, a new field of inquiry provides a new perspective. And when you venture into new territory, you see things without the ingrained prejudices of those around you. This phenomenon is described by H.T. Kuhn (1970).

Paradoxically, it is by way of the informed layperson that scientists communicate across their disciplinary boundaries. Paralyzed as they are by the rigidities of established science, they address the layperson and, through him or her, reach scientists in related or distant fields. I'm therefore addressing myself not to specialists but to the "honest man or woman" of our time. After accumulating experimental findings on pleasure for about fifty years, I now have answers to some

---

[2] I described this itinerary in La Quête du Plaisir, Montre´al: Liber, 1995. La Quête du plaisir was a book about science, The Fifth Influence is a book of science that hopefully will familiarize its readers with my conclusions, which transcend the boundaries of the contemporary Babel of science.

problems that specialists no longer see.

By training, scientists lack candor except perhaps on political issues, where they very often display the great naïveté of great minds. They're trained to be rational: when one says something to scientists, when one presents new information in their field of expertise, they first ask: "How do you know? What is the evidence for such a proposal or such a conclusion?" In anticipation of such questioning, I've tried to meet scientific standards in preparing this book on the role of pleasure in biology and behavioral decision-making. I present arguments that any reader may verify. Only a few pages are intuitive. They are based on the preceding evidence, but depend more on I believe than on I know. These two statements are separated by a divide that I will clearly announce each time. The body of this work will build on the initial assertion of Chapter I with arguments that may be checked and shared.

A basic postulate of ethology—the science of behavior—is that behavior is always optimal. In other words, it tends to satisfy the most urgent need of the subject, usually an animal in the case of ethological studies (Tinbergen 1950; Baerends 1956). This postulate holds true for human behavior. Although ethologists and ecologists have proposed theories of behavior optimization, they avoid one detail: the immediate mechanism that serves to optimize behavior. In other words, they look into how behavior is optimized, but largely ignore the mechanism that drives the optimization. Yes, biologists have the law of natural selection to explain how a useful function is passed on to succeeding generations, i.e., by favoring the survival and reproduction of the preceding generation (Barrette 2000). Yes, psychologists have recognized that the mind is also a product of evolution and that psychological traits obey this same law of survive or perish (Bunge 1979; Cosmides et al. 1992; Johnston 1999). These mechanisms nonetheless act only over the long term by slowly altering one succeeding generation after another. How is behavior optimized over the short term? This short-term mechanism—how a decision is made—is what my book is all about.

Just a word on what it is and is not about. It is about a mental event: pleasure. Only the mind will be studied in the following chapters. I agree that thinking takes place in the brain. "The brain secretes thought just as the liver secretes bile." But I will largely pass over the anatomical basis of thought and focus more on experimental findings that shed light on how the mind works. Although the techniques in this area are relatively recent, the mass of information available is already huge. Classical neurophysiology has already provided interesting information on animal brains (see for example MacLeod 1992, Nicolaïdis 1992, or Berthoud 2002 for the pleasure of eating). Now we're beginning to access the human brain. A few years ago, the latest brain imaging techniques cost a fortune. Today they cost almost a pittance. It has become possible to experiment with techniques that were hitherto prohibitively expensive and reserved for clinical uses. Imaging devices have become standard equipment in many hospitals.

Brain imaging has shown that the left amygdala is highly involved in pleasure. It is activated when positive or negative verbal stimuli are presented (Hamann and Mao 2002), when amusing or sad films are shown (Aalto et al. 2002), and when food smells are described to hungry subjects (Morris and Dolan 2001). In addition to locating a pleasure center, these findings confirm, through the similarity of responses observed after pleasure and displeasure, that both experiences have a single behavior-motivating function and form a single entity. The same conclusion is supported by EEG recordings before, during, and after (Kotani et al. 2001). They show the strong activating power of pleasant and unpleasant stimuli (Bocker et al. 2001; Carretie et al. 2001). In particular, they show that the painful sensations during intense muscular effort correlate, not with the muscle signals that produce the sensation, but with the EEG (Nybo and Nielsen 2001). They also show specific activation of the frontal lobe or the anterior cingulate cortex in the mechanisms of almost instant decision-making that pleasure/displeasure makes possible before rationality can intervene (Gehring and Willoughby 2002). The same areas are activated when people remember painful emotions, a sign of involvement in hedonic cognition (Shin et al. 2001). Finally, when this type of research is extended to animal experimentation (Shizgal and Conover 1996; Berridge 2000; Peciña and Berridge 2000), which can explore areas off-limits to human experimentation, we see that a variety of rewards activate the same structures (Shizgal 1997). This bears out the findings of human experiments I will describe further on.

Nonetheless, I believe that a huge distance separates our understanding of the brain's anatomy/physiology from our understanding of its mental workings. It is too huge a distance for us to make serious conclusions—an attitude dubbed "functionalist" by Dubrovsky (2003). Of course, we can speculate. MacLean (1993) conjectured that the human brain evolved through three stages: reptile, paleo-mammal, and human. Papez (1937) mused that emotion originates in the convolutions of the brain's hemispheres and began with the evolution of mammals. These speculations have dominated scientific thought and still hold credence in the field. Yet they fail to explain why reptiles display objective signs of emotion, as I will show in Chap. X. Hence, I will speak here of mind/body relations, as Bunge has (Bunge 1980), rather than of the mind/brain relations of Churchland (1986).[3]

The objective study of consciousness is a vast enough field for investigation. Many research teams have now grasped the importance of pleasure and are striving to describe its underlying structures. These structures, however, give rise to conscious phenomena that are still poorly understood, despite a growing number of studies. This is where my interest lies, in what Bernard Baars has neatly called the global workspace (Baars 1983; Baars 1997).

On a final note, let me say that my conclusions have long been anticipated by philosophers through inward examination. Like Socrates, each of us has been familiarized with the contents of this book through personal experience. But to be intuitively familiar is not necessarily to know. The sole originality here is to bring such knowledge into the realm of science. For this, we should thank the experimental method, which turns I believe into I know.

---

[3] On this point, see an interesting discussion in: Dubrovsky B. A comment on three topics in volume 7 of the Treatise: teleology, the mind-body problem, and health and disease. Studies on Mario Bunge's Treatise. P. Weingartner and G. J. W. Dorn, Rodopi.

Last but not least, I wish to thank Marie-Claude and Colin. Through their attentive and patient criticism, they greatly improved the first version of this book.

Chapter I
Why the fifth influence?[4]

> For, finally, what is man in nature? A nothingness with regard to
> the infinite, an everything with regard to the nothingness,
> a middle between nothing and everything.
> Pascal, 1623-1662

> "Pleasure is the object, duty, and goal of all rational beings"
> Voltaire, 1694-1778

Blaise Pascal, a 17th-century mathematician and philosopher (Figure I.1), contemplated the world of his time and spoke of our insignificance before two abysses: the abyss of the infinitely small, the atom, and the abyss of the infinitely big, the universe (Figure I.2).

The next three centuries brought scientific discoveries that made us look ever more insignificant. Indeed, the two infinites grew by several orders of magnitude. Pascal's angst was nonetheless challenged in the mid-20th century by Pierre Teilhard de Chardin (Figure I.3), a paleontologist and philosopher who wished to reconcile biology with physics and astronomy.[5] For him, living things were a third dimension of matter whose increasing complexity culminated in Man— a third infinite as great as the other two. He measured this summit of complexity by counting the number of atoms in a single human body. His estimate: 10^{25} atoms. With 'atoms' replaced by 'centimeters', this was roughly the size of the universe and, inversely, the size of an atom (Teilhard de Chardin 1965) (Figure I.4).

However silly it might seem to compare numbers from different dimensions, Teilhard de Chardin was clearly on to something. Let us revisit his three infinites.

How small is the infinitely small? Elementary particles are defined by their energy rather than by their radius, but it is possible to calculate

---

[4] This chapter is largely based on a paper presented at the 43rd Annual Conference of the International Society for the Systems Sciences: M. Cabanac, R. Cabanac, and H.T. Hammel (1999).
[5] It is often thought that Teilhard's objective was to reconcile science with faith. Yet, in the cited reference, biology and physics are clearly his central theme.

their actual size. A hydrogen atom is about 1 Ångström in radius, a proton (a particle in an atom's nucleus) around 10^{-15} m, and an electron probably less than 10^{-18} m. The three quarks that make up a proton have the same radius as a proton. So in meters the smallest identified particles are on the order of 10^{-18} m.

Figure I.1 Blaise Pascal (1623-1662), physicist and philosopher

How big is the infinitely big? The observable universe stretches out to the farthest object whose light reaches us. It forms a sphere whose radius is the distance that light has traveled since the universe began. This distance is around 3,000 Mpc.[6] In meters—the International System unit that comes closest to the size of a human body—the observable universe has a radius of 10^{26} m. Further out, the expansion of the universe approaches the speed of light and objects become invisible.

---

[6] M = mega, pc = parsec. The parsec is an angular unit of distance. 1 pc (parallax second) is the distance from an object whose apparent motion at infinity is one second of arc over a three-month interval. 1 pc = 30,900 billion kilometers. The radius of the universe is around 3,000 Mpc.

The brain is the infinitely complex

Teilhard de Chardin seems to be in the right ballpark for his estimates of the two infinites.   But his calculation of complexity deserves a second look.

How complex, then, is the infinitely complex? Gell-Mann (1994) has stressed the difficulty of defining this question, let alone answering it.   At first glance, it may seem absurd to make a quantitative comparison between complexity and the dimensions of quarks and the universe. Complexity is non-dimensional. It cannot be compared to something else in terms of some unit, such as a measure of distance. Yet we do need some kind of yardstick, if only to get a rough idea of the astronomical complexity of living things.   Teilhard de Chardin chose the number of atoms in a human. This seems to be a poor choice, there being more atoms in a whale or a sequoia. Nothing indicates that these entities are more complex than we are.

The Pascalian angst

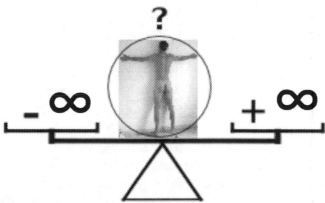

Figure I.2 Pascal's angst of Man balanced between the infinitely big and the infinitely small.

Clearly, the number of atoms is a poor index of complexity, and Teilhard de Chardin himself said as much.   Among other possible candidates, including the genetic code, nowadays the best index is probably the central nervous system—all the more so because our understanding of the brain has advanced considerably over the past half-century. The human central nervous system has nearly 10^{11} to 10^{12} neurons, all of which are organized into a single functional entity. Each neuron can communicate through its synapses with other neurons. Consequently, the number of synaptic connections is probably a better complexity index than simply the number of neurons. The number of synapses varies greatly from one neuron to the next: from 2 in the ultraspecialized bipolar cells of the retina to 150,000 in the Purkinje cells of the cerebellum. We can, however, roughly estimate the number of synapses in the human central nervous system (Kandel and Schwartz 1985). If each neuron conservatively has 10,000 synapses on average, the human brain should have a total of some 10^{15}-10^{16} synapses. This estimate is on the low side. The cerebral cortex alone is said to have 10^{14}-10^{15} synapses (Changeux 1983). The number is mind-boggling. If we assume the universe to be 10 to 20 billion years old, the number of synapses in the human brain would equal the number of minutes since the big bang.

There is yet more to the brain's complexity. Although synaptic transmission of an action potential is binary, the synapse can modulate this signal much more intricately than can the trivial Boolean algebra of our computers. Signal intensity is controlled by vesicles that release neu rotransmitters across the synapse in fixed amounts. The number of vesicles in a synaptic button varies but may be cautiously pegged at 10^2. Our complexity index has now reached 10^{17}, or about the number of seconds since the universe began. We could pursue this metaphor further by delving into the intricacies of the central nervous system. To produce a synaptic vesicle, countless atoms must be coordinated to create the chemical transmitters and the enzymes for making them. At least 10^9 atoms. The nervous system's complexity now stands at a minimum of 10^{26}, certainly an undercount because at each stage of the estimate I have chosen the most conservative assumption.

Keeping the above caveats in mind, we can retain Teilhard de Chardin's response to Pascal's angst if the complexity of the human body is replaced with the complexity of the human brain—now raised to the rank of nature's third infinite, the infinitely complex. A parallel idea is the so-called anthropic principle, which makes humans the center of the universe (Barrow and Tipler 1986; Breuer 1991; Bertola and Curi 1993). But the notion of the infinitely complex differs from the anthropic principle in that it makes us ask *how* agents are driven and not *why*. We can now ask what may be driving this infinitely complex agent, *i.e.*, each thinking brain as an independent anatomical/functional entity.

Before going further, we should recognize that the brain is the locus of the second emergence of evolution (Teilhard de Chardin 1955; Bunge 1979, 1980). I will often return to this concept of emergence. Emergence is said to exist when elements form a system and display new properties that cannot be explained by the individual properties of each element. For example, the H_2O molecule has new physical and chemical properties that are absent from oxygen and hydrogen atoms. Similarly, a car has properties that none of its parts have. Thus, life has emerged from matter, and thought from complex nervous systems (Spencer 1855). Perhaps other forms of mental complexity exist in the universe, but on earth the human brain is, as far as we know, the most advanced locus of thought. In this book, I will confine the infinitely complex to the thinking brain and look into its emergent properties: sensation and consciousness.

In the following chapters, pages of theoretical reflections will alternate with pages of experimental results that have led me to accept pleasure as the driving force behind human behavior. The reflections are based not on intuition and introspection, as with the moralists of the past, but on scientific arguments that can be shared and that will eventually reconcile the moralities of duty and pleasure.

For ethologists, a proximal explanation for behavior may seem unnecessary from the standpoint of phylogenesis and natural selection.

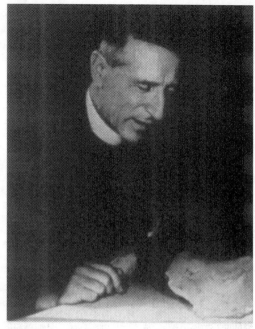

Pierre Teilhard de Chardin
1881-1955

Figure I.3 Pierre Teilhard de Chardin, paleontologist and philosopher.

It is enough to say with Charles Darwin (1809-1882) that natural selection favors the survival of the most effective solutions, arising by chance, to the problems facing the earth's different species in their environments (see Barrette 2000). Yet even from this standpoint an evolutionary explanation is needed. The emergence of thought, consciousness, and self-awareness can and should be examined evolutionarily (Darwin 1872; Lashley 1949; Bunge 1979; Cosmides *et al.* 1992; Johnston 1999; Barrette 2000). Yes, evolution may be understood phenomenologically without bringing consciousness into the picture. But consciousness exists. We should account for it and try to understand its role in nature. For cognitive psychology, in its most hard-line version, consciousness is but an epiphenomenon that may be dispensed with, since robots can reproduce the finest and subtlest of human behaviors and make decisions as complex as those of a chess game, in which they can take on the greatest chess-masters. Robots, however, make decisions that their creators and programmers define. So the problem remains.

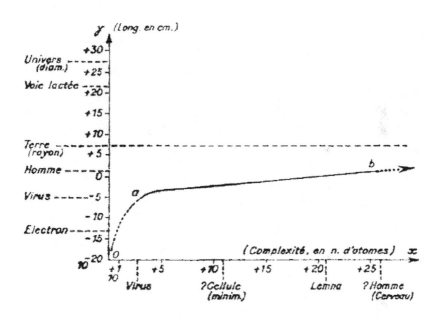

Figure I.4Teilhard de Chardin's complexity curve. Y-axis: lengths of objects/entities measured in centimeters (Homme: human, Terre; earth, Voie lactée: Milky Way). X-axis: complexity as estimated in number of atoms (Cellule: Cell, Homme: Human(brain)). After Teilhard de Chardin, 1965.

A motivation is a modulating and coordinating influence on a behavior's direction, strength, and content (Shizgal 1999). The following chapters will argue that all motivation is a search for pleasure. Not only do humans and higher animals seek pleasure, but they do so continually, in particular by choosing which of several motivations is to be satisfied first. This search optimizes their physiologically oriented behaviors and their mental functioning. For now, I will content myself with this assertion, which will be justified

23

further on.

From this tentative assertion, it follows that pleasure/joy is the motor that drives the human mind. It has the properties of a driving force that pushes humans and higher animals into action. For those animals that acquired it, there was a clear evolutionary advantage: the central nervous system no longer had to store huge amounts of information on the potential benefits of different features of the environment and the appropriate responses to them. Instead of operating in the stimulus/reflex/response mode and storing the reflexes, the nervous system could operate by maximizing pleasure. Pleasure gave flexibility to the behavioral repertoire of any animals that could feel it and pass it on to their descendants. Hedonic decision-making also spared the brain the trouble of having to store an infinite number of automatisms—a clear advantage in terms of economy of information and flexibility of behavioral response. Through an easier and more flexible ranking of priorities, this decision-making process could outperform the prehedonic or reflex process (in living or inanimate agents). It was now possible to make decisions by maximizing pleasure, without weighing the pros and cons. Indeed, this might be the key difference between a conscious agent and a Turing machine. We may have here a means to meet Penrose's conditions for taking the study of consciousness out of the tight framework of artificial robotic intelligence (Penrose 1994).

The four forces

Physicists call a Newtonian force any *influence* that acts on a body and alters it (or tends to alter it). For example, a force applied to a resting body will change that body's total energy, either kinetically (it will change speed) or internally (it will deform or heat up). To date, physicists have found four forces in different contexts: gravity; electromagnetism; strong nuclear; and weak nuclear (Table I). Gravity is the weakest force. Its influence is exerted mainly over cosmic distances and in the presence of large masses. Its range is infinite and all particles with non-zero mass feel its pull.

Electromagnetism is much stronger. It too has an infinite range but acts only on charged particles. It acts on smaller, hot, and dense areas in stars, around planets, in galaxies, and in high-temperature gas clouds in groups of galaxies. On a larger scale, the universe is believed to be electromagnetically neutral.

The strong and weak nuclear forces operate at atomic and subatomic levels, with ranges confined to microscopic distances. They cause radioactivity and nuclear reactions in the cores of stars. The strong force binds quarks together through an exchange of gluons. It behaves strangely. Unlike the other forces, its intensity increases as quarks move further apart.

All of the forces share the property of acting on specific bodies and particles.

Proposal: the fifth influence

- After recognizing that complexity is a characteristic of the universe and that the brain is the locus of the highest organized complexity ever known;
- After accepting that the hedonic dimension of conscious thought necessarily motivates behavior; and
- After reviewing what a force is;
I can now conclude with a proposal:

The hedonic axis of consciousness, *i.e.*, pleasure-joy/displeasure-distress, acts on conscious brains much as the forces of physics influence masses and particles, *i.e.*, it drives them and influences their behavior. Since pleasure can drive the infinitely complex and since no thinking brain can escape the tendency to maximize its pleasure/joy, the hedonic force deserves to be classified as the fifth force of the universe.[7] Because a mental phenomenon has

---

[7] Physicists have advanced the hypothesis that matter was under the influence of a single force when the universe began. As the density of energy decreased over time, the single force divided, through a break in symmetry, into gravitation and the grand unified force (GUF). Next the GUF divided into strong and electroweak, which in turn divided into electromagnetic and weak. It might be interesting to suppose that

no dimensions, it would be more appropriate to call the hedonicity of consciousness the fifth *influence* rather than the fifth *force*.

This proposal is an axiom and, as such, needs no demonstration. Nonetheless, as we shall see in the following chapters, it is supported by experiments that were originally designed to refute it. It therefore meets the criterion of refutability, one of the measures of scientific validity (Popper 1972). Two subsequent chapters will discuss when consciousness and the fifth influence emerged in evolution—probably in the higher vertebrates. At that evolutionary stage, the beginnings of consciousness were guiding the behaviors of our ancient reptilian ancestors.

TABLE I

The four forces recognized by physicists in the universe and the fifth influence

Influence	Subject	Range	Model
Gravitational	Cosmos	Infinite	Planetary systems
Electromagnetic	Charged particles	Infinite	Earth magnetosphere
Weak nuclear	Subatomic	Atom	β radiation and neutrinos
Strong nuclear	Subatomic	Atom	Nuclear reactions
Fifth influence: pleasure/joy	Brain	Infinite (behavior)	Human

With humans and the development of consciousness, the fifth influence has led individuals to discover that rewarding behaviors are not only those that serve immediate biological ends, but also those that serve

---

the emergence of the fifth influence from matter could be the last break in the symmetry of forces. Thus, in the era of living things, pleasure would have finally emerged from complexity as a final symmetry break that arose once the brain had reached a critical level of complexity.

broader social purposes. The fifth influence may now be leading people to ever greater complexity through ever more numerous and closer ties among individuals, the eventual outcome being a network that Teilhard de Chardin has dubbed the noosphere (Teilhard de Chardin 1955).

In the following chapters, I will endeavor to prove the above arguments and develop their implications. I will begin by looking at sensation—the way we receive all of the information we have on our environment.

Chapter II
Sensation

A hypothesis about mental structure cannot be proved merely by
producing an adaptive scenario in which that mental structure
would be advantageous. An empirical demonstration that the
mind is actually structured in that way is also required
Griffiths, 1997

Each of us is surrounded by an immediate environment from which we
take energy and matter and to which we give back an equal amount of
energy and matter. This inflow and outflow is indispensable to life.
Whether we are looking at the whole organism or at organic molecules,
our life processes cannot be understood without understanding this
ongoing exchange between the environment and ourselves.

For physiologists, the exchange is controlled by self-regulating
mechanisms that act independently of volition. For example, breathing
is a two-way flow of O_2 going into the body and CO_2 going out
regardless of what we think or, more to the point, what we want.
Classical physiology stopped there, with no place for behavior. Yet
behavior is actively involved. Breathing supports our voice, a key
channel for social communication. It also determines the intensity of
the muscular effort available for behavior. Although autonomic control
almost exclusively runs the heart and lung system for gas exchange
between the environment and body tissues, our behavior will be only as
intense as our ability to breathe enough oxygen for the muscular effort.
Finally, breathing can be briefly stopped at will, as when we swim
under water.

These relationships between breathing and behavior are ignored by
physiologists, yet they exist.

Aside from breathing, most exchanges between our bodies and the
environment are behaviorally controlled. We decide to eat, to drink, to
defecate, or to urinate. Of course, heat exchange is an exception:
autonomic responses maintain a stable body temperature by continually
excreting the heat we produce through chemical reactions in our

tissues. We do not sweat at will, nor do we consciously constrict or dilate the blood vessels in our skin. Yet, even here, over the long term, behavior plays a major role. We protect ourselves from the cold with clothes, thereby creating a warm, moist, and virtually tropical microclimate next to our bodies (Scholander *et al.* 1957). It is not surprising, then, that behavior has especially intrigued those physiologists who study the balance of exchanges between an organism and its environment.

How does an organism become aware of its physiological needs? Indeed, it must be aware to satisfy them consciously. For a few moments—the time to make a decision and then act—physiology and consciousness interact to produce behavior. This frontier between physiology and psychology has drawn researchers who wish to understand how behavior meets physiological needs.

For psychologists, it is enough to fall back on the concept of motivation and say that motivations adapt behavior to physiological needs. We meet these needs because we are motivated to do so—through hunger, thirst, drowsiness, heat stress, and cold stress. Such motivations are the focus of psychological research, this being a quite legitimate approach to the study of the mental objects.

For biologists, the mind tends to be considered off-limits by their research community, often implicitly. Yet they are better able than psychologists to analyze physiological motivations because they have more relevant information at their disposal.

What, then, is the first condition for adapting a behavior to a need? Information. Organisms must be attuned to the physical and chemical characteristics of their external environment. Can this environment meet their needs for energy and matter? Can it receive the surplus energy and matter they must get rid of? This condition holds true not only for behavior but also for autonomic responses. To control the inflows and outflows of energy and matter between the external environment and itself, an organism must gather information. If the organism is conscious, the information gathering is called sensation or perception.

What is a sensation?

Sensation has always interested philosophers. Plato held that sensation and opinion are two screens that mask truth (Plato, 427-347 BC), but others before and after him thought differently. Heracleitus (Jeannière 1959) taught that knowledge comes to humans "through the door of the senses" and Protagoras (Croiset and Bodin 1955) that all psychic life consists only of sensations. Plato's own pupil, Aristotle (Aristotle a), took up the Sophist view that sensation is the "door to the soul."

This view has persisted down through the centuries to the present. Thomas Hobbes (1651) wrote: "There is no conception in man's mind which hath not at first, totally or in parts, been begotten upon the organs of senses." Étienne Bonnot de Condillac argued that if a statue were progressively given the five senses it would acquire every aspect of the human mind (Condillac 1754). For him, the mind uses the senses to know and understand the world. The senses are thus necessary and sufficient for development of the mind. This notion was also accepted by Immanuel Kant for whom, nonetheless, the senses are but one of the two sources of knowledge, the other being understanding (Kant 1788). According to Edward Bradford Titchener "[s]ensationalism is the theory that all knowledge originates in sensations; that all cognitions even reflective ideas and ... intuition can be traced back to elementary sensations " (Titchener 1909). Likewise, Kenneth Wartinbee Spence argued that "[a]ll science, whatever the realm of application, has a common origin: the immediate experience of the observing person of the scientist himself" (Spence 1948).

After this immediate experience, the next step is to share evidence with one or more other people. This sharing of evidence is likewise channeled through sensation—all the more reason for studying this door of the senses. Indeed, the study of sensations, called psychophysics, is what eventually led to experimental psychology (Geldard 1972). Physicists were the first to put psychology on a scientific basis—Gustav Theodor Fechner (1801-1887), Herman von Helmoltz (1821-1894), and Wilhelm Wundt (1832-1920).

"The concept of the senses as portals of the mind has therefore turned into a commonplace statement among modern psychologists"

(Marks 1974). Nonetheless, there still persists today the Platonic view that sensation is a screen masking the truth. This view today draws support from two problems: the difference between sensation and perception; and the complexity of attributes. Ultimately, the problem is a semantic flaw.

Sensation and perception

Psychologists began to distinguish sensation from perception in the 18th century. Thomas Reid believed that a sensation occurs when a sensory organ is stimulated and that a perception includes not only a sensation but also a conception of the perceived object, as well as an irresistible conviction that the object exists (Reid 1785). Both definitions are still widely accepted. Levine and Shefner clearly define sensation as "the process of detecting a stimulus (or some aspect of it) in the environment," and perception as "the way in which we interpret the information gathered (and processed) by the senses." "In a word, we sense the presence of a stimulus, but we perceive what it is" (Levine and Shefner 1981).

Schiffman considered the distinction between sensation and perception to be somewhat obsolete. He brought a new perspective, equating sensation with physiology and perception with psychology (Schiffman 1982). This may explain why two attitudes have developed in recent times.

The first attitude maintains that a stimulus associated with a context acquires a meaning (Titchener 1909). What makes conscious perception more complex is that a behavioral response well adapted to a stimulus also carries a meaning that may alter the perception (Tolman 1918). This tendency is pushed to an extreme with Gestalt Theory, which by definition considers perception to be a whole in which a sensation and its meaning form a single mental experience (Kofka 1935). While not necessarily holding such a radical view, many psychologists think that the distinction between sensory discrimination and perceptual discrimination is more theoretical than real because the two cannot be dissociated (Pradines 1928-1934; Corso 1967). Thus, pure sensation does not exist. It is always embedded in a complex perception (Merleau-Ponty 1945). Such an attitude, I believe, may reflect the stimuli used. These studies of perception almost exclusively used auditory and visual stimuli (Banks 1991). The eye and the ear, however, are channels for social communication and thus particularly prone to sending contextual messages to the mind. Other sensory inputs, such as tactile stimuli, are less complex and likelier to be described as sensations.

The second attitude accepts the theoretical separation between sensation and perception. Aldous Huxley, experimenting on himself with mescaline, reported that the drug altered his perception but that his sensations remained intact (Huxley 1954).

It is likely that the psychologists who have no problem with equating sensation and perception, like Geldard (1972), Marks (1974), and Levine and Shefner (1981), feel this way because the stimuli they used—light, sound, temperature, skin pressure, or chemicals—are only slightly context-related, or not at all. In my opinion, this equivalence weakens the definition of sensation, just as it weakens that of perception. Sensation should be seen as an entity in itself, simpler than perception and thus different. I will return to this point after discussing the problem of the attributes of sensation.

The attributes of sensation

"A great deal of confusion would be avoided if psychologists at large recognized the fact that the sensation of experimental psychology is a simple, meaningless (or rather non-meaningful) process definable only by an enumeration of its attributes" (Titchener 1909).

"An attribute of sensation, ..., is any aspect or moment or dimension of sensation which fulfills the two conditions of inseparability and independent variability" (Titchener 1908).

From this definition it follows that attributes are always present when a sensation is received and that when the attributes disappear so will the sensation. This definition will become clearer once the attributes are spelled out. Sensation, however, will become less clearly defined.

33

Wilhelm Wundt described sensation as having two attributes, *quality* and *intensity* (Wundt 1902). He added *affectivity* in 1893 in the fourth edition of his treatise on psychophysiology, but withdrew it in the following editions and returned to two attributes. Oswald Külpe added two other attributes, *duration* for the five senses and *extension* for vision and touch (Külpe 1893). Titchener added *clearness* to the list of attributes (Titchener 1908). *Pleasure* and *pain*, initially considered to be sensations (Mill 1869), were later added (Ziehen 1924). For Külpe, pleasure-displeasure is not an attribute because it can have its own attributes (quality, intensity, duration), and especially because a sensation may exist while being neither pleasant nor unpleasant— contrary to the definition of attributes. For Yokoyama, affective content is phenomenologically distinct from usually accepted sensory qualities (Yokoyama 1921). Finally, for Beebe-Center, affectivity is a possible though not required attribute of sensation (Beebe-Center 1932).

Some senses have their own attributes. Vision has light and color, and hearing has pitch and volume, as proposed by Titchener (1908). The list of attributes tends to divide and subdivide more or less indefinitely since attributes can have their own attributes. For example, color has three attributes of its own: hue, brightness, and saturation. Complexity, however, is not the main drawback of this theory of attributes. Edwin Boring listed four (Boring 1942):

1) It is not clear that vision has the attribute of intensity.
2) It is not possible to find an independent variability between visual brightness and visual intensity.
3) Some sensations are too complex to fit within the rigid framework of attributes.
4) It remains unclear whether the attributes are truly inseparable.

TABLE II.1
The five senses of Aristotle

ORGAN	Eye	Ear	Nose	Tongue	Skin
SENSE	Vision	Hearing	Smell	Taste	Touch

Today, psychophysicists are less interested in the attributes of sensation. They have developed a multidimensional scaling method called "cross-modality matching" whereby a single arbitrary unit can measure several, or even all, attributes at once (Ennis and Mullen 1986). This approach tends to duck rather than confront the problem of attribute complexity. In one version, a subject is asked whether two stimuli are similar, an easy task even when the reference stimulus does not evoke the same type of sensation as does the other stimulus. A subject may, for example, be asked to pull a lever with a force equal to the intensity of the sounds presented. As Marks puts it, "multidimensional scaling is concerned with *psychological* relations, the relations of various sensory (psychological) attributes or dimensions to each other" (Marks and Gonzalez 1977).

In conclusion, this field of study now faces two obstacles: a fuzzy distinction between sensation and perception; and an interminable and heterogeneous list of attributes, on the other. We need to redefine our terminology. We need to clarify and simplify.

A simpler descriptive model of sensation

Instead of describing sensation as having attributes, it seems simpler to me, basing myself as much on objectivity and simplicity as on introspective evidence, to describe sensation more mathematically as a 4-dimensional space (Equation II.1 and Figure II.1).

$$\psi = f(x.y[t], z[t]) \quad \text{Equation II.1}$$

These four dimensions of sensation (ψ) are quality (x), intensity (y), hedonicity (z), and duration (t).

Quality is a nominative, scalar, or discrete dimension whose elements may be categorized, e.g., a sweet taste, a lavender smell, or a mechanical stimulus. The nature of the stimulus is thus described. Intensity, hedonicity, and duration are parametric, quantitative dimensions. The intensity of a sensation may vary: stronger or weaker stimuli, higher or lower chemical concentrations, lighter or stronger mechanical pressures, and so on. The hedonicity of a sensation may be pleasant, unpleasant, or indifferent. Duncker listed four types of

35

pleasure, with the first one being sensory pleasure (Duncker 1940-1941). The need to distinguish the affective from the discriminative has been proposed by LeMagnen (1956) for food sensations, by Melzack and Casey (1968) for painful sensations, and by Young (1959) and Pfaffman (1960) for sensations in general. In the case of pain, this distinction may seem unnecessary at first glance, but its potential has proven to be heuristically rich (Rainville *et al.* 1997, 1999, 2000, see Chapter III).

There is thus broad acceptance among psychologists for sensory pleasure as a third dimension of sensation. This dimension measures the utility of a stimulus. What for now is only a postulate will be amply demonstrated further on. It is, in fact, the key argument of this book.

Only the hedonic dimension may be either positive or negative. Pleasure is maximized through positive search behaviors and displeasure is minimized through negative avoidance behaviors. This dimension is also the only one that can have a zero value. If the x, y, or t dimensions are zero, there is no sensation. If the z dimension is zero, there still is sensation. It is simply one of indifference and does not guide behavior.

The qualitative dimension of sensation

It is neither obvious nor simple to explore the X-axis of Figure II.1 and to list the sensations. For Aristotle, animals and humans have five senses (Table II.1) (Aristotle b). This 5-sense model has lasted over two millennia with hardly any challenge. Eighteenth-century philosophers and nineteenth-century psychologists did not add to this short list and modern psychological and physiological treatises on sensation almost exclusively study the five senses. Yet sensation is in no way limited to five senses. On this point, two schools of thought have appeared in recent times.

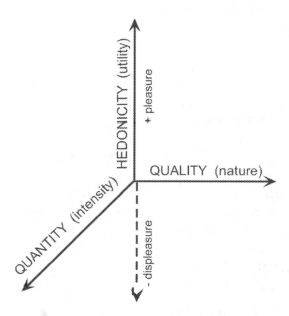

Figure II.1Theoretical model of sensation in response to a stimulus. Sensation is represented as a 4-dimensional mental object, each dimension being analogical to a dimension of the stimulus. The coordinate axes show only the three main dimensions: quality, quantity, and hedonicity. Quality describes the nature of the stimulus and is a non-parametric variable. Quantity describes the intensity of the stimulus. Hedonicity describes the utility of the stimulus and may be positive (pleasure), negative (displeasure), or zero (indifference). The third dimension's existence is for now simply assumed but will be substantiated in the following pages. Pleasure may be altered by one's past experiences or internal physiological state. The fourth dimension, duration, is not represented here (after Cabanac 1979).

The first school may be called physiological. The focus is on the sensory organs—the tongue, the skin, the inner ear, etc.—rather than on sensation as such. Lévy-Valensi, for example, followed this school in a physiological treatise (Lévy-Valensi 1933) and many psychologists have adopted the same view (Geldard 1972). After describing the sensory organs, physiologists more or less deliberately tend to consider them the source of sensation. Because cognition and consciousness lie outside their field, physiologists do not bother to distinguish afferent path from sensation when identifying and studying the structure and function of the many afferent nerves. The sensation list of Table II.2 is the one most commonly found in physiological treatises (e.g., Wolfe 1988b) and tends to lengthen the list of the five senses.

The other school of thought may be called psychological because of its introspective approach. The perceptual aspect of sensation is examined with less interest in sensory organs. Thus, no reference to specific organs is required to describe pain, which may occur on any part of the body, except for a small number of sites like the skin of the center of the cheek and the olecranon, or the nerve tissue of the brain itself.[8] Adherents to this school have lengthened the list of the five senses with several new additions:

-perception of time (Boring 1942; Schiffman 1982)
-sense of orientation (Schiffman 1982)
-kinesthesia (Corso 1967; Geldard 1972; Ludel 1978; Schiffman 1982)
-perception of space (Wolfe 1988a)
-organic sensations (visceral, hunger, thirst) (Geldard 1972).

TABLE II.2
Beyond the five senses

Sensation	Sensory organ
Vision	Retina, eye
Hearing	Cochlea, inner ear
Taste	Taste buds, tongue
Smell	Olfactory neurons, C fibers, nasal membrane
Heat	Free nerve endings, dermis
Touch	Nerve endings on hair bulbs, Paccini, Meissner, and Krause corpuscles, dermis
Space	Labyrinth, inner ear; muscle spindles, muscles, Golgi corpuscles, tendons
Pain	Free nerve endings of C fibers, everywhere

After Wolfe (1988

---

[8] As Dr. Lecter has shown (Harris 2000), p. 481.

All of these additions are vague and imprecise. They seem to be forms of perception, as defined above, rather than forms of sensation strictly speaking.

The two schools can be reconciled by combining the physiological approach with introspection, as recommended by Titchener (1909) and Straus (1963). But such an approach first requires a discussion of semantics. How does sensitivity differ from sensation?

Animals have sensors, *i.e.*, nerve cells that specialize in qualitative and quantitative analysis of their immediate environment. The cells send this information, coded in batches of impulses, to higher nerve centers. In the following pages, *sensitivity* will mean an afferent neuron's capacity to detect physical or chemical changes to the immediate environment around its endings and then to transmit this information to nerve centers. The anatomical and histological structure of the sensors is sometimes not fully known. The sensitive portion of the neuron, the sensor, may be a specific histological organ or a free ending. Some peripheral sensors are still unidentified, such as temperature sensors.[9] The afferent path may be a single neuron but most often it is a chain of neurons.

A precise definition

The brain has properties that cannot be explained by the properties of its neurons, no more than life can be explained by the atomic or molecular properties of a living cell's components (Bunge 1989). Sensation should not be defined in terms of physics or chemistry, or even nerve impulses. It is a form of cognition. It is a mental object. Consciousness is an emergence[10] and sensation may be defined as the emergence of sensitivity in consciousness (Figure II.2).

This definition forbids applying the terms sensation and sensory where no nervous system is present, as some have tried to do with bacteria (Miller *et al.* 1989), the immunological system (Deschaux 1988), or the perception of time—for which no nervous substrate has

---

[9] We are only just starting to grasp how they operate: D.D. McKemy, W.M. Neuhausser, and D. Julius (2002).

[10] See Chapter 9.

been described. Such a definition is consistent with leading English or French dictionaries, which define sensation as a mental process aroused by the stimulation of a sensory organ. The definition does not, however, specifically imply the existence of sensors.

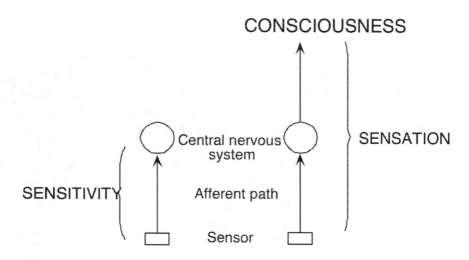

Figure II.2   Diagram of nerve sensitivity (left: a sensor, an afferent path, and a nerve center) and sensation (right). The latter is an emergent property of the nervous system. It occurs when information enters consciousness via nerve sensitivity. Sensitivity then becomes sensation.

The above definition has an important consequence: sensation is no longer limited to the five senses or even to the lengthened list of Table II.2. The next step is to locate the sensory organs. Indeed, the paths of sensation take us beyond the five senses

Pain may come from any point of our anatomy but is not the only sensation from inside our bodies. Stimulation of muscle and tendon receptors arouses sensation (Roland 1975; Gandevia and McCloskey 1977; Rossetti *et al.* 1994). Warming the esophagus produces a sensation (Maule *et al.* 1975). Mere introspection—if I ignore the outside world and focus on my own body—gives me fairly vague information from my members, my chest, my neck, and my head. I can sense obscure messages from my internal organs: heartbeats, abdominal movements and, of course, hunger pangs, colic, or a swollen bladder. Figure II.3 illustrates that point. This example also shows that the qualitative, intensive, and hedonic dimensions may vary independently of each other.

We can therefore propose a new hypothesis: any sensitivity, or afferent nerve discovered by physiologists, is a potential source of sensation. This hypothesis requires four comments:

1) The sensory window so defined is open to the outside world, but it is limited. A bit broader than the five senses, it is still fairly narrow, as seen in the short list of Table II.2. We would undoubtedly benefit from being able to detect and know other variables of our human-altered environment: speed rather than just acceleration (included in the space sensation of Wolfe, Table II.2); ionizing radiation; food ingredients; air pollution levels; and current date and time. Yet, however limited, this sensitivity and sensation window has enabled land vertebrates to survive and our own species to succeed. Of course, this ancient window has now become a hindrance to our understanding of the universe.

2) Besides information from the external environment, our brains are amply informed on the physiological state of the internal environment within our bodies. Table II.3 lists the currently known sensors for our internal physical and chemical status. In most cases, the afferent nerve is just a small bundle containing a few neurons, often C fibers. The contrast is striking between these tiny trickles of information and the large rivers of the five senses. This may be why the "big five" have always dominated psychology. The vagus nerve carries chemical, mechanical, thermal, and pain information for all internal organs of the thorax and abdomen, yet it contains no more than 40,000 afferent fibers. In contrast, the sense of smell uses over 100,000,000 fibers, the optic nerve has 1,200,000 fibers, and a single cochlea receives 30,000 myelinized afferent fibers. The difference is even greater if we take the increased myelinization of the "big five" into account: myelinized fibers conduct larger, faster, and more frequent impulses, whereas C fibers conduct smaller, slower, and less frequent ones. It is hardly surprising, then, that the internal

41

organs provide only episodic and imprecise sensations when compared with the five senses. Nor is it surprising that so little has been known about their sensory function for so long.

3)   The quality of a sensation depends on anatomy and also on the frequency profile of impulses in an afferent nerve. In addition, there is an initial stage of information processing in certain receptors, the retina in particular. The signal that reaches the brain is not necessarily the one that might be expected. The retina records contrasts rather than actual intensities (Wehrhahn 2000). This is also true for the intensity of any sensation, as we will see further on.

4)   A sensation seems to need a semantic basis. If there are no words to describe the sensation, it tends to go unnoticed (Faurion 1993). For example, it has been proposed that the short list of flavors—sweet, salty, bitter, and sour—be lengthened by adding a fifth flavor, *umami* (Ikeda 1909). This Japanese word describes a mixed glutamate/amino acid flavor that is unknown outside Japan, apparently because no word is available.

According to this new definition, sensation clearly differs from perception (Figure II.2 and Figure II.4). Perception is based on sensation but is also supplemented by multiple and simultaneous inputs from the senses and, above all, by input from memory. It is this memory input that gives visual and auditory sensations their sociocultural content. For the same reason, visual and auditory inputs usually evoke perceptions rather than actual sensations.

The intensive dimension of sensation

By defining sensation as the emergence of sensitivity in consciousness, we not only gain a simpler approach but also one that we can use to analyze the link between sensation and stimulus. This link follows a 2-stage physiological path: from stimulus to impulses; and from impulses to sensation. When a stimulus triggers a sensor and produces impulses, the intensity of the resulting sensation will depend on the frequency of these impulses as they travel to the brain (Adrian 1928). In turn, the total number of impulses reaching the brain will depend on the specific frequency of each excited fiber and the number of these afferent fibers.

Most sensors have a firing rate (F) that "adapts" quickly, as physiologists say. The firing rate is time(t)-dependent:

$$F=\delta stimulus/\delta t \qquad Equation\ II.2$$

In other words, such sensors respond mainly to changes in the stimulus. If the stimulus remains constant, the transmitted message will tend to lose strength. The receptor "adapts." Adaptation may be fast, as with olfactory sensors, or slow, as with temperature sensors. This sensor property is transferred to the sensations. Thus, the sense of smell is fast adapting because olfactory sensors detect changes in a smell rather than absolute values. This property amplifies perception of directional gradients and facilitates the appearance of anticipatory regulatory responses.

The above physiological definition of intensity may help resolve certain problems encountered with sensory modalities where the borderline between quality and intensity is hard to define on psychological grounds, e.g., the controversy over the intensity of white, gray, and black (Boring 1942). Some ambiguities have persisted because of inadequate terminology. The best known example is that of the Greek root *thermos*, which means both heat and temperature. But there are many others. According to Cicero, the ancient Greeks used a single word for pain and fatigue (Cicero, 106-43 BC). Newton (1721) equated brilliance with intensity, a source of confusion that Helmoltz (1866) later sorted out.

With regards to the sense of vision, the signal actually captured by the retina seems to be contrast, as pointed out above (Wehrhahn 2000). If we turn a TV set off, the screen looks gray. If we turn it on, some portions of the screen look black. Yet the screen produces no black tones.

We know that sensation intensity depends on the frequency of the transmitted impulses. How this relationship works is still largely a matter of theory. Not enough observations have been accumulated to bridge the gap between a stimulus and the intensity of the resulting sensations. In fact, advances in knowledge have tended to make on sensation intensity harder to understand. Modern physiology has

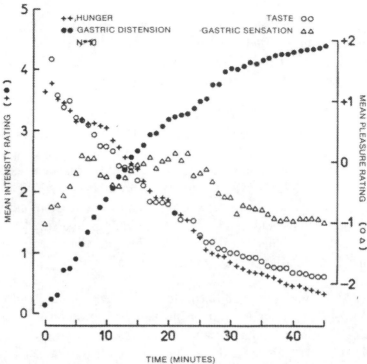

Figure II.3   Example of sensations not on the classic 5-sense list. Alongside taste, one of the five senses, subjects perceived stomach sensations that are not one of the five.   These sensations nonetheless have the four dimensions of figures II.1 and II.5. The above chart shows changes in mean response at a noonday meal where the ten subjects ingested samples of sweetened water (10 g of sucrose in 50 ml).   Each minute, the ten subjects would ingest a sample and give four oral ratings: intensity of hunger (+); sensation of stomach distention (●); pleasure or displeasure of taste sensation (○); and pleasure or displeasure of stomach sensation (Δ).   They had no trouble rating the intensity and hedonicity of their internal stomach sensations. Results: their sensation of taste shifted from pleasant to unpleasant (negative allesthesia) with each ingestion.   Their stomach sensations increased progressively in intensity from 0 to 4.5, with the corresponding hedonicity showing a bell curve (-1, +0,2, -1).   Conclusion: stomach sensation exists independently of the sense of taste and displays

alliesthesia, as does taste itself (E.F. Rabe and M. Cabanac unpublished).

TABLE II.3

List of afferent nerves that monitor an organism's interior

Sensor	Location	Information
Mechanoreceptors	Major arteries: carotid, aorta	Blood pressure
	Heart	Blood volume
	Lungs	Lung pressure/ volume
	Veins	Venous blood volume
	Digestive tract	Digestive tract repletion
	Muscles	Muscle length
	Tendons and joints	Tension
Chemoreceptors	Major arteries: carotid, aorta	Blood PaO_2
	Digestive tract	Digestive tract contents
	Medulla oblongata	Blood pH, PaO_2
	Hypothalamus	Circulating hormones
	Liver	Glucose of portal vein
Thermoreceptors	Hypothalamus	Local temperature
	Spinal cord	Local temperature
	Digestive tract	Local temperature
Osmoreceptors	Hypothalamus	Osmotic pressure
	Liver	Osmotic pressure of portal vein

discovered that feedback loops exist within the central nervous system and that afferent fibers innervate certain sensors. These circuits may and probably do filter the intensity of the transmitted message according to the relative urgency of other mental activities. This being said, sensation intensity is a function of stimulus intensity.

Psychophysics, a word coined by Fechner (1860), is the quantitative measure of relations between stimulus and sensation. Fechner gave the latter word its current meaning while measuring the intensity of "sensory sensations"[11] in relation to stimulus intensity.

---

[11] *Sinnliche Empfindungen.*

Psychophysics is uninterested in the neural basis of sensation. It examines only the relations between a stimulus and its mental object, typically with a view to quantifying stimulus/sensation relations, sensation thresholds, and sensation intensity. To learn more about this field, which cannot be adequately covered here, the reader may consult the following specialized textbooks and reviews: for smell, see Cain (1988); for taste, Bartoshuk (1988); for hearing, Green (1988).

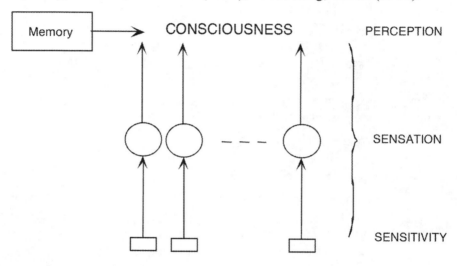

Figure II.4   Consciousness is not just sensation. Beyond sensation, there is perception: sensory input is combined with information from other sensory sources and is continually compared with information stored in memory.

Duration of sensation

The fourth dimension of sensation is duration, which describes how long a stimulus is present. The notion that a sensation has duration should pose no problem other than that of the reality of time itself. The duration of a sensation may sometimes exceed the duration that a stimulus is present, if the stimulus is so intense that some excitation persists once stimulation has ceased. In Figure II.5 below, duration is added to the other three dimensions.

Information and behavior

An organism thus monitors its external and internal environments through inputs that feed into its central nervous system. How, then, does it assess its internal needs in relation to the utility of an external stimulus that may meet such needs?

Suppose an organism has to correct a physiological imbalance by resorting to resources from its environment. The only useful behavior will be one that moves the organism from an unfavorable state to a favorable one. For this to happen, the required resource must first exhibit a gradient in the external environment. Otherwise, there will be nowhere better to move to. The organism would have to create a gradient, either by gathering resources over a wide territory for storage at one location or by creating a microenvironment. Both types of response have arisen in all stages of phylogenesis.

Second, this gradient must be perceptible to the organism. There are two ways to detect an environmental gradient: by using time or by using space. If only one sensor exists, as in microscopic animals, or if many are grouped into one point, as in mammalian olfactory receptors, the organism must use time to judge in which direction to go. As we have seen, many sensors operate in a time-dependent manner: at each passing moment, the current signal is compared with the last one received. Signal strength will change over time, thus showing the organism in which direction the gradient runs. This is how olfactory receptors operate. It will thus be possible to move upstream or downstream along the gradient.

With two or more sensors and enough distance between them, an organism can compare signals from two locations on its body. Signal differentiation may thus be spatial, rather than temporal, with each sensor transmitting a similar but different version of the signal. The difference between the two transmissions indicates the physical or chemical gradient in the environment and the organism can now move in the most useful direction for its physiological needs. The best example is stereophonic perception, which requires hearing with two ears.

These two kinds of gradient detection can guide movements to a stimulus but cannot be used to assess stimulus utility. The organism would have to compare the stimulus with its own internal state. This brings us to the hedonic dimension, a subject that has interested me since the 1960s (Cabanac and Chatonnet 1964; Cabanac and Minaire 1966) and to which we will now turn.[12]

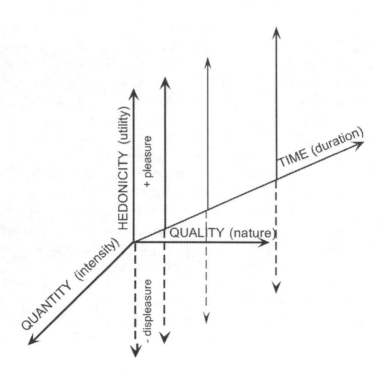

Figure II.5 Complete sensation diagram, with duration added to the three dimensions of Figure II.1. Between brackets: information carried by the axis on stimulus characteristics.

---

[12] At the time, we simply published short papers. It was only later, after work at the laboratory of the J.B. Pierce Foundation, that I understood the need to publish longer and more detailed papers, especially, alas, papers in English (Cabanac 1979).

Chapter III
The pleasure of sensation [13]

"Nature gives us organs to forewarn us
through pleasure what we have to seek,
and through pain what we have to flee."
Condillac, 1754

The dictionary defines pleasure in a somewhat circular way: "A feeling of satisfaction and happiness coming from having experiencing, or expecting something good or to one's liking." The noun *pleasure* describes a state of mind. The adjective *pleasant* describes what causes pleasure. The antonyms of *pleasure* and *pleasant* are *displeasure* and *unpleasant*. According to Young, the hedonic dimension of sensation is a continuum between two extremes: distress (extreme negative affectivity) and delight (extreme positive affectivity) (Young 1959). Midway is indifference. This continuum is implicit even in our language: the word "pleasure" becomes its antonym simply through the addition of a prefix. Pleasure and displeasure motivate us to seek or avoid. Avoiding displeasure is just as motivating, if not more so, than seeking pleasure. When these two extremes are weak and barely perceptible, they give way to indifference.

The terms *affective* and *affectivity* refer to pleasure and displeasure. In keeping with the usage established by Beebe-Center, *hedonic* is replacing *affective* in English, but the two terms were originally synonymous (Beebe-Center 1932). *Affective* is a better word in my opinion because the Greek root *hēdonē* solely means pleasure and excludes displeasure. I will nonetheless use hedonic to avoid the ambiguity of *affective*, which has become synonymous with *emotional* in the current English-language literature.

Titchener went to great pains to refute the notion that pleasure is a peripheral sensation (Titchener 1908). This refutation implies that pleasure may exist not only in sensations but also in all kinds of mental events. For Nafe, "Experience from every sense department may ...

---

[13] This chapter is a development of Cabanac (1979b).

49

become affective experience. ... Pleasure and displeasure are inherently alike, as if made from the same matrix" (Nafe 1924, p. 544). For these authors, pleasure/displeasure is a common denominator that takes place in the brain. Wundt proposed three dimensions for the hedonic process: attractiveness-repulsiveness, excitation-inhibition, and tension-release—a fairly complex model (Wundt, 1902). Titchener showed how direct, easy, and natural it is to estimate attractiveness and unattractiveness (Titchener 1908). Young defined the hedonic process using three attributes: positive or negative sign[14] (because cognition may be pleasant or unpleasant), intensity, and duration (Young 1959). All of these distinctions become unnecessary and obsolete once sensation itself has been defined, as in the 4-dimensional model of the previous chapter (Figure II.4).

Not all stimuli evoke pleasure or displeasure. Of the countless data that reach the brain at any moment, most arouse neutral sensations, as noted by Külpe (1893). For example, we usually feel neither pleasure nor displeasure on seeing most objects. If we do, it is for reasons of cultural or emotional aesthetics and not for truly sensory reasons. As Pfaffmann pointed out, "there is almost no limit to the range of previously neutral stimuli that, by one method or another, can be made pleasurable or unpleasurable" (Pfaffmann 1960). We will return to this point, as well as to the dominant function of indifference. Pfaffmann uses the term *primary reinforcers* for all stimuli that give a sensation of pleasure or displeasure even when first encountered. Most are negative reinforcers, *i.e.*, they arouse displeasure. Concentrated quinine solution, for example, tastes unpleasant because it is bitter. A sound may be unpleasant because it is loud. A stimulus can therefore be unpleasant by nature or simply, as Wundt has proposed, because of its intensity (Wundt, 1902) (Figure III.1).

Thus, most stimuli evoke indifference and, among primary reinforcers, most are unpleasant. The most effective positive primary reinforcers, with all conditions of intensity being satisfied, are thermal,

---

[14] Other authors use the term "valence."

olfactory/gustatory,[15] or mechanical. There are probably no other positive primary reinforcers.

Do we all perceive pleasure the same way?

The answer lies beyond the limits of science, and probably always will.

The first step of the scientific process is to share evidence. For this, it is important to grasp the distinction between public and private data. The former may be shared by more than one observer and come from measurable and replicable phenomena of the external world. The latter are mental phenomena and may be shared by more than one observer only through very indirect information. Sensory pleasure is an example of private data, as is sensation itself. Our sole access to it in the mind of others is what they tell us through their behavior or through oral accounts. We can agree with someone that something is delightful, this feeling being a characteristic of the stimulus, but we are never sure our pleasure is shared. Behaviors and oral responses are examples of public data that we each broadcast. They do not reveal the intrinsic nature of the underlying mental substrate, which forever remains private. Such data, however, can be compared from one subject to another and, for the same subject, from one moment to another. The results are replicable and thus amenable to scientific study. This is the very principle of psychophysics, as we shall see.

EXPERIMENTAL STUDY OF SENSORY PLEASURE

Measurement of pleasure

How, then, can pleasure—a form of private data—be studied scientifically? In the 20th century, objective measurement of pleasure

---

[15] According to Matti Chiva (in a lecture given for the Nutrasweet Award), odors are not inherently pleasant or unpleasant. People learn these affective associations. But this view is not universally shared. See Barthoshuk (1991).

lagged behind the spectacular development of other fields of science. One reason may be that scientific psychologists, in reaction to psychoanalysis, wished to be objective and tended to avoid introspection. They preferred to investigate motivation by measuring animal behavior, without resorting to so-called mentalistic cognitive notions. The very term "mentalist" was long considered pejorative among scientific psychologists. It may still be. This is unfortunate because animal experimentation loses in precision what it gains in objectivity. I will return to this point (Chapter X).

Introspection

Private data can be accessed through introspection. "He who knows himself also knows others; for each man bears the entire form of the human condition" (Montaigne 1965). Mental phenomena, though impossible to share, are undeniably objective to anyone who thinks them. They seem as real as genuine objects. So I will use the term *mental object* for any presentation taking place in the mind at a given moment. It is through the methods of psychophysics and the measurement of behavior that we may bring mental objects into the ambit of scientific study.

As we have seen, psychophysics involves presenting a standardized stimulus (identified and quantified in terms of its public physical and chemical characteristics) and asking subjects to describe their private sensations. A simple yes or no might suffice if the aim is only to study a perception threshold or whether pleasure is present or absent. One can go a step further by asking for a number that describes the intensity of the stimulus quantitatively. Or one may record not the oral response but an analogous behavior that the subjects provide to describe their sensations. This method, called "multidimensional scaling" or "cross-modality matching," may be applied to any mental object, sensation, perception, or experience. Further on in this book, examples will be given of its use to measure sensations and other forms of satisfaction involving mental activity, such as video games or poetry reading.

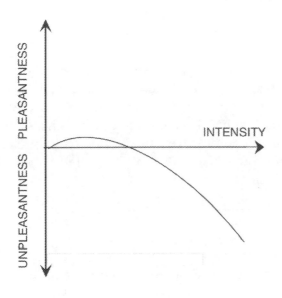

Figure III.1   Wundt, considered pleasure and displeasure of sensation as depending upon the stimulus intensity. Freely adapted from Wundt (1902).

The behavioral method is conceptually even simpler. It involves measuring the quality and quantity of a stimulus that a subject is seeking, e.g., the concentration and volume of a sweet-tasting solution that a subject consumes.   The approach is the same as in animal experiments, but when applied to humans it has the great advantage of giving the experimenter access to the subject's introspective experience, with the help of prior oral instructions. The experimenter thus has good reason to believe that the subject's pleasure is being accessed.   It is impossible to go further and become absolutely certain. The limit is never reached because subjects can always cheat when describing what they actually experience or which preferences they are seeking.

Introspection suffers from two main obstacles. First, a conscious experience may be hard to communicate in words. Any effort to communicate assumes that the subject and the experimenter share a common perception and vocabulary. If they do not, the mental phenomena are not communicable. How do you describe a yellow color to someone blind from birth?

The second obstacle is paradoxically the opposite. Because everyone perceives sensation and pleasure, we conclude a bit hastily that scientific analysis will be easy and the results obvious. This impression is misleading because common knowledge is not necessarily science. Each of us has but an imperfect notion of the laws that determine our own sensations of pleasure. Alliesthesia will provide a good example.

Alliesthesia

The third dimension of Figure II.4 runs from negative to positive. A stimulus need not be at a fixed point of the hedonic axis to evoke a constant sensation. On the contrary, it may evoke a sensation from different positions at different times. The same stimulus may be perceived as pleasant or unpleasant according to the conditions of the moment. This is the phenomenon of alliesthesia (Cabanac 1987). The word,[16] from the Greek roots αλιοσισ (modification) and εσθεσισ (sensation), means that the hedonic dimension of sensation can be modulated to suit the circumstances. Positive alliesthesia occurs when the sensation moves on the hedonic axis toward less displeasure or more pleasure; negative alliesthesia when it moves in the other direction. The causes of alliesthesia are either physiological or intrinsic to the subject's personal history.

Causes of alliesthesia

Human alliesthesia has been known and studied especially when it comes to heat stimuli and the senses of smell and taste during eating.

---

[16] Created in conjunction with S. Nicolaïdis.

Internal signals

Internally generated data are mainly responsible for changes to the pleasure from a sensation. A subject will perceive cold stimuli on the skin as unpleasant when body core temperature is low, *i.e.*, hypothermia. The same subject will perceive the same stimuli as pleasant when body core temperature is high, *i.e.*, hyperthermia. The sensation's hedonic dimension therefore reflects the body core temperature (Cabanac 1969; Cabanac *et al.* 1972; Mower 1976; Marcus and Belyavin 1978; Attia and Engel 1980, 1982; Strigo *et al.* 2000). Over the range of skin temperatures between the two pain thresholds of 15°C and 45°C, body core temperature determines the pleasure and displeasure from thermal stimuli on a hand (Figure III.2). Attia and Engel have shown that this phenomenon is not specific to the hand's skin (Figure III.2), but exists simultaneously over the whole skin surface (Attia and Engel 1981).

Likewise, pleasure from the sense of taste varies with one's satiety and physiological status. Eating food will turn the pleasure of a sweet sensation into displeasure (Cabanac *et al.* 1968; Gilbert and Hagen 1980; Barthoshuk 1991; Scott 1992; Fantino 1984, 1995). Figure III.3 provides one example. We will come across many such examples further on, in relation to body weight. In the case of food stimuli, the signal leading to taste alliesthesia is neither general glycemia nor glycemia in the portal vein but is normally triggered by the passing of highly concentrated chyme through the duodenal opening (Cabanac and Fantino 1977), a signal identified in rats (Smith and Young 1974; Cabanac and Lafrance 1992). Not unexpectedly, cerebral imaging techniques show signs of negative alliesthesia when people repeatedly eat delectable stimuli, like chocolate (Small *et al.* 2001).

Clear-cut alliesthesia was demonstrated in mecanokinetic sensations aroused by muscular exercise. Pleasure was present as long as exercise was aerobic. Displeasure took place as soon as muscular work became anaerobic (Ekkekakis and Hall 2005).

The sense of smell is also strongly hedonic. Few odors are greeted with indifference (Bartoshuk 1991). Most evoke displeasure. Alliesthesia exists for food odors before and after a meal, but not for non-food odors (Duclaux *et al.* 1973). It is innate and present in infants, whose degree of satiety is measurable by their facial expressions in response to milk odors.[17] Soussignan *et al.* have shown that infants display expressions of attraction to food odors before breastfeeding and expressions of aversion after (Soussignan *et al.* 1999).

In response to a stimulus held constant, negative alliesthesia occurs when a sensation becomes less pleasurable or more unpleasurable. But alliesthesia is not always negative. It may be positive, that is, there may be a shift toward more pleasure or less displeasure. Temperature sensation offers examples of both kinds of alliesthesia because internal temperature may easily move either way during an experimental session. With taste sensations, negative alliesthesia is more easily shown, this being the normal trend during a meal. As satiety fades, food stimuli again evoke pleasure, *i.e.;* positive alliesthesia. Experimental studies have shown other clear examples of increasing preference (Jacobs 1958) or even positive alliesthesia for sweetness after administration of insulin, a hypoglycemic hormone (Briese and de Quijada 1979), or 2-deoxyglucose (a non-metabolizable analogue of glucose, leading to tissue hypoglucia) (Thompson and Campbell 1977). Positive alliesthesia for saltiness has been observed after intense muscular exercises and the resulting loss of sodium chloride through sweating (Leshem *et al.* 1999), after a salt-free diet (Beauchamp and Cowart 1985), or after kidney dialysis treatments that reduce the body's concentration of electrolytes (Leshem and Rudoy 1997). Another example of positive alliesthesia is the increased palatability of alcohol when one is on a low-calorie diet (Söderpalm and Hansen 1999).

Finally, pain sensation itself may vary in displeasure according to one's internal state (Melzack and Casey 1968; Cabanac 1969; Nelkin 1986; Rainville *et al.* 1999).

Setpoint
Sensory pleasure requires a signal from inside the body, but this signal

---

[17] For information on this technique, see J.E. Steiner (1977), "Facial expressions of the neonate infant indicating the hedonics of food related chemical stimuli", *Taste and Development*, J.E. Weiffenbach, Bethesda, MD, U.S. Dept. Health Educ. Welfare: 173-189.

is not simply information from a deep sensor that monitors temperature or intra-duodenal concentrations. It is a complex signal that resembles what regulatory physiologists have described in studies of autonomic responses. All regulation is characterized by what is called a *setpoint*— a benchmark that the regulation seeks to maintain (see Cabanac and Russek 1982). In your home heating system, the setpoint is the temperature you select on the wall thermostat. If the room temperature dips below that setpoint, your heating system will kick in to set things right—by turning the furnace on or by activating the radiators. Physiological regulation works the same way. When the level of calcium in extracellular fluid drops, the parathyroid gland secretes a parathormone to help transfer calcium from the bones to the body's fluids, thus reestablishing a normal calcium balance. Other kinds of physiological regulation operate on the same principle. Regulation specialists use the term *error signal* for the difference between the setpoint value and the actual value:

Error signal = |value of regulated variable| - |setpoint value|

The function of all regulation is to eliminate the error signal. To this end, responses are activated to bring the regulated variable
back to normal, *i.e.*, to the setpoint. To go back to the example of calcium regulation, the body prevents hypercalcemia by excreting calcium through the kidneys and depositing calcium in the bones, thus lowering the level of calcium in the blood. Conversely, the body prevents hypocalcemia by transferring calcium from the bones to the extracellular fluid. These regulatory responses are carried out by circulating hormones, which in turn are secreted into the bloodstream by endocrine glands—the thyroid, and the parathyroid. These glands monitor the level of calcium ions in the blood.

It is sometimes difficult to recognize the existence of a regulatory setpoint and to find its value. A setpoint is a piece of information and not an organ. It may be inferred from an organism's response to an internal imbalance. The organism should respond in a way that counters this deviation from its normal state, *i.e.*, by trying to cancel the error signal. Such a response provides the best way to find the setpoint value for any biological system of regulation. In the case of excess blood

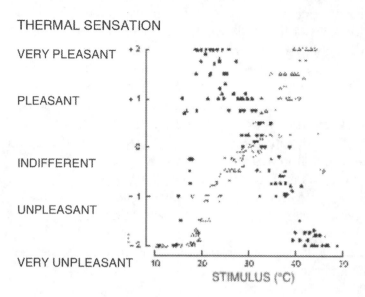

THERMAL SENSATION

Figure III.2 Responses describing a subject's pleasure (positive ratings on the Y-axis) or displeasure (negative ratings) while being thermally stimulated (X-axis) on a hand. Each point is a response to a stimulus during 30 s. The white points were obtained in hypothermia and the black ones in hyperthermia. Below 15°C and above 45°C, virtually all stimuli are described as being unpleasant. This is no surprise: the two temperatures correspond to the pain thresholds for cold and heat. For in-between temperatures, the subject uses the entire range of available responses from very unpleasant to very pleasant. Two clouds of points appear clearly. Under hypothermia, warm temperatures are pleasant and cold ones unpleasant. Under hyperthermia, the reverse is true: cold temperatures are pleasant and warm ones unpleasant. The same stimulus may be perceived as pleasant or unpleasant depending on the subject's internal state. Note: circles are used when the subject is immersed in a warm bath and triangles when in a cold bath. The effect of bath temperature on the skin is negligible: the pattern of white circles produced by a warm bath resembles the pattern of white triangles produced by a cold bath. The same resemblance may be seen with the black circles and black triangles (Cabanac 1969).

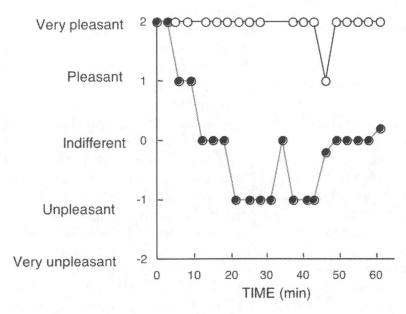

Figure III.3 Verbal responses describing a subject's pleasure (positive ratings) or displeasure (negative ratings) after tasting and spitting out samples of sweetened water. These are the results of two sessions. In the control session (white points), the subject receives the same stimulus every three minutes, spits it out, and gives a consistently pleasant rating over an hour. In the other session (black points), the second taste stimulus is followed by injection into the stomach, via a tube, of 50 g of glucose dissolved in water. The injection quickly shifts the sweet sensation from pleasant to unpleasant. The unpleasant response begins to disappear around 40 min after the stomach injection. The same stimulus may be perceived as pleasant or unpleasant depending on the subject's internal state.

calcium, the setpoint is the level where calcitonin secretion appears or disappears, this hormone being an antagonist to parathormone. In the human species, the setpoint for regulation of blood calcium is about 2.5 mM/l. When the error signal is positive, e.g., a blood calcium level of 3 mM/l, the subject is hypercalcemic and secretes calcitonin while ceasing secretion of parathormone (the hormone that raises blood calcium levels). When the error signal is negative, e.g., a blood calcium level of 2.2 mM/l, the subject is hypocalcemic and ceases secretion of calcitonin while secreting more parathormone.

Strikingly, we see exactly the same kind of regulation with pleasure from heat or food. In both cases, an error signal combines two pieces of information: the setpoint and the regulated variable. And in both cases, the signal triggers a compensatory response: the search for pleasure. As a driving force for behavior, pleasure is nothing less than a physiological response on behalf of a regulatory system.

This observation applies to all of the different sensory pleasures. Any sensation that supports homeostasis is pleasant. Any sensation that threatens homeostasis is unpleasant. For example, pleasure encourages healthy subjects to maintain their body core temperature at 37°C, as seen above. When the setpoint is altered, so is the error signal, and sensory pleasure follows suit. In the case of fever, the biological thermostat is adjusted upward. The pleasure from heat sensations encourages feverish subjects to maintain a higher body temperature (Figure III.5). The search for pleasure helps defend not so much the internal temperature but rather the temperature setpoint of a biological thermostat. When the setpoint rises, as in fever, behavioral preference will defend this higher value.

The same is true for food palatability. In Figure III.6, food sensations show the same pattern as we saw with fever. Body weight looks as if it were being regulated in both subjects. When in a normal state, they found tastes or smells to be pleasant on an empty stomachand unpleasant after swallowing 50 g of glucose (negative alliesthesia). When this simple experiment was repeated after several weeks of a draconian diet with much weight loss, the same 50 g of glucose could not make the food sensations unpleasant. The alliesthesia had gone. Several months later, the subjects had regained their initial weight and the alliesthesia had reappeared. The pleasurability of food stimuli seemed to vary according to the difference between their actual weight and their weight setpoint. They seemed to have a *ponderostat*. The search for pleasure in and of itself guided their behavior toward a stable body weight. With alliesthesia being absent after eating, or appearing later, underweight subjects will eat more and regain their initial weight (Cabanac *et al.* 1971; Gilbert and Hagen 1980; Kleifield and Lowe 1991). As with a thermostat, the autonomic responses defend the ponderostat setpoint (Steffens *et al.* 1990).

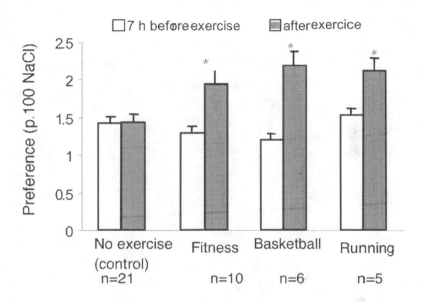

Figure III.4   Appetite for salt after intense sweating produced by 40 min of various exercises. Salt loss due to sweating leads over the next few hours to positive alliesthesia for saltiness. After Leshem et al. (1999).

In Figure III.5, we saw how thermal pleasure can defend a higher temperature setpoint during fever. Similar examples are known for the senses of smell and taste during eating. In such situations, the pleasure has been adapted to defend upward- or downward-shifted setpoints. Forced overeating is followed by a spontaneous return to normal weight when subjects can eat as much as they wish (Fantino *et al.* 1983). In obesity, the ponderostat is adjusted upward and taste alliesthesia defends a high setpoint (Guy-Grand and Sitt 1974; Doassans-Wilhelm 1978). In anorexia nervosa, the situation is the reverse: at a low body weight, patients almost perpetually feel no hunger. Their alliesthesia defends a low body weight setpoint

(Melchior *et al.* 1990). Both situations are presented theoretically in Figure III.7. In addition to pathological conditions, the ponderostat may also be altered by drugs. Nicotine, for instance, lowers the body weight setpoint of smokers (Perkins *et al.* 1995; Cabanac and Frankham 2002).

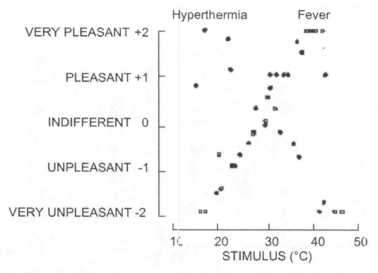

Figure III.5 Pleasurable (positive) or unpleasurable (negative) responses to thermal stimulations on the hand, from a subject immersed up to the chin in a tepid bath at 33°C. The results are for two sessions that were identical except for one point: in one case, the subject's internal temperature is raised by prior immersion in a warm bath; in the other, by illness (flu). The subject's response profile is hyperthermia when healthy and hypothermia when feverish. The search for sensory pleasure and the avoidance of displeasure produce opposing behaviors. Both, however, are thermoregulatory. In one case, a healthy subject defends a temperature of about 37°C. In the other, a feverish subject defends a temperature of about 38.5°C. After Cabanac (1969). This phenomenon was implicitly described by Aristotle when he wrote: "The ill man and the healthy man do not feel heat in the same way" (Aristotle, 384-322 BC).

Illnesses and drugs are not alone in affecting the regulatory setpoints of various physiological functions. Over a lifetime, body weight will increase as the setpoint drifts upward. Over the menstrual cycle, the temperature setpoint will vary, falling before ovulation and rising after (Cunningham and Cabanac 1971). Nicolaïdis uses the term *homeorhesis* and Mrosovsky *rheostasis* for these slow readjustments of regulatory setpoints (Nicolaïdis 1977; Mrosovsky 1990).

Sensory pleasure seems to depend on the difference between the regulated variable—body core temperature for heat sensations and body weight for food sensations—and its regulatory setpoint. We will see other examples of sensory pleasure being adapted to ensure the organism's integrity and proper functioning.

Learned aversion: the Garcia effect

While studying the toxic effects of nuclear radiation, John Garcia discovered a new phenomenon: the irradiated animals rejected certain food stimuli. For them, these stimuli seemed to have acquired aversive properties (Garcia *et a*l. 1985). After systematically analyzing this rejection, he found that the aversion for a new taste was determined not by the radiation, but by the radiation-induced digestive illness—nausea or diarrhea. This mechanism is crucial in teaching what foods are safe to eat, since it makes an animal reject anything that has previously caused food poisoning. The learned aversion must be for a new flavor that the animal has never encountered in its life, and it must be followed by digestive disorders, nausea, or diarrhea. No aversion will develop if the sickening sensation is perceived only in subsequent contacts with a flavor (Pelchat *et al.* 1983). This feeding mechanism is thus narrowly specific. Curiously, when nausea is created by administering lithium chloride to an animal, aversion may develop even if this substance is administered under general anesthesia (Bermudez-Rattoni *et al.* 1988).

Such avoidance of food poisoning exists not only among rats but also among all other vertebrates going back to the reptile stage (Paradis and Cabanac 2002), including of course the human species (Pelchat and Rozin 1982). This long-term and potentially permanent negative alliesthesia may explain the food aversions of some individuals after poisoning, after pregnancy nausea (Revusky and

Bedarf 1967; Letarte *et al.* 1997), or after radiation illness in the case of cancer patients (Schwartz *et al.* 1996). Although learned aversion was discovered for the sense of taste, it also exists for the sense of smell (Frank 1985). In both cases, it always applies to sensations associated with food stimuli.

Learned pleasure

Altering the hedonic dimension does not always mean a decrease in pleasure. Sometimes, it may mean an increase. Berridge (2001) has reviewed all of the known cases where a pleasure response can be acquired through learning. Here, I will make do with a few examples to show that the link between pleasure and a stimulus is not necessarily rigid and permanent. A neutral or even unpleasant stimulus may become pleasurable if associated with a pleasant stimulus. This mechanism is known especially in the case of food flavors. It may be recognized in the following examples:

- Positive Garcia effect. This is the reverse of learned aversion, which may be called a negative Garcia effect. Just as nausea and diarrhea will make a preceding new flavor unpleasant, improved health and sense of well being will make a new, and initially neutral, flavor pleasant. Any new flavor encountered during recovery from a digestive illness will acquire a pleasant affective tone (Garcia *et al.* 1974). This may explain certain positive idiosyncrasies, just as the Garcia effect explains negative idiosyncrasies (Figure III.8).

- Postfeeding effect. LeMagnen injected either insulin or a control saline solution into rats while presenting them with new food marked by a strong odor, such as menthol or eucalyptol. The insulin eliminated the meal effects and strongly lowered blood sugar levels. The insulin-treated rats now avoided eating the scented food. The control rats continued to eat this food (LeMagnen 1953). These are only animal experiments, but we may cautiously conclude that postfeeding satiety made the preceding stimulus pleasant and that the insulin-induced absence of satiety kept this stimulus-response association from developing. It is likely that the same mechanism has produced our widespread appreciation for the smell of coffee or tea (Cines and Rozin

1982). The coffee flavor precedes the postfeeding mood-altering effect of caffeine and thus acquires a pleasant dimension.

Specific sensory satiety

A final type of alliesthesia is encountered with the smells and tastes of food. When a food item is consumed, satiation specific to it develops during the meal (Rolls *et al.* 1981). Subjects not only stop eating it but also say it is less palatable. Satiety is thus faster for the flavors of already consumed food and slower for new flavors. A similar process may be at work in sexual arousal, *i.e.*, the Coolidge effect.[18] In both cases, alliesthesia is produced by peripheral stimuli.

Vision and hearing

> "When we have undergone privation and suffering, the satisfaction given to our needs causes us pleasure. Yet the same is not true for all of our pleasures ... those that very often concern hearing and vision ... are free from pain. ... They are not preceded by any privation for which they would somehow be the satisfaction" (Aristotle, 384-322 BC).

After Aristotle, Ovsich noticed that innate pleasures are generated only by what he termed "contact" sensations—warmth, pain, taste—and skin sensations (Ovsich, book in preparation). He classifies smell as a contact sensation because it is highly hedonic, even though it picks up remote stimuli, as do vision and hearing. Innate pleasures may be unlearned primarily because, as we shall see, contact sensations are closely linked, on the one hand, to the stability of the body's internal environment and, on the other, to the utility of the pleasure-generating behavior. The corollary is that the pleasures we get from vision and

---

[18] The term *Coolidge effect* is used to describe how variety, in terms of new sexual partners, seems to boost sexual arousal and performance. It is said that President Coolidge and his wife were visiting a chicken farm when his wife was told that the rooster copulated several times a day. "Tell that to my husband," she said. President Coolidge was thus informed and he asked: "Same hen?" The answer was no. The rooster, in fact, copulated with very many hens. "Tell that to my wife," he replied.

hearing are usually learned because these sensations are not closely linked to our internal environment. We use vision and hearing, more than we use the other senses, as channels of social communication. Certainly, visual and auditory sensations can be rich in hedonicity, but the signals that arouse these pleasures seem to be cultural in nature rather than biological. With Ovsich, it is hard to see what dimensions of the internal environment could be changed when one listens to music or looks at pictures. Something might be optimized by maximization of visual and auditory pleasure, but this something remains to be identified. It is likelier that most visual and auditory pleasures are learned at some point in an individual's past by being secondarily associated with the primary pleasures of biology, food, warmth, and body movement.

Vision may nonetheless arouse some innate aversions and pleasures. In such cases, however, the signal is complex and carries an inherent meaning. Infant apes show fright on seeing a snake, with no social contamination to explain this displeasure. In humans, the sight of young, nubile faces is pleasurable (Johnston 1999). Men prefer to look at female faces rather than masculine ones (Aharon *et al.* 2001). Pleasure is aroused when subjects view images of appetizing food while on an empty stomach (Huffman *et al.* 2000). Likewise, it is pleasant or unpleasant to see faces expressing emotions, depending on the emotion being expressed (Russell 1987). Whatever the emotion expressed, or the sensation evoked, a visual signal held constant can be made more pleasurable or less pleasurable if the subject is satiated or if the image of another emotion is presented alongside. Clearly, some innate visual pleasures do exist and alliesthesia may occur with visual stimuli.

Indeed, the literature does reveal a few examples of alliesthesia with visual sensations. Such sensations may be altered by signals from deep within an organism, *i.e.*, by signals that are responsible for hunger and satiety and that produce smell/taste alliesthesia. On an empty stomach, subjects feel more pleasure watching normally colored images of food on a computer screen than they do watching the same images with abnormal coloring. The hedonic difference between normally and abnormally colored images disappears after satiation (Huffman *et al.*

2000). Seeing palatable food causes more pleasure or less pleasure depending on the subject's degree of hunger. A similar effect exists with water: transparency—a characteristic quality of water—is perceived better by dehydrated subjects in ambiguous stimuli than by normally hydrated subjects (Changizi and Hall 2001). Visual preferences for differently colored fabrics vary in the evening with the lighting intensity experienced during the day. Kim and Tokura (1998) have described this phenomenon and argue that the thermostat setpoint is affected by lighting during the day.

Russell and Fehr (1987) have shown that observers perceive the same photos of human faces as pleasant or unpleasant according to the cultural context surrounding the photo presentation. So vision does seem to display alliesthesia, just like the sensations that monitor constant variables in the body's internal environment. Indeed, when systematically looked for alliesthesia can be found in visual and auditory sensations that originated from the environment (Brondel and Cabanac 2007).

Nonetheless, most of the vivid pleasures from vision or hearing appear to be learned rather than innate. Works of art in particular seldom leave people indifferent. In this case, the pleasure results from a lengthy learning process—a long chain of mental associations with other innate or learned pleasures. Whenever there is pleasure, there may apparently also be alliesthesia.

Pain

It may seem strange and artificial to dissociate the discriminative and hedonic components of pain. For anyone, pain means displeasure, so much so, that the words are synonyms in everyday language. Yet the 4-dimensional schema of sensation also applies to pain. Some pains may be pleasant. Examples include repeated tickling of a sore tooth or slightly painful thermal stimulations, just beyond the pain thresholds (15°C and 45°C), which correct body core temperature while being perceived as painful but pleasant (Figure III.2 and Strigo *et al.* 2000). Melzack and Casey (1968) were the first to propose that pain be

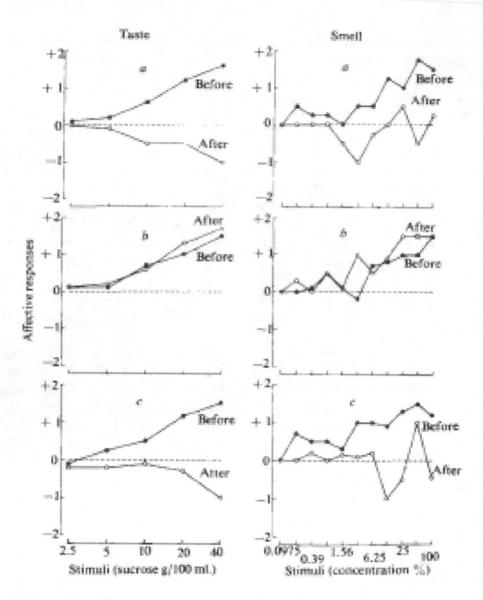

Figure III.6   Hedonic responses from two subjects describing the pleasure or displeasure of food sensations: the flavor of sweetened samples for the subject on the left, and a food odor (orange syrup) for the subject on the right. For each subject, the results of the three sessions are given from top to bottom. In the top boxes the subjects are on empty stomachs (before) and perceive the food stimuli as pleasant at

all concentrations. When concentrated glucose is injected into their stomachs, the resulting negative alliesthesia turns these pleasant sensations into unpleasant ones (after). In the middle boxes, the same experiment was tried on the same subjects, who had now lost much weight after a draconian low-calorie diet of several weeks. The alliesthesia had gone. When the subjects began to eat again as much as they wished, they regained their initial body weight in several months and the alliesthesia due to the glucose stomach injection reappeared. Body weight seems to be regulated by an early or late satiety effect depending on whether the subjects are at their body weight setpoint or below. After Cabanac et al. (1971).

separated into a discriminative dimension, which they call sensory, and a hedonic one, which they call affective-motivational. This concept covers a reality fruitfully studied by Rainville and his team. These authors have shown that the discriminative dimension of painful sensation activates the somatosensory cortex (Hofbauer *et al.* 2001) whereas the hedonic dimension activates the anterior cingulate (Rainville *et al.* 1997). These centers are therefore highly dissociated from each other. This dissociation of pain sensation is confirmed by study of pain under hypnosis (Rainville *et al.* 1999 and Figure III.9), with a further study showing selective inhibition of centers involved in either dimension of sensation (Rainville *et al.* 2000).

Physiological role of sensory pleasure

We will now turn to the relationship, already alluded to, between the hedonic dimension of sensation and behavior, or between sensory pleasure and the effects of seeking such pleasure. This relationship should already seem evident after the examples on the previous pages. More could be provided, and the conclusion would be the same: the motivation to approach and consume a stimulus, or to avoid it, is as strong as the pleasure or displeasure aroused by the stimulus. Approach and consumption behaviors are triggered by and for pleasurable sensations relating to food, heat, or sex. The end-purpose of pleasure appears to us through motivation, in the primary sense of

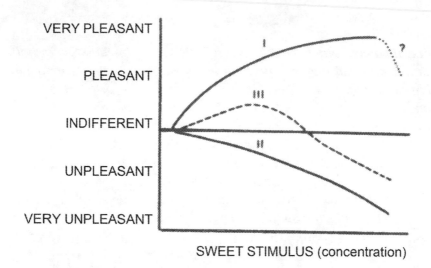

VERY PLEASANT

PLEASANT

INDIFFERENT

UNPLEASANT

VERY UNPLEASANT

SWEET STIMULUS (concentration)

Figure III.7 A theoretical and partly hypothetical presentation of the hedonic dimension of sweet sensation for stimuli of increasing concentrations. Three responses are possible on the basis of satiety and actual weight in relation to the ponderostat setpoint.

Type I

— *normal or obese subjects, on an empty stomach but not on any diet;*

— *subjects who have lost weight and are on an empty stomach;*

— *subjects who have lost weight, after a meal (absence of negative alliesthesia). Dotted line on the right is hypothetical.*

Type II

— *normal or obese subjects (not on any diet) after a meal: negative alliesthesia in relation to their response (I) on an empty stomach;*

— *anorexic subjects on an empty stomach: the subjects are perpetually above their ponderostat setpoint because they are overfed by their therapists*

— *overfed subjects, on an empty stomach: certain cultural practices involve overfeeding (e.g., before marriage[19]);*

Type III

---

[19] Some societies have a custom of requiring individuals to fatten themselves, e.g., before marriage. The artificial weight gain disappears once they can eat only as much as they wish. M. Fantino, F. Baigts, M. Cabanac, and M. Apfelbaum (1983), "Effects of an overfeed regime on the affective component of the sweet sensation", *Appetite*, 4:155-164.

— this intermediate response is sometimes observed in certain subjects. It may be seen in subjects who are slightly below their ponderostat setpoint after a meal or are slightly above their setpoint while on an empty stomach.After Cabanac (1979).

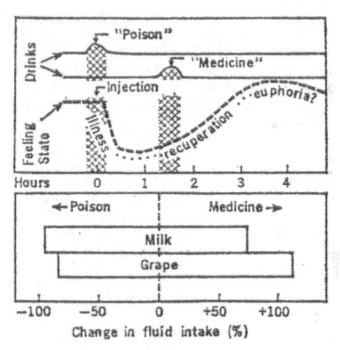

Figure III.8 Influence of presenting a new flavor never encountered previously: before a digestive illness (poison) and after the illness, during convalescence (medicine). The illness is caused artificially by giving the animal an emetic. The bars below indicate the rats' behavioral changes in response to two flavors (milk and grape) administered either before (poison) or after (medicine) the digestive illness. Depending on when these new stimuli are presented, the animals tend either to avoid them or to overconsume. After Garcia et al. (1974).

the movement or force it gives to an organism. Pleasure and displeasure immediately indicate whether a stimulus should be sought or avoided.

Evolution shows us that if an organ and its function solve a problem advantageously they will tend to persist in the succeeding generations that inherit them. This is the very basis of natural selection. Such Darwinian thinking has been applied not only to anatomy and physiology, but also to psychology by the psychologists Bunge (1980), Cosmides, and Tooby (Cosmides *et al*. 1992). The same approach may help us understand sensation, and its special hedonic dimension. I believe that hedonicity had from the outset a strong selective advantage: animals that possessed this faculty were able to multiply at the expense of those that did not, thus ensuring its persistence to the present day. We have seen that the hedonic dimension may be learned. It is thus a function that gives its possessors flexibility and adaptability. Instead of operating through rigid reflexes, or through selection of empirical rules that sooner or later prove to be maladaptive, pleasure enables the central nervous system to operate on a case-by-case basis. Above all, pleasure eliminates the need to store huge amounts of information that would result from associating all stimuli in the environment with all possible behavioral responses to them.

As we examine the different senses and the way they operate, a basic law of psychophysiology will emerge, the equation:

PLEASANT = USEFUL

This law appears only indirectly in the experiments described on the previous pages.

Optimization

Ethologists postulate that animal behavior is always optimal. Natural selection operates generation after generation not to eliminate the less adapted but to favor the reproduction of the more adapted (see Barrette 2000). Ultimately, survival belongs only to those animals that have inherited the right behaviors. An optimal behavior is one that provides the best fit to an animal's ecological niche—no need to bring either consciousness or pleasure into the picture. Yet sensory pleasure does exist and we have seen how it points directly to a clear biological goal. In this analysis, can we go further than simply observe acorrelation between pleasure and utility? We first need to distinguish between distal utility and proximal utility. Distal utility is a behavior's propensity to favor an individual's long-term survival and to ensure the survival of numerous descendents. Proximal utility ensures an individual's immediate survival. Of course, the former needs the latter, at least until the individual has reproduced and, in higher animals, raised its immediate descendents.

In the above examples, the stimuli were useful because they could improve the subject's physiological functioning, *i.e.*, correct a problem or a deficiency. The utility[20] is proximal and the pleasure is useful primarily over the short-term. Again, however, proximal utility is a prerequisite for distal utility, so pleasure also enhances survival value over the long term. Sexual pleasure, for instance, is a powerful driving force for reproductive behavior and aids the species over the long term, rather than just the individual.

We will now turn to the experimental arguments for the equation:
pleasant = useful.

Thermal optimization

If a stimulus is pleasant when it corrects an internal deficiency, the search for thermal pleasure should help maintain the constancy of the body's internal environment. Such is the case. Let us recapitulate: as long as the body's core is too hot or too cold, corrective stimuli to the skin will be pleasant and the search for pleasure useful. For a subject with hypothermia, cold is unpleasant to the skin and warmth pleasant. Conversely, for a subject with hyperthermia, cold is pleasant to the skin and warmth unpleasant. Sensory pleasure seems to be a motor for bringing behavior into line with physiological need. Thus, pleasant stimuli tend to narrow the gap between body core temperature and optimal temperature, whereas unpleasant stimuli tend to widen the gap.

---

[20] Using the current meaning of the word *utility* and not that of economists.

When thermal pleasure is sought and thermal displeasure avoided, the resulting behavior should be better for an organism. This is how behavior can adapt itself to physiological needs. Does it?

There is a way to answer this question quantitatively. The approach, however, is not to ask subjects about the pleasurability of stimuli presented to them, as in the previous experiments. Instead, they are told to go and look by themselves for stimuli they find most pleasurable. At the same time, physiological data are collected. The utility of pleasure may thus be quantitatively measured. Such an

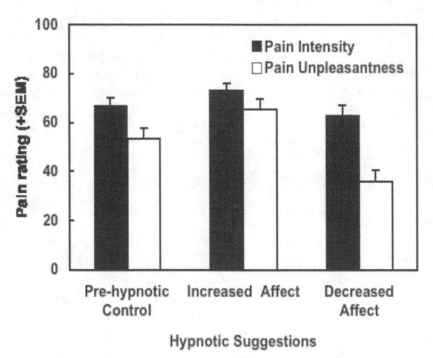

Figure III.9 Mean rating (+ sem) of magnitude of pain sensation by a group of subjects when their hands are soaked in water at 46.5°C (pain threshold is 45°C). The magnitude of the discriminative dimension is relatively unaffected by a hypnotic suggestion that the pain has increased or decreased. In contrast, the affective dimension (hedonic) is significantly influenced by the hypnotic suggestion. These findings point to alliesthesia (personal communication by Pierre Rainville).

experiment is presented in Figure III.10. A subject is immersed up to the chin in an agitated thermostatic bath, to control the temperature over most of the skin. The bath also slowly reduces the core body temperature because of the high thermal conductivity of water, 25 times higher than that of air. The subject's left hand is fitted into a rubber glove that receives a water current at a temperature that he or she can control. The subject is simply told to maximize pleasure for the left hand by using the right hand, which is immersed in the bath, to manipulate a switch that controls electrically operated valves. For a couple of hours, the bath temperature is varied so that a wide range of skin and body core temperatures may be investigated. The subject meanwhile responds and maximizes pleasure for his/her left hand. The temperature chosen is recorded at each moment by means of a thermocouple attached to a finger on the left hand. It is thus possible to get a continuous recording of body temperatures and preferred temperature.

Minute-by-minute analysis of the recordings leads to a mathematical model[21] that summarizes the mean thermal preference of several subjects (T_{pref}):

$$T_{pref} = -0.3T_{bath}(T_{es} - 36.3) + 44 \qquad \text{Equation III.1}$$

T_{bath} and T_{es} are the temperatures of the bath and the body interior (esophagus). Temperatures are expressed in degrees Celsius. We can quickly check the model's validity by assuming that the subject has hypothermia and an esophagus temperature of 36.3°C. The first part of the equation is zero, so the model predicts a preferred temperature of 44°C. This is very hot but still lower than the burn threshold.

---

[21] A model of physiological function is a simple description. Physiologists use two types of mathematical model. The first one is a theoretical description of the functions under study; it includes assumptions and its predictions are compared with the experimental results. The second one merely describes the observed phenomena. The model presented here belongs to the second type.

A related equation has been similarly obtained by Bleichert *et al.* (1973):

$$T_{pref}=a + bT_{es} +cT_{mskin} \quad \text{Equation III.2}$$

Where T_{mskin} is the skin temperature of the entire body.

The focus here is on the subject's perceived pleasure, *i.e.*, a subjective psychological variable, a mental event, and not on an objective physical or physiological variable that can be shared with an observer. The model highlights an important complementary piece of information: the subject's mean skin temperature, which is close to the bath temperature and plays a role in modulating thermal preference. This role is minimal in comparison with that of body core temperature, for which a few tenths of a degree Celsius can reverse the subject's thermal preference. But it is real.[22]

Two conclusions may be drawn from the results of this experiment. First, when equations III.1 and III.2 are compared with the equations for sweating and shivering, we see a strong similarity between behavior and autonomic responses. For example, under experimental conditions, production of human heat and sweat obey the following equations:

Shivering, in watts (Nadel *et al.* 1970):

$$Q_M=42(36.5 - T_{es})(32.2 - T_s) + 8(32.2T_s) \quad \text{Equation III.3}$$

Sweating, in watts per square meter of skin surface (Stolwijk *et al.* 1968):

$$Q_{Evap}=132T_{es} + 20T_s - 5500 \text{Equation III.4}$$

Q_M is defined as the increase in metabolic heat production above the resting baseline value, and Q_{Evap} as the increase in evaporatory thermolysis. T_{es} is body core temperature and T_s the skin temperature of the entire body.

There is a striking similarity between Equations III.1 or III.2 (which describe behavioral responses for seeking thermal pleasure) and

---

[22] Skin temperature seems to have altered the thermoregulation setpoint: warm skin lowered the setpoint while cold skin raised it. This may account for the rise in body core temperature when a subject is suddenly exposed to cold.

equations III.3 and III.4 (which describe the autonomic responses of thermogenesis or thermolysis), despite minor differences in the parameters. The variables are the same, including mean skin temperature (bath temperature in the behavioral experiments). This similarity confirms the physiological nature of sensory pleasure and its biological end-purpose, at least in the case of thermal sensation.

Beyond the form of the equation and the values of the parameters, we come to a second conclusion: the search for pleasure can be predicted from physiological variables, such as mean skin temperature and body core temperature. Thus, pleasure is not an abstract superstructure. It is not a mental experience that science cannot investigate. On the contrary, it is a measurable variable that emerges out of biological complexity. In addition to studying it quantitatively, we can measure the way it is determined both quantitatively and qualitatively. The search for pleasure leads to a fully thermoregulatory behavior that works more efficiently than the autonomic responses it supplements. If a man is suffering from hyperthermia, he can immerse just one hand in cold water at 20°C and thereby remove over 70W from his body, *i.e.*, more than his own heat production (Figure III.11). So this search for pleasure costs nothing in terms of energy expenditure. It simply adapts behavior to a physiological end-purpose. This is so true that the skin's degree of comfort or discomfort provides an index of heat load in the workplace (Attia and Engel 1980, 1982).

A final example, pathological in nature, further supports this conclusion. Congenital indifference to pain is a rare syndrome and is accompanied by loss of sensory pleasure with respect to temperature.[23] Subjects display completely maladaptive behavior in a cold environment. They have no sensation of thermal comfort or discomfort and endanger themselves in potentially harmful thermal environments (Cabanac *et al.* 1969).

---

[23] It is likely that the absence of pleasure occurs in other areas of sensation. I invited one of these subjects to a good Lyon restaurant and he ordered a steak and French fries instead of the delicacies available. At the time, however, I was not yet interested in the sense of taste.

Optimization of food intake

Our study of the sense of taste confirms what seemed obvious to us with heat sensations: pleasure means useful (Bartoshuk 1991; Booth 1991; Sclafani 1991; Shulkin 1991). Some caution, however, is warranted. Food preferences seem to establish themselves slowly, and relatively little work has been done on the subject. Excellent reviews on food pleasure may be found in Giachetti (1992), Bellisle (1992), Fantino (1992b), Nicolaïdis (1992), Boggio (1992), and also Fantino (1995).

Pleasant sensations are but a tiny fraction of all potential sensations that result from chemical substances on the tongue. The overwhelming majority of taste stimuli produce an either unpleasant or indifferent response, due to their intensity or to their very nature. Evolution has favored pleasant taste response to useful molecules, in particular to energy-carrying ones. This observation also holds true for other animal species. Rats consider sweet sensations to be synonymous with food (Mook 1974). Alkaloids, which are either useless or dangerous, are bitter-tasting. Sodium chloride is the saltiest substance we are familiar with and is useful for the organism, at least at concentrations where saline solutions are pleasant-tasting[24] (Figure III.4). Pleasant tastes are thus associated with edible substances and displeasure with inedible ones.

Post-intake alliesthesia and the few examples of selective appetite we have already seen confirm that pleasure is adapted to the quantitative and qualitative food needs of humans and animals (Fantino 1995). Many more examples could be provided, but the example of Figure III.12 alone seems proof enough, all the more so inasmuch as animal experiments corroborate the human data. The intense pleasure that the Addison's subject felt when tasting saline solutions (which were life-saving) confirm that the selective appetites discovered by Richter are mediated by the hedonic component of the sense of taste (Richter 1942-1943). A complete review of the literature is available in Fantino (1995) and Aagmo and Marroquin (1997).

A bitter taste is considered unpleasant. Yet beer and other bitter drinks (e.g., with cinchona bark extract) are consumed in copious

---

[24] In Mexico, a hot country, people drink tequila with salt.

quantities and deemed pleasant by millions of people. This pleasurable taste is an acquired one, beer being aversive to children. The preference is probably acquired whenever a dehydrated and perhaps overheated subject consumes beer. By meeting the body's need for water, and by tapping into an alcohol-induced euphoria, such consumption may give beer a pleasant taste. The same mechanism may account for the popularity of other bitter-tasting drinks. With some caution, it may also account for consumption of spicy foods in many cultures. Spicy foods are *a priori* aversive for humans and animals alike. Yet, when consumed, they come to be gradually preferred in some countries (Rozin *et al.* 1980, 1982). There is thus positive alliesthesia. Interestingly, these countries all have hot climates. The active agent of cayenne pepper, capsaicin, stimulates sweat secretion, so learned pleasure from spicy foods may result from a beneficial thermoregulatory effect. Admittedly, it has proven impossible to teach animals to like pepper, but none of the species used—rats, dogs, pigs—can sweat. They lose heat through evaporation (rats, pigs) or panting (dogs). For these species, capsaicin would be useless.

Pica is a mental disorder that makes a person eat non-nutritive substances, such as chalk or clay. Though considered pathological by psychiatrists, it might be a response to the pleasure of ingesting trace elements. In fact, the most common occurrences are during growth and pregnancy, when nutritional requirements are higher(Cooper 1957). This behavior may also occur during times of nutritional deficiency, typically iron deficiency (Sontag *et al.* 2001). Nothing indicates that it is a response to a sensory pleasure, but this view seems highly plausible.

Olfactory pleasure likewise serves to guide behavior toward optimal food intake, as seen in the previous pages. It may also serve as a sexual and reproductive signal.

Equation III.1 shows that thermal preference is a function of mean skin temperature. This peripheral sensory signal is instrumental in adjusting the body's thermostat. Cold skin raises the thermostat setpoint; warm skin lowers it. Such a function anticipates the organism's future requirements in a hostile environment. The same is true for food sensations. If highly palatable diets are offered to rats

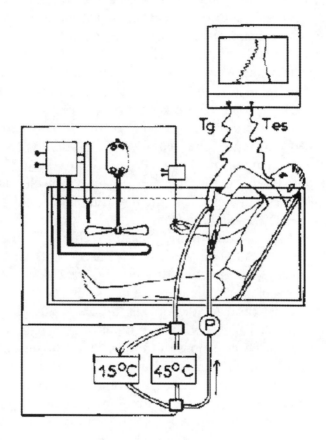

Figure III.10 A thermocouple is inserted into the esophagus. One end is placed behind the heart and records the body core temperature (T_{es}). The subject's left hand lies outside the bathtub inside a large rubber glove. Each glove fingertip is pierced by a tube through which water is continuously pumped into the glove. The water flows back to where it came from, i.e., a temperature-controlled tank. From the bathtub, the subject can activate electrically operated valves with his right hand to regulate the flow of water into the rubber glove. In this way, he feeds the rubber glove with either boiling or ice-cold water. After Cabanac et al. (1972).

(LeMagnen 1960; Sclafani 1978; Sclafani and Springer 1978; Rolls *et al*. 1980) or to hamsters (Tomljenovic-Borer 1974), their food intake will increase so much that they will become obese. Access to abundant (and inexpensive) palatable stimuli may raise the ponderostat setpoint, an effect that perhaps accounts for the epidemic of human obesity today. Indeed, when food intake is made less palatable, subjects seem to adjust their ponderostat setpoint downward (Hashim and Van Italie 1965; Cabanac and Rabe 1976).

Reproduction
In the area of reproduction, scientific experiments are not legion. They nonetheless suggest, as would common sense, that pleasure is adapted to reproductive behavior and that erotic sensations display alliesthesia (Aagmo 1999). Body odors serve as messages and communicate information that guides reproductive behavior. Both male and female subjects can tell a person's sex solely from the smell of his or her shirt (Russel 1976). This olfactory message is not greeted with indifference: the smell of one's spouse is usually liked (Holt and Schleidt 1977), whereas the smell of a stranger is very much disliked (Schleidt *et al*. 1988). Alliesthesia may affect body odors and thus increase one's chances of reproduction. Vaginal odor and its hedonic component are less intense at the time of ovulation (Doty *et al*. 1975). LeMagnen showed a sex difference in the perception of the odor of exaltolide, a highly musky substance. Only adult women perceive this odor and their sensitivity increases strongly at ovulation. Similarly, women are more sensitive than men to the smell of the male hormone testosterone. These differences depend on the hormonal state of the subjects and may vary accordingly (LeMagnen 1952).

Infants are attracted by the smell of compresses impregnated with mother's milk. At six weeks of age, they markedly prefer the milk of their own mother (Russel 1976). This attraction may be seen as part of reproductive behavior broadly speaking, rather than as a simple feeding behavior.

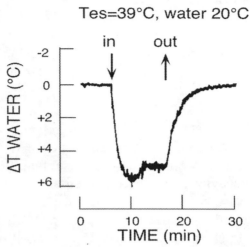

Tes=39°C, water 20°C

Figure III.11 Direct recordings of the temperature difference between water entering and leaving the glove of Figure III.9, as a function of time on the X-axis. 0 to 6 min is the control recording, without the subject's hand. The difference is zero, the water leaving the tank is the same temperature as the water entering. At the first arrow, the hand of an overheated subject (esophagus temperature=39°C) is slid into the glove. For the subject, the cold water of the glove is very pleasant. Immediately, the difference becomes positive: heat leaves the hand and warms the water. When the difference stabilizes, the plateau corresponds to a heat flow of 70 W from the hand. At the second arrow, the subject pulls his hand out of the tank and the difference returns to zero. After Cabanac et al. (1972).

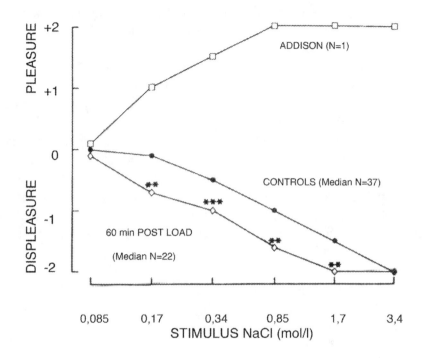

Figure III.12 On the Y-axis, oral responses on a scale of -2 to +2 describe the pleasure (positive) or displeasure (negative) when subjects tasted the saline solutions on the X-axis. The two lower curves indicate the median of N healthy subjects before and after having salt injected directly into their stomachs. There was a negative alliesthesia in response to the stomach injection. The asterisks indicate significant differences. The most interesting curve is the one for a subject suffering from Addison's disease. Because this illness destroys the adrenal glands, the patient no longer had any mineralocorticoids, his kidneys could no longer concentrate urine, and his body was losing sodium. He felt increasing pleasure as salt concentration rose. The most highly concentrated solution caused a very unpleasant sensation in the controls and a very pleasant one in the patient. Such an appetite for salt (positive alliesthesia) would help keep the patient alive in the absence of any other therapy. After Cabanac and Duclaux (1973).

A certain number of studies have dealt with conscious perceptions during orgasm. One point that often preoccupies the public is how the two sexes compare in their sensations. Their autonomic responses during orgasm are measurable but, of course, the approach here is no longer one of asking: "What do you see when I present a yellow light?" The findings should calm the war of the sexes, the respiratory and circulatory autonomic responses being identical in women and men (Bartlett 1955; Fox and Fox 1969). This conclusion is bolstered by an interesting study in which each subject was asked to write a page describing his or her orgasmic sensations. These texts were stripped of all anatomical details that might identify the author's sex and then submitted to groups of readers of both sexes, some of whom were sexologists. The readers could not discern the author's sex from the texts (Vance and Wagner 1976).

Body movement optimization

Body movement sensations can also generate the pleasure/displeasure signal of utility/harmfulness, with no connection at all to the body's internal environment. In the case of these sensations, pleasure or displeasure indicates optimal functioning, as we shall see further on. A movement seems pleasurable more because it is useful to the organism. To date, science has hardly shown any interest in the pleasure of caresses, for which solid empirical knowledge is nonetheless available.[25] The comfort of skin sensations is transmitted by time-dependent (rapidly adapting) mechanical receptors, the pleasure being thus movement-related rather than simply contact-related. This type of pleasure may have been key to species survival.

Body movement is minimized by minimizing effort or, alternately, by maximizing comfort. When a task involves pointing a finger at a target, eye and movement coordination optimizes the accuracy of target coding. Optimal performance clearly correlates with minimization of discomfort (Figure III.13) (Rossetti *et al.* 1994). Aside from the movement itself, intense muscular effort, as in athletic training, produces euphoria (Folkins 1976) through production of opioids in the

---

[25] Thy caress is sweeter than wine" (Cant. 4:10).

brain (Sforzo 1989). This euphoria may strengthen the organism's optimal functioning and thus be a mechanism for the long-term survival of humanity (Sher 1998).

A characteristic form of alliesthesia for sensations from the entire body has recently been reported by Hall *et al.* (2002) and Ekkekakis *et al.* (2004, 2005). Subjects were asked to describe their sensation of work intensity (on a scale of 1 to 6) and pleasure/displeasure (on a scale of -5 to +5) while walking. Work intensity rose, not surprisingly, from 3 to nearly 5 and then sharply fell to 3 just when walking stopped. Hedonic response stood at 2 before the walk began and changed little during the walking session, only to fall and become disagreeable at -1.5 near the end of the session. Rest was almost instantly accompanied by a rise to +3. It is worth noting that during the resting state, *i.e.*, in the absence of any mechanical stimulation from muscle/joint receptors, the pleasure rating rose significantly from +2 (before rest) to +3 (after rest). There is thus a real positive alliesthesia for this kind of perception, with the same resting state being differently rated (Ekkekakis 2003, Ekkekakis *et al.* 2004, 2005).

Finally, another mechanical sensation seems to be subject to alliesthesia. In hypercapnia, the lungs appear to be fuller than they actually are. In normocapnia, the sensation is closer to reality. In sum, this is a case of pulmonary alliesthesia. The discomfort of hypercapnia-induced dyspnea leads to a slower pace of exercise and restoration of a normal internal environment (Katz-Salamon 1986).

Conclusion

This brief review of the literature reveals that sensory pleasure acts as an indicator of the right behavior. Pleasant stimuli are useful; harmful stimuli unpleasant. By seeking and maximizing sensory pleasure for things as different as food, heat, and movement, an organism is driven to optimize its behavior to meet physiological ends. This observation leads to four logical inferences, whose crucial importance will be discussed further on:

If pleasure points behavior in the right direction for energy, nutrition, and reproduction, an organism cannot keep on seeking and consuming the stimulus indefinitely. Once the internal variable has been reset to its setpoint value, the pleasure will disappear. The stimulus that used to be pleasant becomes uninteresting or even unpleasant. Sensory pleasure is thus always transitory. It was no accident that vomitoriums were placed close to Roman orgies. Once relieved of a full stomach, people could return to the pleasures of eating.

Conversely, for the same reasons, displeasure can last indefinitely. If a stimulus arouses displeasure, there is a malfunction or a source of harm. As long as the source of harm has not been eliminated or the malfunction corrected, the feeling of displeasure will remain useful. It may thus be permanent. My friend Édouard Briese, of the Universidad de los Andes in Venezuela, told me about a man from the Andean highlands who suffered all his life from endless headaches, probably because of the low oxygen pressure at high altitudes. On traveling to the coastal lowlands, his headaches disappeared. He did not want to go home.

Stimuli with no physiological impacts are treated with indifference, arousing neither pleasure nor displeasure. If pleasure is felt, it must have been acquired through learning.

The search for sensory pleasure optimizes behavior. Optimization is not a vague concept. On the contrary, it is precise and may be judged on physical and physiological criteria. It is improvement in productivity, *i.e.*, more work is produced over the same length of time. Here time comes into the picture. I will often come back to this notion in the following chapters.

In this chapter, I have discussed primary pleasures from basic sensations and merely touched on pleasures acquired through learning. Older findings were reviewed rapidly, being addressed in greater detail in Cabanac (1979b), and more weight was given to later data and aspects. Pfaffmann (1960) in particular has shown that almost any neutral or even unpleasant sensory stimulus may become pleasant if associated with beneficial effects. Pleasure is thus indirectly confirmed as an indication of utility. Any sensation may eventually display alliesthesia, but alliesthesia is most clearly seen with physiological signals.

Finally, pleasure is not limited to sensory pleasure. I will further on examine the role of these other pleasures that are not closely related to sensations. We will see that the role of pleasure as a driving force for behavior goes beyond the framework of basic sensations, which has been the limit of my discussion so far. There are forms of cognition that simultaneously involve not only several sensory modes but also decision making. Before reviewing the experimental data, I will first cover the theoretical groundwork of McFarland and Sibly and venture into ethology to discuss the concept of the behavioral final common path (McFarland and Sibly 1975).

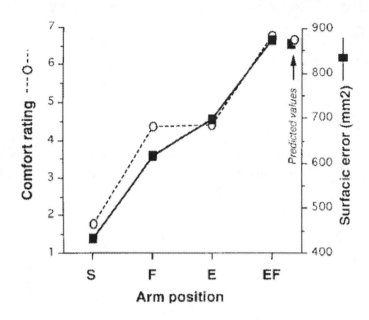

Figure III.13   Subjects were given relatively easy movements and mechanical tasks: point your finger at a target while your arm is in different positions. The researchers recorded the subject's rating of position discomfort (left-hand Y-axis: Affective response) and the geometrical accuracy of the movement (right-hand Y-axis: Surface error). On the X-axis, the letters indicate the positions of the working arm: S= standard spontaneous position; F=maximum twist of the wrist; E=maximum elevation of the arm; EF=combination of E+F. Discomfort increased from S to EF.   At the same time, movement inaccuracy increased from S to EF. Finally, performance and discomfort for EF can be predicted by simply adding the ratings (○) or the performances (■) for F and E. Thus, not only does pleasure optimize movement, but the hedonic dimension is also additive. After Rossetti et al. (1994).

Chapter IV

The common currency of exchange[26]

> When a research program is well developed,
> confirmations and verifications, and not
> efforts of refutation, are what assumes
> importance. ... Thus, a vigorous program
> leads to new predictions.
> Roy, 1998

In nature, a stimulus seldom appears alone. At every moment our senses are bombarded by visual and auditory signals, some of which require a fast response. Meanwhile, motivations are also present with varying degrees of intensity. Hunger, thirst, fatigue, curiosity, various forms of appetite, and physiological, mental, and social urgencies are all competing against each other for satisfaction. But we can do only one thing at a time ... well. Humans and animals alike have to prioritize their actions to satisfy competing motivations.

Behavioral final common path

To describe this convergence of motivations on a single output, McFarland (Fig. IV.1) uses the term "behavioral final common path." He adapted this term from the one that the great physiologist Sherrington had coined for the spinal motor neuron—"final common path." The analogy is a close one. This neuron is the point of

---

[26] After publication of the article on which this chapter is based (Cabanac 1992), the "hedonist" current of behavioral psychology won the support of several writers in the field and became academically respectable by the time the French edition of this book came out in 2003. The same article, however, had been rejected by three other academic journals between its first submission in March 1989 and its publication in the *Journal of Theoretical Biology*. The rejections were accompanied by such flattering comments as "totally lacking in importance and originality." This 3-year hiatus reflected the prevailing attitude at that time to the scientific study of hedonism and consciousness.

convergence for countless excitatory, inhibitory, or reinforcing messages. Such messages—either information or commands—come from points higher up or lower down in the nervous system. They come from the muscle that the motor neuron itself innervates, from antagonistic muscles of the same member, from muscles of the opposite member, from antagonist or synergistic muscles of the entire organism, from various tendon stretch receptors and, evidently, from cerebellar and cortical excitatory and inhibitory inputs. The motor neuron integrates all of these inputs into a common output: a change in membrane potential that will or will not excite the innervated motor unit. This common output may determine muscle tone, reflex motor responses (posture, balance) and, of course, voluntary motor control.

Behavior is similarly determined by a convergence of countless motivations—some complementary, others synergistic, and still others competing against each other for attention. In the last situation, a "motivational conflict," the brain selects the most urgent motivation on the basis of all incoming information. Motivational conflict takes two main forms. In one form, similar positive motivations may enter into conflict. Read a book or watch TV? Chips or salad? This kind of conflict is readily resolved: one of the stimuli is consumed and the corresponding motivation is satiated.

In the second form, two opposing motivations are at loggerheads. One leads to consumption, the other to avoidance. If a fire breaks out at a movie theater, it won't take long to choose the appropriate response: skip the movie and leave the building. But the choice isn't always so clear. Should I ask my boss for a raise … and risk losing my job? Should I put down a fascinating book … to do some chore that can wait? Should I do volunteer work that I love … but takes up all of my free time? Should I get up to breastfeed my child … who's crying in the middle of the night? We have to make decisions at every passing moment because behavior cannot serve more than one motivation at a time. In the case of positive motivations, conflicts may be resolved easily enough, but a decision still has to be made.

Motivational conflicts, especially those involving physiological needs, have become easier to resolve with human progress. A modern home spares us the need to look for habitats with drinkable water and suitable temperatures. Refrigerators make food storage possible, so that we no longer have to go looking for more food after every meal. Clothing maintains a microclimate around our bodies much like that of our remote African ancestors, even at the highest latitudes (Scholander *et al.* 1957). Other techniques and technologies have further freed us from basic survival behaviors. As well, by dividing and specializing labor, we have greatly shortened the time to find and prepare food—from most of the day among our forebears to only a few hours per day.

Nonetheless, we still have to choose among tasks to be done or leisure activities to be enjoyed. At every moment we rank our priorities more or less consciously.

"The necessity for comparing the merits of different courses of actions [implies] that there must be some trade-off mechanism built into the motivational control system. Since the trade-off process must take into account all relevant motivational variables, it is clear that the mechanism responsible must be located at a point of convergence in the motivational organization ..." (McFarland and Sibly 1975).

I have already stated, and will often repeat throughout this text, one of the founding postulates of ethology: animals continually try to satisfy their most urgent motivations by their behavior. Hence, at any moment, behavior is optimal because it has already been tried and tested by natural selection (Tinbergen 1950; Baerends 1956; see also Barrette 2000). This level of optimization is distal. It proceeds indirectly by gradually eliminating suboptimal behaviors with each passing generation. Optimization also takes place at a more proximal level. Ethologists have ignored this level but it will be central to my book.

In their theoretical study of the behavioral final common path, McFarland and Sibly argue that the central nervous system must have a way to prioritize co-occurring motivations. It must translate them into a "common currency" that serves to rank their urgency and compare their trade-offs (McFarland and Sibly 1975; McNamara and Houston 1986). Motivations are thus bumped up or down as they gain or lose priority for behavioral satisfaction. Without a common currency, their different natures would keep them from "speaking to each other." Such

91

prioritizing especially explains a decision to choose unpleasant behaviors, such as doing without food or engaging in tiring muscular work. The same circumstances that produce "negative" currency units might also produce enough "positive" ones to keep the balance positive. Animals choose not to feed when they see a predator or a potential mate because they give higher priority to immediate survival or the chance to procreate.

Figure IV.2 illustrates the way such a mechanism could operate and how it may lead sometimes to displeasurable behaviors being chosen. There are two behaviors:

- The first behavior (1) generates pleasure. Will it be chosen? Yes. The search for pleasure is a positive motivation.
- The other behavior (2) generates displeasure. Will it be chosen? No. The search for displeasure is a negative motivation that leads to avoidance or abstention.
- If, however, behaviors 1 and 2 are closely interlinked and if the net resulting sum of pleasure 1 plus displeasure 2 is positive (*i.e.*, the pleasure of 1 exceeds the displeasure of 2), both behaviors, 1 + 2, will be performed.

Thus, these two motivations can "speak to each other" through the common currency of pleasure, the result being a conscious choice to do something unpleasurable. Of course, such a choice will be made only if the net result of *pleasure - displeasure* remains positive.

Pleasure/displeasure, the common currency of exchange

We have seen how sensory pleasure is closely adapted to physiological needs. Since such needs are often satisfied by a behavioral response, their relative importance may be ranked in terms of their pleasurability, i.e., the common currency postulated by McFarland and Sibly. Imagine how this ranking would work. In situations of motivational conflict, pleasures and displeasures aroused by sensory messages from different neural pathways may be compared with each other with a view to minimizing displeasure and maximizing net pleasure. We have seen that pleasure from sensations of warmth, smell, taste, and posture point the way to behaviors for self-defense or self-assistance. Such sensory pleasures may act as a common currency that expresses the relative values of competing motivations: thermoregulation, hunger, thirst, and fatigue. At each moment, priorities could be ranked by adding up the total pleasure and displeasure from all sensations. The net result could serve to optimize behavior by satisfying the most pleasurable and, hence, most urgent motivations.

Let us go back to the previous examples of motivational conflict. Should I ask my boss for a raise? Only if the risk of losing my job is low or if the chance of getting the raise is high. Should I put down a fascinating book? Only if the chore cannot wait. Should I do volunteer work? Only if I still have free time. Should I get up to breastfeed my baby? Only if the pleasure of stopping the crying and fondling the infant exceeds the displeasure of insomnia.

Without some kind of reward, an unpleasant task will probably not get done. An analogy would be the way our cells combine a likely process with an unlikely one in the ATP (adenosine triphosphate) energy cycle. A costly endothermic process is made possible by a co-occurring exothermic process. Without the energy from the latter, the former would be impossible.

The situation in Figure IV.2 is hypothetical. It has been tested, however, by a series of experiments, described in the next chapter, where subjects are placed in situations of motivational conflict to see whether they maximize the net result of their pleasure and displeasure. There are also echoes in the writings of some pensive authors who have come to similar conclusions simply through introspection. This is hardly surprising. If such mechanisms do exist, they must exist in all of us.

Figure IV.1 Oxford's Ethologist David McFarland in 2001.

After studying feeding behavior and its sensory, cultural, and social determinants, Paul Rozin (1999a) concluded that his findings on the pleasure of eating might apply to other pleasures. Eating is a basic need and central to so many emotional and cultural experiences (Rozin 1999b). All of these eating-related motivations have to "speak to each other" because they all converge on a single behavior. For Baars and Newman, the most intense ideas—or any other mental object—occupy the center-stage of consciousness and thus conceal other, less intense ideas. Attention is thus selective (Baars 1994). In other words, all behaviors must pass through a final common path. This view of behavior is also present in the Decision Affect Theory of Mellers *et al.* (1997), which implies that all kinds of signals are incorporated in decision-making. All of these theories are consistent with the hypothesis of pleasure as a common currency.

Resulting hedonic experience	Action

Behavior 1	a ------> A	*Yes*
Behavior 2	B ------> b	*No*
Behavior 1 + *Behavior 2*	a + B ------> A + b	*Yes*

with $a < A$, *and* $B > b$
and with $a + B < A + b$

Figure IV.2   Theoretical representation of the way pleasure, the common currency, is used to compare behavior 1, which produces pleasure, and behavior 2, which produces displeasure. Behavior 2 may be chosen if the overall result of combining it with behavior 1 is pleasurable (Cabanac 1992).

Equally consistent is the theoretical work of Williams (1979). He introspectively defines and describes conflicting social motivations and uses the expression "common currency" to indicate the need for social motivations to speak to each other. He suspects that this common currency could be pleasure. Plutchik and Axe (1967) use the same reasoning to come to the same conclusions. They argue that emotions are mixed states because the underlying motivations are competing with each other. The same concept of emotion as a mixed state has been tested experimentally by Fredrickson and Levenson (1998), who have shown that positive, pleasant emotions hasten recovery from the aftereffects of negative, unpleasant emotions. It looks as though dissimilar emotions cannot coexist on the center-stage of consciousness. Fredrickson (2000) even suggests that positive emotions not only counter negative emotions and gloom, but also broaden the thinking processes of individuals, apparently because such processes involve the same final common path. I will discuss this point further on (Chapter XI). Recently, when Price *et al.* (2001) studied the role of emotion in decision-making during motivational conflict, they concluded that it played a central role. In particular, they propose that decision-making is emotional and depends on adding up the positive and negative of desire, expectation, and (hedonic?) experience. These authors do not define emotion. If we use the definition I propose further on,[27] their article fully confirms the central place of hedonicity in decision-making.

> "A major challenge confronting the decision paradigm is the generally poor fit achieved in empirical analyses of behavior that are guided by decision theory. In attempts to use decision models to explain or predict such wide-ranging behaviors as job choice, migration, contraception, criminal activity, and self-protective measures against health, home and work-place risks, the fraction of explained variance has generally been low" (Loewenstein 1996).

By way of explanation, Loewenstein suggests that the authors ignore "visceral" influences on behavior (hunger, sleep, fatigue, etc). Such influences would explain cases of apparently maladaptive behavior. I believe he's right, and this comes back to my proposal of pleasure as a common currency. The experimental bases for this proposal will be discussed further in the next two chapters.

In recent years, several authors have unequivocally expressed similar views on the place of pleasure in decision-making.

Fazio (2000) calls attitude a positive or negative bias toward something or someone and sees it as having functional value. Attitudes facilitate decision-making and improve decision quality, thus freeing the subject to deal with other sources of stress. For this author, however, attitude is harmful when the object has changed somewhat or when attention should focus on an object that is not the current focus of an attitude. Zernicki (2002) similarly defends the idea that the hedonic dimension of consciousness is the dimension of decision-making and that it's along this dimension that the different influences leading to action are added up. Finally, Finucane et al. (2003) argue that decision-making rests on a subtle dialogue between rationality and affectivity.[28]

---

[27] Chapter XI.

[28] They use the word "affect" with its former connotation of "good/bad." Lately, English-speaking authors have been equating it with "emotion."

These authors implicitly recognize that different signals have to speak to each other. This conversation, I would add, is made possible by the common currency of pleasure. Such a conclusion was made by Wolf (1996) and has been formally adopted by Ovsich (1998) and Mellers (2000). Ovsich propounds the concept of "pleasantness of the condition of a subject," which would be the sum of all vectors that make up the stream of consciousness. Though differently expressed, this concept is consistent with those of the final common path and of pleasure as a common currency, to Ovsich, "pleasantness plays the role of a common and integrating orientational measure." Mellers has reviewed the place given to pleasure in the psychological literature and agrees that pleasure is key to predicting which decision is chosen.

In the next chapter, we will review findings from human experimentation. But we should first mention that animal experimentation has already provided indirect support for this hypothesis. Do animals feel pleasure? That question will be examined in Chapter X. The evidence is indeed indirect and subject to caution. Nonetheless, rats seem to perceive a taste as pleasurable or not by adding up all of the different taste sensations, these being an array of multiple and distinct inputs (Young and Christensen 1962). When rats perceive or anticipate sensory pleasure in different situations, they release a neurotransmitter, dopamine, that might be the common currency that mediates pleasure.[29] There may thus be a similar adding up of sensory inputs for all senses taken together, the common output being a behavior that tends to maximize the net result: total pleasure + total displeasure.

We will confront this theoretical model with experimental evidence in the next chapter.

---

[29] S. Nicolaïdis. Seminar at Université Laval, November 5, 2002.

Chapter V
Physiological motivations in conflict: How pleasure integrates sensations and optimizes behavior

O that you would kiss me with the kisses
of your mouth! For your love is better
than wine
Song of Solomon, 1:2

Chapter III showed us the close fit between sensory pleasure and physiological needs in each example so far examined. Since many physiological functions are fulfilled through behavior, pleasure may be the common currency in choosing behavioral responses. Such is the hypothesis of many ethologists. After reviewing the theoretical background in the last chapter, we will now present experimental evidence from situations of motivational conflict. In each case, we will look for the role of sensory pleasure in decision-making and will examine whether subjects choose the behavior that comes closest to being physiologically optimal. The experiments will focus on three types of conflict. The first and simplest type will pit two tastes against each other. The second one will involve the different sensory motivations that walking generates in the body, *i.e.*, several physiological signals from different parts of the body will be in conflict for the performance of a simple task: physical exercise. The third and most complex conflict will take place between two very different sensations: fatigue and thermal comfort.

All three experiments will use the same 3-step approach:
- explore pleasure or displeasure from one of two stimuli in conflict along a continuum of increasing intensity, e.g., increasingly cold ambient temperatures;
- do the same with the other stimulus, e.g., fatigue from walking on a treadmill with steeper and steeper gradients. The resulting data are used

to plot a 2-dimensional "pleasure map." The X- and Y-axes represent the two sensations in conflict;

- simultaneously present the two stimuli and let the subject alter either variable until an optimal position is reached on the pleasure map.

First conflict: sweet *vs.* sour

The simplest conflict is between two sensations from the same sense of taste: sweet and sour. The approach is outlined above. During the first session, the subject tastes a series of increasingly sour samples and rates the pleasure/displeasure of the taste, either a positive number for the intensity of pleasure or a negative number for the intensity of displeasure. During the second session, the subject tastes a series of increasingly sweet samples and rates the pleasure/displeasure of the taste. During the third session, the subject is no longer asked for an opinion. A series of increasingly sour samples is presented and the subject may adjust the sugar concentration to get the most desirable taste. A series of increasingly sweet samples is then presented and the subject may adjust acidity to get the most desirable taste.

When the experimenters (Chantal Ferber and myself) presented a sample that was both sweet and sour, the pleasure of sweetness was not always independent of the pleasure of sourness. For example, when presented with several samples of constant acidity and increasing sugar concentration, the subject was not asked to rate the combined pleasure of acidity and sugar concentration. The two variables were rated independently, the same sample being presented twice without the subject knowing that it was the same. The two ratings could be highly dissociated from each other. An acidity of pH 3.5 tasted best at a sugar concentration of about 0.4 mole/l. At the same pH, the sugar concentration tasted best at about 2 mole/l (Cabanac and Ferber 1987).

Once all pH levels and sugar concentrations had been fully investigated, a 2-D pleasure map could be plotted. The subjects were free to make their own mixtures. For a given acidity, the sugar concentration could be freely adjusted, and vice versa. In this search for taste pleasure, an optimal mixture might reflect the preferred pH, the preferred sugar concentration, or a compromise between the two.

This initial experiment led to two conclusions. First, the subject could clearly distinguish between sensations from two different though related sensory modes (tastes), the pleasure from each sensation being exchangeable. Second, if allowed to choose freely, a subject would just as likely seek pleasure from either sensation.

Thus, both tastes seemed to be tapping into the same pleasure. This finding is consistent with the use of a common currency by competing motivations, as postulated by McFarland and Sibly (1975). Here the competing motivations were pleasure and displeasure from different pH levels and sugar concentrations.

Nothing indicates, however, that taste choice was being optimized. Chapter II presented us with a law of psychophysiology: pleasant = useful. Ultimately, the subjects should have been optimizing the utility of the stimulus, yet their preference for sweet or sour had only a remote relationship to utility. This shortcoming will be corrected in the next two experiments.

Second conflict: legs *vs.* chest

Chen *et al.* (1999) recently studied fatigue. They placed subjects on an exercise bicycle for 10 min and measured oxygen consumption, shortness of breath, and leg effort while gradually raising the pedaling speed to a maximum power output of 180 W. As pedaling speed rose, so did oxygen consumption, *i.e.*, physiological cost. Perception of leg effort also rose, but not at the same rate. Oxygen consumption was least at 60 rpm and higher at slower and faster speeds. In contrast, shortness of breath and leg effort were least at 80 rpm. Leg effort intensified at higher and lower pedaling speeds and shortness of breath peaked at 100 rpm. A conflict thus developed between minimizing oxygen consumption and minimizing leg effort at power outputs less than 180 W. What was optimal for one was less so for the other. Is this inconsistent with the idea of pleasure as a common currency? Two points:
- The experimenters imposed all of the physical exercise parameters. These constraints probably interfered with perception of comfort since shortness of breath, leg effort, and oxygen consumption increase

differently at increasing speeds. It would have been interesting to let the subjects choose at least one parameter and study their sensations;

- The exercise lasted only 10 min, not long enough to reach stable exercise conditions. In particular, it was after 10 min that the core temperature began to rise and that major circulatory adjustments were being made for muscular effort. It would have been better to observe subjects under stable exercise conditions.

Both shortcomings were avoided in my 1985 study (Cabanac 1985). The subjects had to ascend a 300-m rise in elevation on a treadmill whose angle of slope could be varied and whose speed determined the time they took to ascend the 300 m. A 3-step approach was used, similar to the sweet vs. sour experiment. Each subject was tested in 25 successive sessions, with either slope angle or treadmill speed being varied over a wide range of slopes and speeds. During these sessions, the subjects were periodically asked to rate the pleasure/displeasure they felt in their chest and legs. The ratings were used to plot pleasure as a function of two dimensions: legs and chest.

Changes to treadmill speed or slope tended to cause specific responses in different parts of the body. When speed increased, unpleasant sensations of fatigue would appear in the leg muscles. When slope increased, the sensations would appear primarily in the chest: tachycardia and shortness of breath, both equally unpleasant. During each session, I periodically asked the subject to focus on either part of the body and verbally rate the degree of local discomfort in the chest or the legs. The lines in Figure V.2 represent the ratings at the end of each session, *i.e.*, under stable exercise conditions.

Leg discomfort is plotted in the top graph (Figure V.2) for different combinations of treadmill slope and speed. The -1 line is the discomfort threshold and the -2 line is the discomfort rating. Leg discomfort varies almost linearly.

Chest discomfort is plotted in the middle graph and combines shortness of breath and tachycardia. There seem to be two thresholds perpendicular to each other and parallel to the coordinate axes. The top graph and middle graph were combined through simple addition to generate the bottom graph. These composite curves roughly correspond to an equilateral hyperbola.

The three response profiles can now be compared with the actual behavior when one variable (speed or slope) was held constant and the other freely adjusted by the subject. This was the third step of the experiment. In a series of eight sessions, the subjects were simply told to adjust the speed with slope held constant or the slope with speed held constant. They were not asked to focus on their sensations. They could freely move about on the pleasure map, as plotted from the results of the preceding sessions. Regardless of whether slope or speed was held constant, these sessions had remarkably similar outcomes. The subjects adjusted the free variable to make the 300-m ascension last the same length of time from one session to the next (Figure V.1).

These behavioral choices were recorded at the end of the sessions, when the discomfort thresholds were recorded, and plotted on each of the three graphs of Figure V.2. The choices are indicated by black dots on the pleasure maps, *i.e.*, the three graphs of the figure. Clearly, the last graph shows the best fit between behavior and sensation—the algebraic sum of displeasure in the legs and chest. This impression is confirmed by statistical analysis. Leg and chest sensations thus seemed to speak to each other. This finding not only confirms the previous results on exchanges between taste pleasure and displeasure, but also shows that the body seeks to optimize effort. The subjects made their bodies work at a constant power output, the 300 m being ascended in a constant time (ca. 40 min for the subject in Figure V.1). Yet they had no stopwatches and no awareness that they were keeping time. So how did they do it? By listening to their bodies and minimizing leg or chest discomfort.

As with the sense of taste, we again see the exchangeability of hedonic sensations—in this case, negative ones from the legs and chest. Yet these sensations differ much more from each other. The ones from the legs are muscle pains and the ones from the chest are a pounding heart and shortness of breath. Nonetheless, this difference did not prevent the subjects from comparing them on a common hedonic dimension. We also see that pleasure maximization—or rather displeasure minimization, which amounts to the same thing—optimizes behavior. By superimposing muscular effort choices and hedonic thresholds, we find that the thresholds determine a constant power output. Yet walking conditions varied considerably for both slope and speed.

The next example will use the same approach. Sensations will differ even more, however, and will come from walking and from increasingly cold ambient temperatures.

Third conflict: Ambient temperature *vs*. muscular exercise

The third experiment pitted very different motivations against each other: muscular effort and thermal conflict. Not only were the sensory modes radically different, but subjects also had to manipulate two highly different environmental variables: ambient temperature and treadmill slope, and not just intensity of muscular effort as in the last experiment. Here again, we used a 3-step approach. First, we collected subject ratings of pleasure or displeasure at various ambient temperatures.   Second, in another series of sessions, we collected ratings of pleasure/displeasure from subjects walking on a treadmill with varying slopes. The subject walked at a constant speed and we simply altered the slope to increase or decrease intensity of effort. With these two series, we were able to plot a pleasure map in two dimensions (Figure V.3). The figure presents the algebraic sum of the two ratings   (pleasure/displeasure of muscular effort and ambient temperature). The isohedonic lines mark off pleasure areas (white) and displeasure areas (gray with shades that darken with increasing displeasure).

The pleasure map shows a third series of ten sessions: five sessions where the subject could choose treadmill slope with ambient temperature held constant and five where, inversely, ambient temperature could be chosen with treadmill slope held constant. The two environmental variables were antagonistic. When walking speed was constant, an increase in treadmill slope meant more muscle power output and, thus, more body heat. The subject would tend to heat up. When ambient temperature decreased, more heat was lost and the body cooled down. The heat loss could be countered by a steeper treadmill

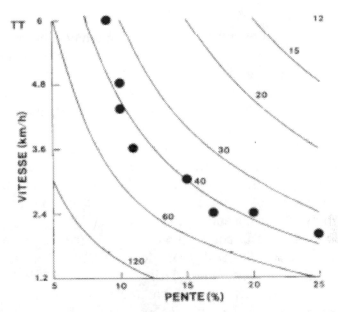

Figure V.1 Subjects were placed on a treadmill whose slope (PENTE) and speed (VITESSE) could be adjusted. Over eight sessions, slope was held constant at 10%, 15%, 20%, and 25% and then speed was held constant at 2.4, 3.6, 4.8, and 6 km/h. When slope was held constant, the subject could choose the speed and, conversely, when speed was held constant, the subject could choose the slope. Subjects knew they could periodically alter their choices. The only instruction was to climb a rise in elevation of 300 m. On the figure, numbers above the equilateral curves indicate how long the subject took to climb 300 m for different slope/speed combinations. Dots indicate actual behavioral choices over the eight sessions. The dots all fall along a curve corresponding to a duration of about 40 min. Subjects behaved identically for a wide variety of speeds and slopes, thus choosing to make their muscles, circulation, and respiration work at a constant power output. After Cabanac (1985).

slope or facilitated by a lower ambient temperature. Depending on which variable was held constant, subjects could respond to cold by increasing treadmill slope and intensity of muscular effort or by raising ambient temperature. Conversely, subjects could respond to heat by lowering ambient temperature or by decreasing treadmill slope.

Lightly shaded areas on the map have a positive total of the two ratings for muscular effort and thermal comfort. Within these 2-dimensional spaces, the overall feeling is one of pleasure and the subject chooses behaviors that will maintain this hedonic state.

Choices are indicated by black dots on the pleasure map. As can be seen, subjects always positioned themselves in a lightly shaded area. Their choice of behavior integrated all hedonic information from completely different sensory modes. This 2-dimensional pleasure was their motivation. Nybo and Nielsen (2001) have shown that the electroencephalogram of subjects working under hot conditions integrates both hyperthermia and fatigue.

This experiment tells us something else. As in the last experiment, optimality was inferred from physiological sensations, and behavior served to maintain optimality. For each subject, muscular effort was proportional to loss of heat to the environment and, according to electrocardiograms, the pace of walking was adjusted to keep heart rate within the zone of aerobic efficiency. Clearly, the subjects had no other information than the sensations from their own bodies. The search for sensory pleasure thus brought their behavior into line with optimal thermoregulation and cardiopulmonary activity. The three experiments of this chapter have provided highly instructive findings:
- experimental proof that the hedonic dimension is exchangeable among different sensations. This is true not only for a single sensory mode, such as the tastes of related flavors, but also between sensations as different as muscular effort, shortness of breath/tachycardia, and thermal comfort;
- evidence, in the last two experiments, that behavior is optimized by a search for 2-dimensional sensory pleasure, as mapped by physiological criteria.

The experiments created a conflict between strictly physiological motivations of homeostasis and thermoregulation. Decision-making, however, has to consider not only physiological motivations, but also motivations on other levels of mental life. Eating food, for example, is both cognitive and affective (Cantin and Dubé 1999). Because behavior is not limited to serving physiological needs and because most of our time is actually used for non-physiological tasks, one might ask

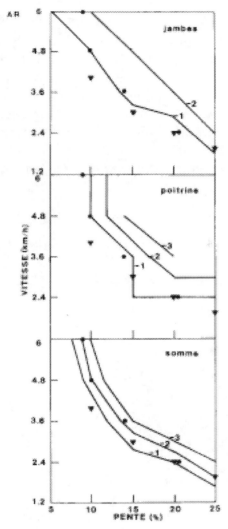

Figure V.2 a) Example of verbal responses in a conflict situation—legs (jambes) vs. chest (poitrine). In each of a series of sessions, the subject had to climb the equivalent of 300 m of altitude on a treadmill of varying slope (PENTE) and varying speed (VITESSE). Over a series of twenty-five sessions, the five speeds on the Y-axis were combined with the five slopes on the X-axis. The three graphs show the isohedonic curves plotted by interpolation, based on personal ratings of discomfort

in the legs (top) and chest (middle). The bottom graph is the algebraic sum of the other two graphs.

b) On each of the three maps, black dots represent the choices in eight new sessions where the subject could choose one variable while the other was held constant. Triangular dots indicate that slope was held constant and speed varied. Round dots indicate that speed was held constant and slope varied. Subject choice was more intercorrelated when the two sets of results are added together (bottom) than when they are presented separately (top and middle). After Cabanac (1985).

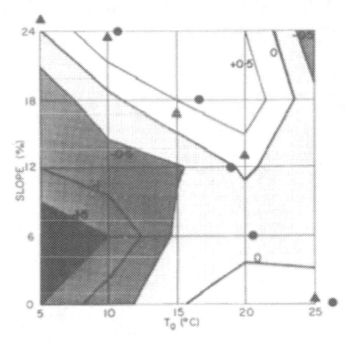

Figure V.3 Example of a map for one subject, showing how pleasure and displeasure are added up over a 2-dimensional sensory space. The Y-axis is treadmill slope and the X-axis is ambient temperature. The isohedonic lines, and the shading between them, indicate subject rating of pleasure/displeasure following a 1-hour walking session. The lines were obtained by interpolation between grid intersections. The darker the shading, the lower the comfort rating. White areas indicate an overall positive rating for both dimensions.

108

This map represents slope and ambient temperature chosen by the subject following an hour of walking when either slope (round dots) or ambient temperature (triangular dots) was held constant. As may be seen, the triangles and the circles form a single population of dots. Subjects thus adjusted either variable to produce the same outcome. Eight out of ten dots are in the white area. The other two are either on a boundary or in an area where pleasure is impossible but displeasure is minimal. The subject thus tended to maximize 2-dimensional pleasure. Finally, we see that intensity of effort increases almost linearly with decreasing ambient temperature. The effort chosen by the subject, when maximizing sensory pleasure, is optimal for thermoregulation. After Cabanac and LeBlanc (1983).

whether this schema could also encompass curiosity, gambling, love of money, and any other motivation. In other words, do these conclusions apply to other sorts of pleasure? Do they apply to "mental pleasures" as opposed to the sensory pleasures of our previous examples? This question will be addressed in the next chapter.

Chapter VI

Non-physiological motivations in conflict: Pleasure still optimizes behavior

Man does not live by bread alone.
Deuteronomy, VIII:3

The last chapter showed the exchangeability of pleasure from different sources: taste, muscle fatigue, shortness of breath, heart rate, and body temperature. All of these pleasures were sensory in origin if we define sensation as in Chapter II. In addition, the underlying motivations (fatigue, comfort) led to behaviors with strictly physiological aims. When our subjects varied muscular effort or ambient temperature, their choices directly affected their respiratory, circulatory, and thermoregulatory functions. They behaved in a way that altered the supply of energy-carrying metabolites in their blood, muscles, and liver, as well as such internal constants as their oxygen level and core temperature.

Other motivations, however, also jostle for access to behavior. Our daily lives are full of behaviors with no direct physiological impacts, e.g., working at a desk, reading a book, listening to the radio, or conversing with someone. The physiological costs are negligible, yet such behaviors generate much pleasure or displeasure. Are these feelings similar in nature to the sensory pleasures of the previous chapters? Do they display the same exchangeability? To answer this question, we will examine the non-physiological, 'mental' pleasures of such activities as winning money or playing video games.

Pain and cold in exchange for money

The first experiment pitted pain against money. To produce pain, you can tie a tourniquet around your arm or leg to cut off circulation and starve downstream tissues of oxygen. The pain is acute. Though ideal for finding the pain perception threshold, this method is dangerous for

111

seeing how long you can withstand the pain, for lesions may develop in the oxygen-starved tissues. Yet this was the aim of my experiment. I thus chose a safer method, isometric contraction, where you have to adopt a sitting position with your back against a wall and your legs at right angles, but without a seat. Such a position can be maintained only by keeping your extensor muscles fully contracted.[30] You don't move and the contraction keeps blood from irrigating your muscles. A painful ischemia soon appears and steadily increases to the point of becoming intolerable. This was the pain that my subjects endured for a monetary reward (Cabanac 1986).

The subjects could halt the session at any time by sliding to the ground. A counter was placed in front to show how much money was being accumulated with each passing second. It would stop counting once the subject had halted the pain by sliding to the floor. The longer the session lasted, the larger the final amount of money, but the rate of accumulating the money varied from one session to the next When the rate of accumulation was slow, the pain soon became intolerable and the subject would quickly put an end to the session, to the pain, and to the increase in the reward. When the rate of accumulation was high, the pain took longer to become intolerable and the session could last twice as long (Figure VI.1). To keep session sequence from affecting the results, each subject was given a different sequence of sessions by means of a Latin square.

With Ken Johnson, we conducted a similar experiment with the temperature falling progressively during the session (Johnson and Cabanac 1983). The longer the subjects chose to stay, the more money they earned. But the money accumulated at different rates in different sessions. Two experiments—pain vs. money and cold discomfort vs. money—produced almost the same results. Both showed a logarithmic exchange between discomfort/pain and money. The reward had to increase exponentially to produce a linear increase in pain tolerance. The duration (D) of the session is described by equation VI.1:

$$D = k \cdot Log\tau + c \qquad \text{Equation VI.1}$$

(Johnson and Cabanac 1983; Cabanac 1986)

---

[30] This exercise is part of the training for competing downhill skiers.

Note: τ is the rate of monetary reward per unit of time and k and c are constants.

This relation is consistent with the diminishing value of money, as first proposed by Bernouilli (1738) and repeatedly confirmed by the economists Lipsey *et al.* (1984). Indeed, when Stevens (1959) measured the desirability of money by a questionnaire, the answers confirmed the micro-economist belief that successive increases in money have progressively less value even though each increase is identical to the next.

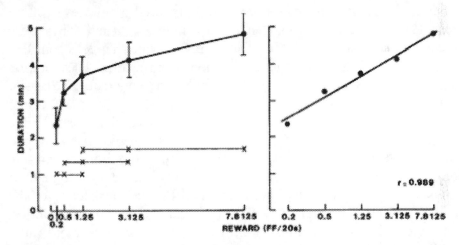

Figure VI.1 Outcome of pain vs. money conflict for a group of ten subjects. The X-axis displays how much money (French Francs) was accumulated for each 20 s of pain tolerance, using a linear scale on the left and a logarithmic scale on the right. The Y-axis displays how long (minutes) the pain was tolerated. On the left, the bars above and below each dot indicate standard error. Means differ significantly if not joined by a common line (x-x). On the right, the same results are presented on a logarithmic scale (X-axis). The correlation coefficient is r. The response follows an exponential curve with an exponent of 0.5 (less than 1). After Cabanac (1986).

These three experiments provide several significant findings:

- When the subjects were placed in a real situation, they had no trouble comparing physiological discomfort (pain or cold) with a purely mental reward (money). These physiological and mental signals could speak to each other, one being traded for another. Not only did they speak to each other, they also expressed themselves in mutually understandable quantitative terms.

- Besides being quantitative, this internal dialogue came about in the absence of any conscious calculation. The subjects acted on the strength of their sensations, without thinking about the outcome. They made their decisions on the fly and ignored memories of other sessions, or even of what happened a few minutes earlier. They were unaware that their response to discomfort or pain changed from one session to the next as a function of monetary reward. They had no idea that their decisions followed a simple mathematical law, that of equation VI.1.

- After the last session, while analyzing the results, we told the subjects about their behavior. Some were convinced that they had ruined the experiment because they had carefully monitored their pain or discomfort, as requested, but were evidently unable to analyze their physiological states. They were stupefied by the consistency of the actual results. Although they willingly endured thermal discomfort and the pain of ischemia from one session to the next, their willingness was barely conscious and not rational, strictly speaking. Of course, they consciously chose their behavior and they were aware of their discomfort and the increasing monetary reward. But they were not reasoning. Their thoughts went no further than whatever was agreeable or disagreeable. Unbeknownst to them, a natural dialogue was going on between the motivation of money and those of discomfort or pain. Decisions were being made consciously but not rationally.

David McFarland repeated this experiment at Oxford, while adding a third dimension: family attachment. The subjects earned money that went not to themselves, but to family members. The outcome was similar but with an extra twist: the closer the kinship with the family member, the more the subjects would suffer for money.[31] In this study, as in the last one, they willingly suffered for this social and clearly non-sensory pleasure.

These experimental findings raise two questions:
- Money is like energy in the way it functions. The similarity is learned of course—young children have no idea of the power of money—but is nonetheless quite real. Could it be that this similarity contaminates the desire to earn money? The motivation for money would then be closely related to biological motivations. To answer this question, other motivations need investigation.
- Although pain is very disagreeable and clearly hedonic in nature, one may wonder whether this dimension of consciousness is where conflicting motivations are arbitrated. To answer this question, we must investigate the actual life experiences of subjects.

The following experiments investigated not only subject behavior, as above, but also perceptions of pleasure or displeasure. These pleasure ratings were compared with actual behavior. We will see that similar laws seem to govern physiological and mental pleasure. Besides money, the pleasure of video-game playing was also used as a reward. The experiments followed the same approach as the one in the last chapter for sensations. In two stages of investigation, the subject rated the pleasure/displeasure of each motivational conflict by choosing from a range of possible perceptions. In a third stage, the two motivations were simultaneously presented and the subject had to choose a solution to the conflict. The choices were then compared with pleasure/displeasure ratings from previous sessions.

Palatability *vs.* money

This experiment tested the hypothesis that pleasure is the common currency for money, mental pleasure, and tastiness—a sensory pleasure. It broke new ground by investigating conflict between the pleasure of tasting food and the displeasure of losing money. Tastiness is a complex piece of information that describes food acceptability and

---

[31] Paper at the Prerational Intelligence conference, ZIF-Bielefeld, 1994.

includes flavor, texture, smell, appearance, etc. (Letarte *et al.* 1997). The overall sensation, however, is easily obtained from subjects. As for money, adult subjects readily agree on the pleasure of winning and the displeasure of losing.

Ten subjects had four meals in our laboratory on four different days and each time were paid a lump sum for their participation (Cabanac 1995). At each meal, they were served ten different kinds of small canapés (open-faced sandwiches served as appetizers) on ten plates.[32] On the first day, during the first meal, each subject ate one canapé from each plate and rated its tastiness. A second canapé was taken from each plate to confirm the ratings. Each time, the experimenter carefully recorded how the subject rated each plate. Next, the subjects were allowed to eat as many as they wished and the total number each of them ate during this first meal was discretely recorded. The exercise was repeated over the next three days at noon, but now the subjects had to pay for each canapé, the price being higher for reportedly tastier ones. This price increase varied over the three meals (Figure VI.2, left). Of course, the subjects were never short of cash because the total price never exceeded their payment for participation. In addition, they were asked to eat as many canapés as they had eaten the first time, so they would not have saved money by eating less.

Not surprisingly, the results (Figure VI.2, right) show that the subjects preferred high tastiness and low prices. When the two were in conflict, subjects preferred the less tasty canapés. They returned to the tastier ones when the price was not high. Subject behavior depended so much on these two variables that it could be predicted from estimated tastiness and canapé price.

Hsee (1999) shows that people do not necessarily choose to get what they like. They also factor in rational data on financial cost. Such behavior is considered inconsistent by the author, yet it is very similar to the way the subjects behaved in the above experiment.

This outcome confirms that the sensory pleasure of taste is processed by the same path that processes the purely mental displeasure of

---

[32] Tastefully prepared by Pierre Samson.

spending or saving money. The same pattern holds up in the next experiment where a physiological motivation is pitted not against money but against the pleasure of video-game playing.

Video-game playing *vs.* cold ambient temperature

This experiment pitted the mental pleasure of playing a video game against the sensory displeasure of steadily falling ambient temperature during the session. The aim was to test the hypothesis that all behaviors are motivated by a pleasure-maximizing tendency, which would here involve both sensory and mental pleasure. We chose video-game playing because, as already mentioned, people see money as being like energy in the way it functions and this similarity might make it more of a physiological motivation than a mental one. By comparison, video games are a more purely mental motivation and one that fascinates teens of all ages, gluing them to computer screens for days on end.

First, each motivation was separately experienced by means of a cold chamber and a video game. The subjects periodically rated the pleasure or displeasure they felt during an hour of exposure. Next, the two motivations were presented simultaneously and we recorded the time the subjects spent in the cold chamber. Actual behavior (tolerance of cold) could then be compared with pleasure/displeasure ratings of the two variables in conflict. In particular, we wanted to find the combined hedonic rating, *i.e.*, video-game pleasure minus cold discomfort. Although games become more enjoyable the faster an action produces the desired result (Hsee and Abelson 1991), this speed factor did not enter into the ratings. Subjects were simply asked periodically to rate the pleasure they currently felt and they could also choose the game they preferred from a list at their disposal. It's known that video-game playing is accompanied by dopamine production (Koepp *et al.* 1998) and that dopamine is released in the brain under a certain number of generally pleasant circumstances.

Twelve subjects, six men and six women, were individually placed in this motivational conflict between the pleasure of video-game playing and the increasing discomfort of an ever colder environment

(Cabanac 1989). Figure VI.3 shows results from subjects who stayed the shortest (left) and the longest (right) in the cold.

Discomfort steadily increased with time spent in the cold chamber. In addition, the pleasure of playing was low for the subject on the left whereas it was high and increasing for the subject on the right. The arrow indicates the time when each subject chose to halt the conflict. This length of time is close to the one predicted from the combined rating of cold discomfort and game-playing pleasure.

Figure VI.4 shows results for all subjects. The results raise a problem: the time actually spent in the cold chamber (solid line) always exceeded the theoretical duration (dotted line), *i.e.*, the time until the negative rating of the cold equaled the positive rating of the game playing. Initially, I thought that this finding contradicted the working hypothesis. I expected the subjects to halt their sessions once the discomfort had become equal to the pleasure, yet they stayed about 5 min longer in the cold. After some thought, I realized that this difference actually confirmed the working hypothesis. When discomfort and pleasure were equal, there was no longer any reason to stay in the cold, but there was no reason to leave either. The decision to leave took place a few minutes later once cold discomfort had *exceeded* video-game pleasure.

This result clearly supports the starting hypothesis. Pleasure is the common currency that serves to compare, and exchange, motivations as different as thermal discomfort and game playing, not to mention tastiness, money, and pain, as shown previously.

A remark is needed on the methodology. The experiments of this chapter are at the crossroads of experimental psychology and microeconomics. They draw on the methodologies of both disciplines. Subjects must receive real and not symbolic rewards, they must not be misled, and the procedure must be free of ambiguity (Hertwig and Ortmann 2001). These criteria were met. The experiments sought decisions and real choices, rather than answers to questionnaires as is often true for studies in microeconomics. Nonetheless, at first glance the conclusion may seem self-evident.

The decisions people choose are the ones that maximize pleasure. So what? I can answer this objection in two ways:

- First, the link between pleasure and behavior is not automatic. Some subjects maximize one source of pleasure more than others do. This flexibility in itself is significant. To understand why one behavior is chosen and not another, we must add up all of the costs and benefits. Otherwise, we will find that some subjects surprisingly fail to choose what they like (Hsee 1999).

- Pleasure maximization seems self-evident to us because we each experience this mechanism in our daily mental lives. The above experiments, however, provide an objective view of what is happening in our minds and those of others. We personally experience decision-making, but the underlying mechanisms are not self-evident. Hence the surprise of my subjects on learning the results. They had fitted their behavior quantitatively to the costs and benefits of each situation they had been placed in. What is interesting and new is not this behavior, long known to micro-economists, but rather its being accomplished through pleasure maximization in two dimensions, *i.e.*, the algebraic sum of the pleasures and displeasures of two conflicting variables. This finding is confirmed by electroencephalography. EEG records show that the frontal lobe is activated in proportion to loss of money. The activation occurs immediately after one learns about the loss (265 ms) and may be involved in mental states of decision-making (Gehring and Willoughby 2002).

We first observed the laws of pleasure maximization in situations of sensory conflict. We have now seen that they also apply in conflicts beyond the realm of physiological motivations, in the realm of money or game playing. In such situations, decision-making maximized the pleasure of the moment. Each subject's past certainly determined the value attached to the money or the game playing, but the influence of time seemed to stop there. The subject's immediate past or memory did not seem to affect the pleasure experience that led to decision-making. This finding is consistent with the Decision Affect Theory of Mellers *et al.* (1997). For these authors, decision-making incorporates experienced pleasure, reward expectations, and risk assessment in a total hedonic perception.

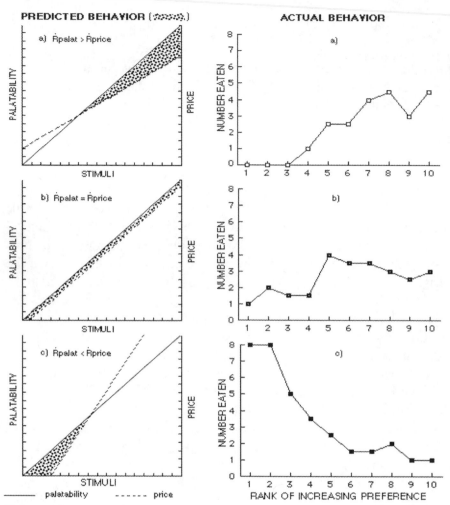

Figure VI.2   Left: Theoretical presentation of money vs. tastiness conflict and expected results. X-axis: in a), b), and c) canapés are ranked by increasing tastiness. Y-axis: continuous line is the mean tastiness rating; broken line is cost of each canapé. Cost rises more slowly than tastiness in a), at the same speed as tastiness in b), and faster than tastiness in c). Shaded zones indicate more pleasure than displeasure.

Right: Results - Y-axis: number of canapés eaten. X-axis: the ten canapés ranked in order of increasing tastiness. In a) the subjects mainly ate tastier canapés. In b) they ate all of the canapés. In c) they mainly ate less tasty canapés. Actual behavior in a), b), and c) on right matches theoretical prediction (shaded zones) on left. After Cabanac (1995).

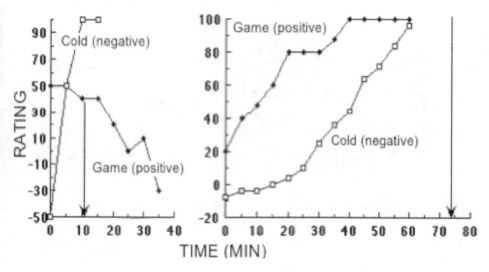

Figure VI.3   Results from subjects who stayed the shortest (a psychology student, left) and the longest (a physics student, right) in the cold chamber during their conflict session. Positive ratings of video-game playing were obtained during one session (♦). Negative ratings of cold discomfort were obtained in another session (□). At the beginning of this session, the warm ambient temperature was pleasant and rated positively. To make comparison of the two ratings easier and to superimpose one curve onto the other, the ratings of cold discomfort were multiplied by -1 on the figure. During the third session, the video game and the cold were presented simultaneously. The arrow indicates the duration actually tolerated by each subject. After Cabanac (1989).

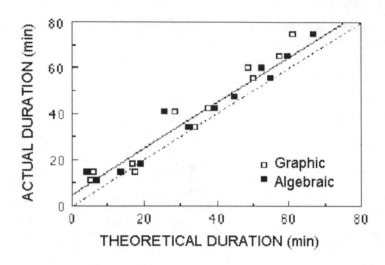

Figure VI.4 Actual duration of conflict sessions of 12 subjects as a function of theoretical duration. The predicted (theoretical) duration was calculateded in two ways: 1) by a graph, the first intersection of the two curves for rating of game-playing pleasure and rating of cold discomfort; and 2) by calculation, using two equations: game rating = f(time) and cold rating = g(time) and assuming: game rating+cold rating=zero. The straight line is the regression line of actual duration vs. theoretical duration. It is obtained algebraically (y = 0.99x + 5.2, with r = 0.96). The regression line obtained by the graph method is virtually the same and is not represented. The dotted line indicates the theoretical case where actual duration would equal theoretical duration. For this group of subjects, actual duration was equal to theoretical duration plus 5.3 min. After Cabanac (1989)

One question remains open. The sensory pleasure experiments have shown that the search for pleasure optimizes behavior. Such optimization may be measured by using objective physiological criteria: power output, internal temperature, heart rate, etc. We have now seen that mental pleasures are similar in nature to sensory pleasures and are equally important in shaping the decisions that people make. Does it follow, then, that mental pleasure optimizes mental functioning just as sensory pleasure optimizes physiological functioning? The question will be addressed in the next chapter.

Chapter VII
Mental optimization

> We have begun to discern that it is not only in his rational life that man's soul is intelligible and that a new order may be discovered even in his actions and feelings that are in appearance the least reasoned.
>
> Oppenheimer, 1972

The preceding chapters have shown that an organism understands the physiological utility of a stimulus through the sensory pleasure that this stimulus releases, whether in a simple situation or in a conflict between physiological motivations. With the key concepts of behavioral final common path and common currency, this line of reasoning has already taken us from physiological motivations to other motivations like money and game playing. We will now go further. If identical laws and mechanisms govern pleasures from motivations as different as game playing and thermal discomfort, these pleasures may be fundamentally alike. Furthermore, if physiological pleasure optimizes physiological functioning, mental pleasure should have a similar effect on purely mental functioning.

A series of experiments will test this hypothesis. We will first see whether pleasure is produced when our minds are functioning efficiently.

Video games

In the first experiment, subjects were no longer placed in a situation of motivational conflict, as before. They were given a video game and we simply collected the pleasure/displeasure ratings of their game playing (Cabanac *et al.* 1997). Next, we correlated the ratings with the subject's objective performance, using the game results. For this experiment, a computer golf game was chosen because it required neither physical dexterity nor speed. Just thinking. player had to choose all kinds of parameters: golf club length, striking direction, striking force, and foot position. The player also had to consider topography, wind speed and direction, and so on. No instructions were given so as not to bias the results (Navarick 1985). After each (fictitious) hole, we simply collected a verbal rating of the pleasure or displeasure of playing.

According to the results, perceived pleasure was directly proportional to game playing success. The closer the number of strokes was to par,[33] the higher the pleasure rating (Figure VII.1). Pleasure was thus attached to optimal performance. Of course, such a finding may seem self-evident. A game is supposed to be pleasurable; otherwise no one would buy it. For now, we will simply accept that this purely mental pleasure is closely correlated with a feeling of optimality. Beyond this simple correlation, it's possible, and likely, that the subjects were experiencing a pleasure that indicates optimality.

Poetry

In a second experiment with Chantal Pouliot and James Everett, we investigated a related kind of play satisfaction: the pleasure of poetry reading (Cabanac *et al.* 1997). Poems were chosen from a French poetry anthology (Pompidou 1964). Twelve poems were selected on four themes: woman, death, eternity, and pessimism. For each theme, the experimenter chose three poems using a subjective criterion: the experimenters' own trouble in understanding the poet's message. This difficulty was then calibrated by two independent referees. For the experiment, the poems were read by two groups of subjects: science students and music students. It was expected that the second group would have a liking for poetry and would understand its messages better than the first group. After reading each poem, each subject rated the pleasure or displeasure felt while reading. Next, the subjects reread the 12 poems and gave a new rating after each one. This time, they rated not their pleasure but their comprehension of the poem's message.

---

[33] "Par" is the number of strokes a player makes to send the ball from the starting line to the hole. A "hole in one" is a difficult result that only professionals can pull off.

The 12 pleasure ratings were then compared for each subject with the 12 comprehension ratings.

The results were surprising. The music students had a disarming sense of fantasy and their pleasure ratings seemed to correlate positively with their comprehension, but the correlation reached statistical significance ($p<0.05$) for only one subject. In contrast, the correlation was significant for most of the science

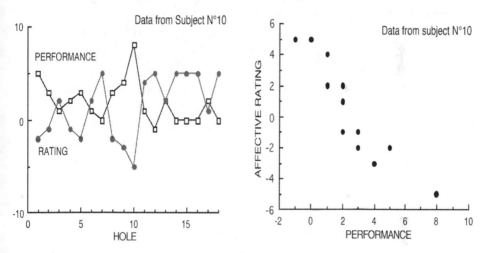

Figure VII.1 Correlation of pleasure with success for a mental activity. Example of results for a subject who completed the 18 holes of the golf game. Left: subject performance and hedonic ratings for the 18 holes of the golf video-game. The rating scale was left to the subject's discretion. Positive means pleasure, negative displeasure. Right: pleasure/displeasure ratings (dependent variable) correlate with performance (independent variable). r=-0.92, p<0.001. Performance is measured by the difference between the number of strokes and par. It may be seen that pleasure increased with good results. The above example features the subject with the highest correlation between pleasure and performance. Nine other subjects took part in the experiment. All but one correlation was significant at the p<0.05 level, the one exception being significant at the p<0.1 level. After Cabanac et al. (1997).

students. The results from the science students show that pleasure may correlate with efficient mental functioning, as predicted by the working hypothesis. Again, some caution is warranted before concluding that the laws of hedonic logic apply to mental functioning in the arts. It might seem self-evident that reading pleasure correlates with reading comprehension. It's less self-evident, however, that the correlation should be weaker among artists. This finding neither proves nor disproves the working hypothesis, but it is interesting.

These two experiments thus support the hypothesis that pleasure is linked to mental efficiency. The link, however, is neither automatic nor self-evident.

How, then, is pleasure related to mental activity? I think it's a function of perceived performance. The key point is that these studies establish a relationship between our intellectual performance and an apparently innate scale of pleasure. Csikszentmihalyi (1990) believes we find tasks to be agreeable when done correctly and disagreeable or indifferent when done poorly, the agreeable impression being called "flow" by this author (it seems to me simpler to speak of pleasure). This view is echoed by findings that a happy personality correlates with academic performance among students (Talbot 1990). Along the same lines, Carver and Scheier (1990) consider that agreeable or disagreeable emotion is part of a positive feedback system that controls behavior in two ways: as an indicator of favorable behavior and as a reward for behavior. Finally, Kubovy (1999) argues that virtuosity in accomplishing a task or behavior is a source of one of the greatest mental pleasures.[34] Such a view is consistent with the results of the above experiments.

As I previously pointed out, some authors link the hedonic dimension to awareness of the *rate* of progress of the behavior (Carver and Scheier 1990; Hsee and Abelson 1991; Varey and Kahneman 1992). The faster the reward is acquired, the happier will be the subjects. Analogous findings have been produced with direction of hedonic change, *i.e.*, an increase or decrease in displeasure. Patients will more positively remember disagreeable or painful testing if the

---

[34] In opposition to the pleasures of the body.

126

testing (and the pain) lasts longer, providing that the pain decreases during this extra time.   These observations seem consistent with the above experimental results and the hypothesis that pleasure is linked to the efficiency of current thought processes.   Such an interpretation would be easy to test experimentally.

So far, we have found a significant correlation between pleasure and efficiency of mental activity.   Does this pleasure actually indicate optimal functioning? Or is the correlation fortuitous?

We have seen an example where pleasure, which I call "mental" to set it apart from sensory pleasure, correlated with presumably optimal psychological functioning.   Clearly, it's hard to judge the optimality of mental functioning.   Objective criteria, such as speed of decision-making or closeness of fit between choice and social rule, may not correspond to distal biological or physiological end-purposes that lie beyond our discernment.   Some caution is therefore advisable. Nonetheless, we do have some objective or at least likely criteria of optimality and they will be used in the next three experiments. In each case, the criteria will measure the behavior's success and efficiency.

Grammatical decision-making

This first experiment was designed by Marta Balaskó.[35]   She spoke quite fluently in French but it was not her mother tongue and she had a French textbook with countless multiple-choice exercises. This book provided us with the material for our experiment. Twelve non-native French-speakers were presented with a list of 200 sentences of varying grammatical correctness.   The list had 50 basic sentences that each appeared 4 times with minor variations, the variants being separated from each other by 40 other sentences. Only one of the 4 variants was grammatically right. Figure VII.2 gives an example. Subjects read and rated the pleasure or displeasure of reading each of the 200 sentences (Balaskó and Cabanac1998).

Next, the 200 sentences were presented again, but this time the 4

---

[35] From Pecs University in Hungary, on a postdoctoral fellowship at Université Laval.

variants were grouped together, the same basic sentence appearing 4 times with only one correct variant. The grouped variants were thus multiple-choice questions and the subjects had to choose the right answer for each question. The hedonic ratings from the first questionnaire could then be compared with the actual choices on the second questionnaire.

The results (Figure VII.3) revealed several findings:

On the second questionnaire, subjects chose the sentences they had most highly rated on the first questionnaire. The similarity was highly significant and well above chance for the 12 subjects.

This similarity of response did not seem to correlate with proficiency in French. On the right-hand graph, we see that grammatically wrong choices were just as likely to be similar to pleasure ratings on the first questionnaire.

The choices thus showed a tight fit with mental pleasure. Subjects tended to behave in a way that would maximize their pleasure even when not knowing the right answer. The correlation was just as strong for the wrong answers. This approach was, for them, a way to optimize their behavior when answering questions about a language they knew imperfectly as non-native speaker.

Prince and Smolensky (1997) have proposed that grammar may correspond to some kind of optimal functioning of the nervous system. In our experiment on the grammar of a second language, pleasure ratings coincided with the choices, right or wrong, that subjects subsequently made. The close similarity between choice and pleasure rating seems to confirm both the Prince/Smolensky hypothesis and the hypothesis that pleasure optimizes mental functioning just as it optimizes physiological functioning. Such optimization of mental functioning, indicated by the perception of pleasure, is also suggested by the experiments with video-game playing and poetry reading.

Mathematical decision-making

The second experiment was done in conjunction with Jacqueline Guillaume, a specialist in mathematics teaching.[36] It was similar in

---

[36] Université de Grenoble, France.

design and methodology but the problems presented to the subjects were simple high-school math instead of grammar (Figure VII.4). The problems were thus relatively easy. A difficulty remained, however, in that the subjects had to solve them mentally and were not allowed to write. An equation is not always easy to solve mentally, even a simple one, so the subjects chose some answers without being able to make a rational calculation. All subjects were university students recruited on the Université Laval campus.

Questionnaire I	Questionnaire II
Question 27: C'est le feu rouge, arrêtez-le	Question 27: C'est le feu rouge:
Question 77: C'est le feu rouge, l'arrêtez	A) arrêtez-le
Question 127: C'est le feu rouge, arrêtez-vous	B) l'arrêtez
Question 177: C'est le feu rouge, vous l'arrêtez	C) arrêtez-vous
	D) vous l'arrêtez

Figure VII.2 Left: example of a basic sentence with four variants A, B, C, and D on questionnaire I. Subjects rated the pleasure of each variant. The numbers 27, 77, etc. indicate the rank order of the sentence on Questionnaire I. Right: the same sentences are presented on Questionnaire II (multiple-choice). Subjects had to check off the right answer. After Balaskó and Cabanac (1998).

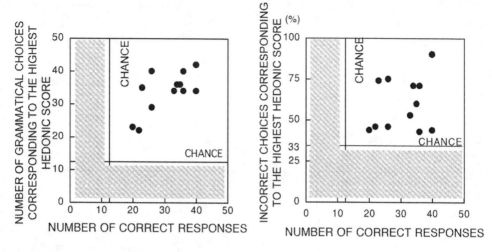

Figure VII.3   Non-native speakers were presented with 50 basic sentences in French. Each sentence was presented in 4 variant forms that were separated from each other by 40 other sentences in the series of 200 sentences, as shown in the previous figure. Only 1 of the 4 variants was grammatically right. The 3 others had minor grammatical or syntactic errors. Subjects read and rated the pleasure or displeasure they felt when reading each of the 200 sentences. Next, they were again presented with the 200 sentences, but now the 4 variants of each basic sentence were grouped together. The same sentence would appear 4 times in succession in 4 different ways, with only one being right. The subjects were thus given a multiple-choice exam and had to choose the right answers. This figure presents the results for the 12 subjects. On the Y-axis: number of right choices that had been most highly rated for pleasure. On the left, the 12 subjects behaved in a way that was well above chance. On the right, their behavior was still well above chance even for wrong choices (on the Y-axis: chance is 33% because, out of 4 possible answers to each question, 3 are wrong). Each subject is represented by a ●. The X-axes give the number of right answers (Balaskó & Cabanac 1998).

Questionnaire I

Question 5: If $n = 4x^2 - 7x + 2$, and $x = 2$, then $n = 2$

Question 55: If $n = 4x^2 - 7x + 2$, and $x = 2$, then $n = 4$

Question 105: If $n = 4x^2 - 7x + 2$, and $x = 2$, then $n = 6$

Question 155: If $n = 4x^2 - 7x + 2$, and $x = 2$, then $n = -8$

Questionnaire II

Problem #5 If $n = 4x^2 - 7x + 2$, and $x = 2$, then:

A) $n = 2$

B) $n = 4$

C) $n = 6$

D) $n = -8$

Figure VII.4   Above (Q I): example of a short problem presented in four variants .on Questionnaire I. The subject rates the pleasure of solving the problem. The numbers 5, 55, etc., indicate the rank order of the question on the questionnaire.

Below (Q.II): this problem is presented on questionnaire II as a multiple-choice question. The subject has to indicate the right answer (B). After Cabanac et al. (2002).

Figure VII.5 provides an overview of the main results, which closely match those of the previous experiment. Clearly, subjects did not choose solutions to the multiple-choice questions at random, this being true not only for the right solutions but also for the wrong ones.

They chose the most pleasurable solutions, whether true or false. Figure VII.5 also shows that the probability of choosing an unpleasant solution (be it true or false) was significantly less than random choice. Subjects therefore chose pleasurable solutions and rejected unpleasurable ones. Moreover, they did so without objectively knowing the correctness of the solution they chose. No subject was a math student or exceptional in mathematics.

Ethical decision-making

"A morality is a system of principles and values concerning people's behaviour, which is generally accepted by a society or by a particular group of people."[37]   Although decision-making and mental pleasure may coincide when the questions are grammatical or mathematical, the overlap may be less when the questions are based on moral imperatives.   With Adriana Fleury, we investigated how pleasure interacts with morality. The experimental design was similar to that of the two previous experiments. An initial questionnaire presented a list of statements to be read and the subject had to rate each statement on a pleasure/displeasure scale. A second questionnaire was then presented. All of the first questionnaire situations were now presented as multiple-choice questions where the subject had to choose one of four possible solutions to a single ethical problem. Each time, the solutions ranged from perfect honesty to shameless dishonesty. For example:

I've found a wallet on the street.
- I'll take it to the lost and found.
- I'll take it with the cards it contains to the lost and found, but I'll keep the money for myself.
- I'll leave it where I found it.
- I keep it for myself.

Another example:
My baby wakes me up every night with its crying:
- I'll see what's happening each time.
- I'll let my spouse take care of the child.
- I'll ignore the crying so that the child will learn not to wake me.
- I'll give it a sleeping pill.

---

[37] Collins Cobuild English Language Dictionary. London, HarpersCollins, 1993.

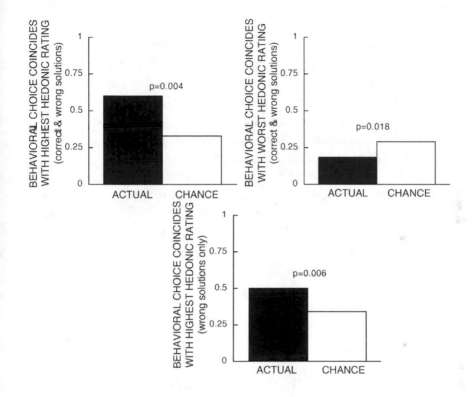

Figure VII.5 Subjects were asked 200 simple high-school-level math problems like the one in Figure VII.4. First, each subject had to rate the 200 problems and their solutions in terms of the pleasure of reading the problem and its solution. Only 50 problems were followed by correct solutions. Second, each subject was presented with 50 problems and each problem was followed by 4 possible solutions, with only 1 of the 4 being correct. The subject had to choose the right solution. Left: subject choices (solutions to multiple-choice questions) matched the problem/solution with the highest pleasure rating, at a level very significantly above chance. This was true regardless of whether the solution was true or false (below). Right: the probability of choosing the problem/solution with the lowest pleasure rating (regardless of whether it was true or false) was significantly less than chance. Subjects thus tended to choose solutions that pleased them and reject solutions that displeased them. After Cabanac et al. (2002).

For this experiment, we recruited students on the university campus. To ensure complete anonymity, they were asked only for their consent and their identities were not recorded. They could thus answer freely without feeling constrained by prevailing social conventions. The Questionnaire II results showed that all subjects mostly chose solutions they had rated on Questionnaire I as pleasurable (Figure VII.6). They did so regardless of whether the solutions were ethical or dishonest. The subjects were fully aware that they sometimes chose dishonest solutions. When asked afterwards, they easily identified which ones were honest, which were less so, and which were frankly dishonest. It was not out of ignorance that they had chosen immoral, and more pleasurable, solutions.

Aggressive decision-making

"The search for pleasure is at the heart of any violent action," says Thierry Lévy. Further on, he adds: "It is a pleasure to avenge oneself. Who would disagree?" (Lévy 1984).

To study aggressive motivation, we used the same approach as in the previous experiments. Subjects had to rate the pleasure/displeasure of aggressive solutions to minor social conflicts (Ramírez et al. 2003).

Four questionnaires were presented to subjects of both sexes ranging in age from 19 to 80. The first questionnaire presented 17 unpleasant situations with five possible responses for a total of 85. The subjects had to rate the pleasure/displeasure of each situation. The second questionnaire grouped the variants of each situation into blocs of 5 to produce 17 multiple-choice questions. The other two questionnaires investigated moral attitudes to aggression and tested subject impulsiveness.

Situations rated as disagreeable were the ones that ended in passive or peaceful responses. On a scale of 1 to 5 of increasing aggressiveness, only class 4 responses generated pleasure, all other ones being unpleasant. A negative rating was given to both the most passive and the most aggressive responses, but clear-cut aggressiveness was pleasant.

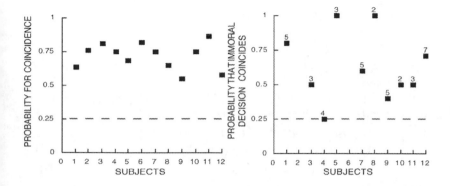

Figure VII.6 Pleasure and morality of behavior. Left: probability is equal to 1 if all of each subject's choices (12 subjects on the X-axis) on the entire multiple-choice questionnaire (50 choices with 4 possible answers each time) match the subject's highest pleasure ratings for the 200 corresponding solutions on the previous questionnaire. Dashed line indicates probability of matching due to chance. Results are well above chance. The solutions the subjects chose were the most pleasurable ones.
Right: Probability that all immoral solutions on the multiple-choice questionnaire match the most highly rated solutions on the previous questionnaire. The X-axis indicates the 12 subjects. Dashed line indicates probability of matching due to chance. Above the data point for each subject, a number indicates how many clearly immoral solutions were chosen by the subject. There are only ten data points because subjects 2 and 6 chose no immoral solutions. Subject 4 chose immoral solutions at the level of chance. When the other nine subjects chose immoral solutions, their choices coincided with a high pleasure rating. After Cabanac et al. (2002).

This finding was confirmed by responses to the second questionnaire: the responses chosen were the most pleasurable ones, *i.e.*, fairly aggressive responses. This result was independent of sex, but increased with age. The tendency to maximize pleasure decreased with impulsiveness.

Aggressiveness coincided with pleasure, thus following the law of pleasure maximization we had previously seen for behaviors with physiological aims and for decision-making in situations of motivational conflict.

***

In all of these experiments, subjects were told to rate the pleasure of reading a grammatical, mathematical, or ethical item. We cannot rule out the possibility that the subjects' ratings incorporated the pleasure they could expect from the response on the questionnaire. If so, the relation of causality would be inversed and less direct: instead of the pleasure causing the behavior, the result of the behavior would cause the pleasure. But this possibility is unlikely. In our lab experiments, subjects could not expect any pleasure from the ethical responses because these responses had no real existence. They existed only as descriptions, contrary to the other experiments (e.g., grammar, mathematics, video-game playing) where the response was a real choice or a real game. Conversely, with the grammatical and mathematical experiments, no eventual pleasure could affect these seemingly rational choices. Yet the subjects behaved in the same way in all situations regardless of whether the choices were real or theoretical or the outcomes real or hypothetical.

Memory

This is my last example of mental function optimization. It deals with memory. If the brain is to operate efficiently, and not run out of memory space, it cannot retain all of the information it encounters. It can only retain useful information. Memory specialists distinguish between encoding (data storage) and recall (reuse) of information or characteristics that may be memorized from stimuli (Tulving 1983; Rubin and Friendly 1986). PET scans suggest that the brain uses newness of information as one of its criteria for information sorting

(Tulving 1985). Another criterion might be pleasure. A highly agreeable or disagreeable stimulus is likelier to be stored in memory for further use than a more neutral stimulus, as shown by the results of the following experiment.[38]

Twelve subjects were presented with a series of 30 smells. Each presentation lasted 5 seconds and was separated from the next by a 3-minute interval. The smells were:

1) imidazole crystals, 2) argan oil, 3) detergent, 4) coconut oil, 5) lemon, 6) cheese, 7) rum, 8) orange, 9) mushroom, 10) chocolate, 11) tobacco, 12) casamino acid, 13) methol, 14) oil of cloves, 15) mothballs, 16) cooking broth extract, 17) coffee, 18) cigarette butts, 19) thyme, 20) tea, 21) rotten meat, 22) lavender, 23) ammonia, 24) geranium, 25) pure alcohol, 26) vinegar, 27) formaldehyde, 28) dental cement, 29) oil of rose, 30) tar.

We presented each stimulus in a glass vial, opened it in the subject's presence, and stated the name of the stimulus. After each presentation, the subject rated first the intensity of the smell and then its hedonicity (from extreme displeasure to extreme pleasure). To control for the intensity of the smell, each pleasure rating was divided by the intensity rating. The resulting ratio "r" for each smell was an index of hedonicity. Strongly agreeable or disagreeable smells had high r ratings, either positive or negative. Intense smells resulted in low r ratings.

For the next ten minutes, subjects played a video game of their choosing. They were then asked to write down a list of stimuli they could remember.[39] Next, 24 of the initial stimuli were again presented,[40] as well as six new smells (Javel water, almond, phenol, maple syrup, pine, cypress) and the subjects were asked whether they recognized the stimulus.

Without assistance, the subjects remembered 12.3 ±0.9 (mean ± standard error) stimuli and had forgotten 11.7 ± 0.9. The r of the

---

[38] I wish to thank Endel Tulving for his assistance and advice in preparing this experiment.
[39] Free recall test.
[40] Memory better retains the initial and final items of a series, so we ignored the results of stimuli 1 to 3 and 28 to 30.

memorized stimuli was 1.14 ± 0.19 and that of the forgotten stimuli 0.86 ± 0.16. The difference between the two was significant (paired Student t test, 3.27, p=0.008). Highly hedonic stimuli, whether agreeable or disagreeable, were better retained in memory than indifferent stimuli, independently of intensity of the smell.

On the recognition test, subjects correctly recognized 14.0 ± 1.0 stimuli, and wrongly rejected 2.1 ± 0.3. Mean r (±s.e.) of correct recognitions was 1.17 ± 0.17 and mean r of wrong rejections 0.64 ± 0.12. The difference between the two was significant (paired Student t test, 2.75, p = 0.021). Thus, recognition followed the same pattern as unaided recall. Independently of smell intensity, the most hedonic stimuli tended to be better memorized than the neutral ones.
Time is one variable of memory storage. Pleasure/displeasure is another. This second variable differs from the first in adaptation level theory, which holds that you compare your life experience at one moment with those of preceding moments (Helson 1964). I will discuss this point further on. For now, we will simply keep in mind that the results of different experiments show that subjects can readily assess their pleasure or displeasure and that these assessments are independent of stimulus presentation sequence or of questions asked and past subject experiences.

Convergence

Pleasure is central to mental life, as shown by the results of the previous experiments. We make decisions in a wide range of areas by maximizing pleasure and this mechanism is a factor in optimizing performance. The psychologist Victor Johnston (1999) has come to similar conclusions through completely opposite reasoning. With a background in computer modeling of mental performance, he sees hedonism as an evolutionary driving force, *i.e.*, natural selection has improved behavioral and mental performance by acting via pleasure. Like previous hedonist philosophers, he has used his own introspection and intuition to ascertain the role of pleasure—an approach that is accessible to any layperson. But he has gone further. Interested in the modeling of mental phenomena, such as facial trait recognition, he has created a computer model called "Sniffer" that can follow a prey's odor trail on a route randomly generated by a computer screen. The model uses the following function to represent pleasure:

Magnitude of hedonic perception = (H) x (S)^a Equation VII.1

H is the hedonic dimension, which may be positive or negative. S is the strength of the smell and the exponent $a \geq 1$.

Sniffer is simply programmed to get onto the odor trail as often as possible in order to refuel and thus be able to survive and reproduce. From one generation to the next, its performance improves to the level that may be seen in the example on Figure VII.7. Pleasure seems to increase Sniffer's adaptability. Over repeated trials, through a kind of natural selection, it brings Sniffer's path closer and closer to the odor trail.

With the success of this model, Victor Johnston went on to simulate decision-making in the famous "prisoner's dilemma." You and a friend have been caught with a stolen car. Both of you are now being held in separate cells and involvement in a more serious offence, but have no proof. They offer cannot communicate. The police suspect you a deal: if you tell them about your friend's other crime you will not be charged with stealing the car. You surmise that your friend has been offered the same deal. What do you do? If you both stay silent, both of you will be charged with the lesser crime. If both of you talk, both will go to jail for a more serious offence, on the evidence of each other's testimony. But if you alone stay silent, you will be punished for both offences while your accomplice walks free. Researchers have imagined all sorts of tactics to get the lightest possible sentences for both prisoners. Computer simulations can greatly improve the results by introducing analogues of pleasure and displeasure (Johnston 1999).

Of course, nothing is proven by modeling the hedonic dimension of consciousness. A model is only a representation, an image, a system. Computers have no other consciousness than the one that humans program them with. Nonetheless, we can see that pleasure *may* optimize behavior, so we can reasonably hypothesize that it does.

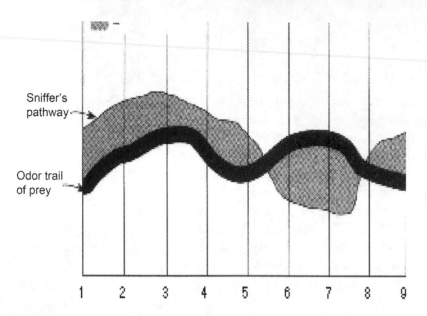

Figure VII.7 Performance of Sniffer computer model in following a randomly generated odor trail. Sniffer's program maximizes its "pleasure." The thick black trail indicates Sniffer's target path and the narrow line its actual path. The gray area indicates error (deviation from target). Sniffer is programmed to respond to simulated pleasure. This model works only because a conscious being (Victor Johnston) built the program and assigned it a task. After Johnston (1999).

Conclusion

As J.R. Roy stated, in the quote introducing Chapter IV, a theory's utility lies in its predictive value. In the experiments with the golf game video and memory of smells, we tested the hypothesis that pleasure optimizes mental functioning even in the absence of direct physiological benefits. The results seemed positive. Indeed, they showed a close correlation between pleasure, decision-making, and optimal performance of mind or memory. This finding is needed if we wish to show that pleasure optimizes not only physiologically oriented behaviors but also mental functioning. It isn't, however, sufficient proof. Real proof may be impossible because the evidence lies in the realm of consciousness. Yet reasonable certainty is possible if more and more results are consistent with our hypothesis. For Popper (1972), the scientific process should try to falsify working hypotheses and each experiment is an attempt to invalidate a theory. In this chapter, each experiment was an attempt to falsify the hedonic hypothesis, but these repeated attempts failed. The hypothesis remains consistent with the results.

When faced with problems of varying nature—video games, grammar, mathematics, ethics, or the pure esthetics of poetry, our subjects behaved in such a way as to maximize their pleasure, since they clearly chose those solutions that would provide the most pleasure. This repeated pattern in different situations is, in itself, proof. It therefore strikes me as reasonable to infer that pleasure is a guide—and even *the* guide—of behavior in such decision-making situations. Ovsich (1998) has recently come to the same conclusion.

If we turn to the results of other experiments in this chapter, we find that the pleasure experienced when reading descriptions of behaviors, or when solving mathematical and grammatical problems, correlated with the subjects' final decisions. Pleasure/displeasure seems to indicate the correct solution to a problem or behavior when a choice has to be made and the correct or rational solution is unknown. This point is particularly evident when subjects chose behaviors known to be immoral or false solutions to mathematical problems. Such choices also had the highest pleasure ratings. These results thus support the hypothesis that decisions are made with a view to maximizing pleasure and minimizing displeasure.

Of course, I am not suggesting that rationality plays no role in mathematics, grammar, or ethics. But pleasure too plays a role, as shown by the above results. Rationality matters more if a problem can be reasoned out, and in such a situation the choice of behavior reflects cultural differences. Japanese, for instance, will behave differently from Chinese or Americans. But cultural differences disappear if the problem cannot be reasoned out (Yates *et al.* 1998). The process of choosing and deciding then becomes the same for all humans. This universal mechanism is, I think, hedonicity. Rationality prevails when enough information is available to make a decision; hedonicity, when much is still unknown or when an emergency requires a snap decision and leaves no time for rationality. Evidently, the hedonic mechanism is the more archaic one, witness its cross-cultural universality in places as different as Japan, China, and North America. It may be what Penrose

(1996) calls intuition.

Pleasure thus seems involved in optimizing behavior, either as a cause or as a result. A causal role is strongly suggested by findings that satisfaction and joy speed up the recovery of patients from the cardiovascular sequels of negative emotions (Fredrickson and Levenson 1998).

As with physiologically oriented behaviors, we can measure optimization of mental functioning. Such optimization aims for a maximum of work in a minimum of time. Again, as with physiological optimization, time is of key importance and may be the fundamental variable underlying all of our mental life. I will return to this point further on. We will simply note here that immediate memory does not seem to influence decision-making. In the experiments, questionnaires were presented to half the subjects from 1 to N, and to the other half from N to 1. Both groups produced similar results every time. Decisions were made without recall of previous decisions.

In conclusion, decisions are guided by the search for pleasure, even in the realm of morality. This decision-making guide is universal and acts as a shortcut for rationality. When we cannot reason out a problem, or when not enough time is available, the search for pleasure provides a response that is fast and, all things considered, efficient.

Chapter VIII

Pleasure and decision-making: The morality of pleasure and the pleasure of morality

> Life and pleasure, as we see it now, are not
> separable, for without behavior there is no pleasure
> and pleasure improves behavior.
> Epicurus, 241-170 BC

> We would often be ashamed of our loveliest actions
> if people could see all of the motives that produce them.
> de la Rochefoucauld, 1613-1680

This chapter will review the previous chapters. I will begin with a short recap and end with several pages from an earlier book of mine, *La Quête du plaisir*. This material is especially fitting here and will be somewhat expanded on.

First, sensory pleasure serves physiological needs. It measures the usefulness of stimuli. By seeking sensory pleasure and avoiding displeasure, we get an optimal mix of behaviors that best serves physiological needs—in other words, a dynamic homeostasis. Pleasure, or conversely displeasure, also indicates what should stay in memory. An important corollary is that we should feel indifferent to neutral sensations and more easily forget them. Thus, indifference too is key to optimizing behavior because it keeps us from dispersing our energies on unnecessary stimuli and activities. I will return to this point in Chapter XII. For now, we can state that indifference is a specific response of the human brain. It can even be visualized. Brain imaging has shown that indifferent perceptions scarcely alter blood flow in cortical areas whereas heightened attention produces visible signs of local activation (Rees and Frith 1998).

Second, when pleasure arises during purely mental activities, it seems to optimize such functioning. Pleasure maximization is thus instrumental in resolving the little problems of daily life: game playing, ethics, mathematics, grammar, and even aggressiveness. This wide range argues for a similar functioning and role in all areas of life.

Third, pleasure is a common currency that prioritizes access of competing motivations to the final common path of behavior. When motivations are in conflict, priority goes to the one with the highest algebraic sum of pleasure and displeasure. Thus, by seeking pleasure and avoiding displeasure, we optimize decision-making and satisfy our most urgent needs first. We may still choose a behavior that does not give pleasure if it is twinned with one that does and if the net balance is positive. We thus learn by association to accept disagreeable behaviors. Such mental algebra may account for behaviors that involve highly unpleasant or even harmful actions: drug abuse, high-risk sexual behavior, strenuous effort, and self-control. Loewenstein (1996) attributes these actions to "visceral influences on behavior."

Finally, the common currency concept implies that the laws of sensory pleasure apply to mental pleasures that are similar in such properties as utility, optimization, and transience. We should keep these properties in mind when examining any kind of pleasure. Transience, in particular. Sensory pleasure appears only in a dynamic situation where the subject is moving to a better state. With satiation, it disappears. Once the internal problem has been corrected, the stimulus is no longer pleasurable (the pleasure having lost its utility) and now produces a neutral sensation. If the stimulus persists, it becomes unpleasant. This applies to all pleasures.

Long before these experimental findings, philosophers had likewise concluded that the search for and pursuit of pleasure leads to better behaviors—an optimal performance of mind and body. They based this conclusion on their own introspective understanding of pleasure.

Pleasure and philosophers

Since Antiquity, Western philosophers and scientists have had two attitudes to pleasure: one positive and the other negative. This dichotomy may originate in the ambiguity of the idea of happiness. I will criticize this ambiguity in the last chapter and propose a new definition of happiness.

The first attitude was notably articulated by Epicurus (241-170 BC), who recognized the search for pleasure as a useful motivation. According to his school of thought, which already existed before him, pleasure is associated with stimulations or situations that promote the survival of the individual or species. Many moralists thus acknowledged that the search for pleasure is what impels us to act: "man has no good thing under the sun but to eat, and drink, and enjoy himself"[41] (Qoheleth, 900 BC). This relationship between pleasure and behavior seemed self-evident to Aristotle (384-322 BC):

> "Aversion and desire are acts of the same faculty; Man smells odors poorly and does not smell any odor independently of pain and pleasure (II,9); ... where there is sensation there is also pleasure and pain, for appetite is the desire of what is agreeable (II,3)."

Epicurus felt likewise, as seen in the quote introducing this chapter (Conche 1977).

After the Greeks, this view was held by many philosophers and thinkers of the Middle Ages, the Renaissance, and later centuries. St. Augustine (354-430, cf. Lamarre 1986), Thomas Aquinas (1224-1274, cf. Aquinas 1984-1986), Montaigne (1533-1592, cf. Saulnier 1988), Gassendi (1592-1655, cf. Bloch 1971), and Sulzer (1751) gave pleasure a dominant if not exclusive role in motivation.

These moralists based their convictions on personal intuition. For Pascal, "Man is born for pleasure, he feels it, no other proof is needed. He therefore follows his reason in giving himself over to pleasure" (Pascal 1670, 1972). The greatest modern philosopher of pleasure is considered to be Bentham, who founded his "greatest happiness principle" on pleasure "the spring of action" (Bentham 1742-1832, cf. also Bowring 1962). But this conclusion was not solely his own. It was shared by several contemporaries:

> "Nature gives us organs to tell us through pleasure what we should seek and through pain what we should avoid" (Condillac 1754).

Kant (1788) and Mill (1869) were just as clear on this point, though more concise. They too were not alone. "The Creator ... gave us

---

[41] *Ecclesiastes, 8:15.*

the incentive of appetite, the encouragement of taste, and the reward of pleasure" (Brillat-Savarin 1828).

With the dawn of the modern age, this school of thought fell into decline but still had its share of proponents. "Pleasures and pains represent the sole genuine basis for understanding human motives" (Jevons 1871). For Dostoevsky (1821-1881), "pleasure is always useful" (Dostoevsky 1950) and for Freud (1920), evidently, the "pleasure principle" sets our life goals.

Finally, to finish off a review that could be longer, I will cite P.T. Young (1959): "From every point of view the affective[42] processes must be regarded as motivational in nature."

Clearly, if a behavior is motivated, it must be oriented by a rewarding sensation. Yet, aside from a few contemporary psychologists who have recognized the role of pleasure (Killeen 1962; Nutin 1975; Toates 1986; Overskeid 2000), this view is scarcely accepted nowadays among philosophers or psychologists. This Epicurean, or hedonistic, school of thought remains a minority view— almost a politically incorrect one. A second attitude has prevailed since Antiquity. Plato attributed less value to the senses and appetite than to intellect and reason (Plato 427-347 BC). With him arose a dominant philosophical tendency that deemed the mind to be a trinity: appetite, emotion, and reason. According to this school of thought, pleasure is an animalistic motivation. Anima and corpore should be dissociated, with the soul alone having some merit and the body being but an instrument worthy of scorn. Only the pleasure of virtuous conduct should reward people for doing what they ought to do. Thus, because of the example of some extreme hedonists, many people spurned Epicureanism in order to cultivate virtue. Epicureanism lost ground and Stoicism became the dominant ideology of the Roman world and its successors.

"Nature or some god has given nothing better to Man than the thinking soul, and it is true to say that pleasure is his worst enemy; if we cannot be reasonable enough and wise enough to scorn pleasure, we ought to be thankful to old age for compelling us to give it up"

(Cicero, Published 1967).

---

[42] In English, the term affective is ambiguous, meaning both hedonic and emotional.

Interestingly, this division between accepting and rejecting pleasure is found not only in Antiquity, but also in most societies, schools of thought, and churches, probably because it exists in each human being. Again interestingly, the Epicurean, pragmatic, tolerant, and utilitarian view has generally been dominated, often forcefully so, by the Stoic, ideological, puritan, and fundamentalist view. This dominance has alternated with hedonistic revivals, depending on the twists and turns of history and geography, but the Stoic view has usually prevailed, at least superficially, and been considered more moral.

This book will not analyze why pleasure lost out in the dominant currents of contemporary thought. Interested readers will find such an analysis, with a historical review of Epicureanism, in an excellent work by Plé (1982). Further material is available in Toates (1986) and Lea *et al.* (1987). I will confine myself here to a recent cause: for over half a century, the excesses of psychoanalysis have led to the entire mental sphere, including the pleasure principle, being consigned to the limbo of non-science. This disinterest in pleasure is one of the negative consequences of behaviorism, as is the disinterest in consciousness. In most psychology labs, behavior has long been studied in and of itself— as if the mind were a black box whose workings can never be understood.[43]   Pleasure is thus absent from most of the recent psychology treatises and manuals. As early as 1942, it was considered unworthy of mention when Boring published his seminal work on sensation and perception in the history of experimental psychology. This academic disinterest will be further discussed in my next chapter.

There's a short but significant analysis of pleasure and behavior in Duncker (1940-1941):

> "A search for the ultimate motives of human conduct cannot disregard pleasure which many eminent minds have considered to be the fundamental motive, or at least an important one. Others, to be sure, have held that pleasure is the outcome rather than the motive or goal of human striving... There cannot be the slightest doubt that many human strivings bear some kind of reference to

---

[43] Cognition has made a return with cognitivist psychology (see Cosmides 1998), but this field has shown little interest in pleasure.

pleasure, and likewise that many pleasures bear some reference to striving."

Duncker thus divided philosophers into two antagonistic schools: hedonists, for whom pleasure is the fundamental motive, and "hormists," for whom pleasure is but an outcome. He proposed the word "hormism," based on the hormic force (a force that pushes us to act) of McDougall (1923).[44] In hedonism and hormism, we can easily recognize the ancient division between the philosophers of the Garden, the Epicureans, and those of the Portico, the Stoics; or, with reference to Plé (1982), between the morality of pleasure and the morality of duty, the latter always eventually dominating and eliminating the former. The same fracture line is discernible among scientific psychologists, who consider the rejection of pleasure justified because the philosophers of pleasure reached their conclusions through personal introspection, a method despised by science. Dubrovsky (2000, 2003) has analyzed this view and found it to be especially evident in the dichotomy between affective psychosis and schizophrenia—a key influence on all modern psychiatric nosography (Kraepelin 1968).

This rejection was once justifiable. Today, we must recognize that "as new techniques are developed, our ideas often have to be revised to encompass the new information obtained" (Teitelbaum 1964).

Over the last decade, the stream of hedonist psychologists has turned into a more substantial watercourse and introspection has once more become acceptable through the rigorous methods of psychophysics. Strangely enough, pleasure is attracting the most interest among researchers in artificial intelligence (Kiss and Reichgelt 1991; Johnston 1999; Cisek 1999; Cardon 2000).

Among the latest hedonicity researchers, Csikszentmihalyi (1990) speaks of "flow" and Fazio (2000) of "attitude." For Fazio, attitude has a positive or negative valence. An object arouses either pleasure or aversion, which in turn shortens decision-making time and optimizes behavior. There may be a disadvantage. If the object subtly changes, the attitude remains unchanged, though now inappropriate.

---

[44] From the Greek Hormao-o = I am charging ahead with ardor. Hormee = Irrepressible tendency to do or express something. Internal force toward something (S. Nicolaîdis).

Csikszentmihalyi and Fazio both maintain that attitude has functional value and usefully orients visual attention and categorization processes by facilitating decision-making and improving decision quality. For these researchers, such optimization frees up mental resources for other problems. They implicitly argue that the hedonic dimension, which they place at the limit of the unconscious, since attitude underlies consciousness, helps assess environmental stimuli and that pleasure/displeasure is ultimately useful.

Some authors (Shizgal 1997; Berridge 2000) agree that pleasure intervenes in animal behavior. This aspect will be discussed in Chapter X. For now, I will simply note that the long evolutionary history of pleasure may explain certain rigidities when animals acquire food preferences and aversions, as Young (1959) shows in rats.

Three authors have most openly and clearly embraced the hedonist view that I have defended for thirty-five years. They are Dan Kahneman (Kahneman *et al.* 1997), who did some of the experiments cited above (Varey and Kahneman 1992),[45] Victor Johnston (1999), and Alexander Ovsich (1998). The last two have notably developed theory and built models in this field.

Johnston's models are computer-generated. As we have seen, by introducing pleasure analogues into computer programming, it is possible to optimize Sniffer's performance (see Figure VII.7) and produce better solutions to the prisoner's dilemma.

Ovsich (1998) has proposed that motivation for any behavior resides on what I call the hedonic axis of consciousness, the decision-maker. His proposal closely parallels the argument of this book. With mathematical language, he describes mental processes and, in particular, hedonic processes. Attitude, desire, attention, and will are shown to be mathematical functions of pleasure. He thus treats pleasure as a non-mentalist, objective reality that can be modeled through equations.

---

[45] At a lecture in Jerusalem on January 19, 2001, he was kind enough to inform the audience that the recent reorientation of his research toward what he calls "experienced utility," which he acknowledged to be a synonym of pleasure, had been inspired by my 1993 lecture at Princeton University and by previous readings of my publications on pleasure.

The previous chapters addressed only a limited spectrum of motivations: hunger, fatigue, thermal discomfort, pain, money, play, poetry reading, aggressiveness, and some tests of mental performance (grammar, mathematics). We need to examine the full spectrum, especially socially driven motivations: fear, love, and desire to dominate. Nor should we neglect inherent motivations: the need to create, curiosity, and spirituality. Do these other motivations relate to pleasure in the same way? Is pleasure their common currency?

I think so. No behavior, in my opinion, escapes the law of pleasure maximization. Our findings on sensory pleasure should apply to pleasures that may be deemed purely mental. This prediction seems borne out by our experimental findings on video-game playing, grammar, arithmetic, poetry, and aggressiveness. Again, as with sensory pleasure, I would also predict that learning can create new links between initially neutral or even disagreeable behaviors and the pleasure of their eventual outcomes. Hence, some pleasures are learnable and pleasure itself may be anticipated.

If pleasure intervenes in behavior and participates in decision-making, it probably does so at each stage of action: 1) awareness of the need; 2) search for a solution; 3) execution of need-satisfying behavior:

> "We are accustomed to think of pleasure as a response to stimulation rather than as a drive for action. A little consideration will show that [like fear or anger] it is both a response and a drive" (Fuller 1962:59)

The hormist attitude: anticipation of pleasure

Pleasure anticipation probably intervenes in the decision-making process (Rolls 1994). This intervention is not only conscious but also thought-out and deliberate, be it innate or learned. We have some indirect evidence for this in studies by several authors.

Anticipation requires intervention by pleasure in memory. We have seen that pleasant and unpleasant smells are memorized more than neutral smells (Chapter VII). This is likely true for all memory storage. Arnold (1970) agrees that the events stored in memory are the ones that have evoked much pleasure or displeasure. For LeDoux, learning does not necessarily require an alert consciousness and, once learning has taken place, the stimuli do not have to be conscious to evoke an appropriate response. This view of memory corresponds to prerational pleasure. The hedonic axis of consciousness operates to some degree independently of the intensity axis. Ovsich (in preparation) has adopted and developed the same view: pleasant or unpleasant stimuli and events are stored in memory for the sake of future efficiency. They will be the most useful to remember.

Pleasure/displeasure anticipation affected decision-making in a study by Ritov and Baron (1994, 1995). The two authors presented subjects with questionnaires and asked them to choose one of two possibilities: vaccinate to protect a child from illness and risk serious side effects; or not vaccinate and risk a fatal illness? More subjects abstained when informed of the consequences of their choice. There was thus pleasure anticipation, but of a negative sort. Displeasure anticipation especially weighs heavily in medical decisions (Ritov 1996), perhaps because the decision-making is experienced much more personally than in a theoretical questionnaire situation, e.g., "Would I avert a railway disaster at the cost of killing rail employees working on the tracks?"

People may prefer the "I don't want to know" response in general situations of uncertainty. Eckblad (1972) shows that pleasure may result from uncertainty, be it an unknown stimulus, an unknown situation, or an unknown solution. Response to the unknown follows a bell curve over time: initially positive, possibly as an anticipation effect, and then negative. Impact on decision-making is mixed. On the one hand, people may abstain from action because they anticipate an adverse outcome. On the other, they may be pushed to act by the positive feeling that comes from satisfying curiosity, as proposed by Berlyne (1950-1951) and confirmed by Eckblad (1978).

Berridge (2000) has reviewed the influence of pleasure[46] on learning and emphasizes the influence of reward expectancy in feeding behaviors.

According to Mellers' Decision Affect Theory, emotional

---

[46] Which he calls "reinforcement" in order to remain politically correct and thus avoid the mentalist vocabulary still spurned by most scientific psychologists in 2003!

experiences are associated with decision outcomes. This theory incorporates utilities,[47] expectations, and comparisons of outcomes on a hedonic scale. When risk enters into decision-making, choices may be described in terms of affective maximization: people choose risky decisions because they expect to be better off (Mellers *et al.* 1997). For example, in a betting situation, the best strategy is to maximize long-term pleasure from the bet (Mellers *et al.* 1999), for "pleasure has a central role in human life" (Warburton 1996).

LeBel and Dubé have recognized that consumers anticipate the pleasure of future purchases:

> "Beyond the actual experience, consumers derive pleasure from anticipating and reminiscing about pleasant events and are able to identify precise aspects of their experiences as it unfolds. Our findings also reveal that multiple sources of pleasure can underlie a single hedonic experience and that the salience of each of these sources can shift over time" (LeBel and Dubé 1998).

Pleasure/displeasure may thus play a role at this stage. When anticipating pleasure or displeasure, a subject will be oriented to act or, like the Stoics, to abstain. Finally, though no cerebral difference is discernable between anticipated and current pleasure, different nervous structures may be activated (Small 2002). Characteristic EEG readings—slow negative potentials—accompany anticipation of positive/negative events, especially negative ones (Bocker *et al.* 2001).

Pleasure and solution-seeking before an action: decision-making and rationality

Humans do not always behave rationally. Such irrationality bothers psychologists interested in decision-making. After a review of the literature, Shafir and LeBoeuf (2002) conclude that rationality cannot account for some behaviors and decisions. This literature has grown markedly in recent years with studies on impulsive behaviors (Ainslie 1975), maladaptive behaviors such as tics and automatisms observable

---

[47] In the economic sense of the term, *i.e.*, benefits.

even in farm animals (Wiepkema 1985), absurd risky choices (McKenna 1996), and reversals of decisions (Tversky and Kahneman 1981). In some cases, self-deception leads to decisions that defy all logic (Byrne and Kurland 2001).[48] How can we explain such odd behaviors? Some authors lean to hedonicity.

Izard (1977) has shown that happiness accompanies the process of solving a problem. We may thus expect to find this factor in the decision-making mechanism. In the different experiments of the last few chapters, we have seen the arguments for an influence by pleasure/displeasure on the decision-making process. This influence has been recognized by other authors for both animals (Hayes *et al.* 1981; Spruijt 1998) and humans (Einhorn and Hogarth 1981; McKenna 1996).

Evans *et al.* (1993) maintain that, in real-life, reasoning supports decision-making and aims for a goal. But rationality is complex. They argue for two types of rationality:

- Type 1 rationality is reasoning to reach personal goals—within the limits of cognition. This is the type people use in daily life: the rationality of motivation. They seek to reach goals and they reach them.
- Type 2 rationality is reasoning based on logical process. We can make machines function according to type 2 rationality. This type may be called algorithmic: the mathematical rationality of Turing machines. Robots are programmed with this mode.

I am convinced that type 1 rationality is decision-making based on pleasure/displeasure (Cabanac 1996). This mode cannot be programmed into machines.

Mellers *et al.* (1998) have recognized the need for alternative schemas of rationality:

"These frameworks view decisions as more reasonable and adaptive than previously thought. For example, "rule following." Rule following, which occurs when a rule or norm is applied to a situation, often minimizes effort and provides satisfying solutions

---

[48] In their study, Byrne and Kurland nonetheless conclude that self-deception improves performance.

that are "good enough," though not necessarily the best. When rules are ambiguous, people look for reasons to guide their decisions. They may also let their emotions take charge."

Thaler and Johnson (1990) note that participants deliberately place their options in the best framework possible. They call this "hedonic editing." To be sure, any decision will be agreeable in itself because it averts a disagreeable motivational conflict (Shephard 1964).

Khrennikov (1998) propose a mathematical model "not based on the rule of reason." Fantino (1998) states that humans "are practical information processors who select good or useful news but avoid bad news." When this author uses the terms "good" and "bad," he's entering the realm of pleasure and displeasure, contrary to what he himself may say. Closer to my arguments, but with the usual semantic caution of current thinking in modern psychology,   Roth and Erev (1995, 1998) argue that decisions are made with low rationality content, essentially with a view to maximizing reward.

Loewenstein et al. (1999) have experimentally further confirmed an apparent absence of logic in the decision-making process: information from one situation often cannot be used in another one that is nonetheless similarly structured. The authors examined analogical encoding of information transfer in negotiating situations. Subjects were more inclined to propose bargaining strategies and less inclined to compromise if earlier shown an analogical case. Subjects who saw an analogy between the two cases were three times likelier to incorporate the learned strategy into their bargaining than those who were shown these cases for the first time. The comparison process may be an effective way of abstracting logical principles, for later use. Here again, it seems that logic (type 2 rationality) is not immediately spontaneous. Is decision-making first routed through pleasure/displeasure? This seems to me likely.

Tversky and Kahneman (1981) concluded that humans are illogical after their subjects had failed to make the same decision when shown two identical representations of a decision-making problem. This lack of uniformity violates one of the fundamental principles of rationality, invariability, which states that a decision should be unaffected by the frame used to present a situation. Tversky and Kahneman (1986) describe decision-making as a maximization process and conclude that its logic provides a poor basis for a theory that can describe (and predict) decision-making. I would suggest that pleasure is what is being maximized (Cabanac 1996). Tversky and Kahneman considered only type 2 rationality, but their subjects were using type 1, which relies on all information available.

Goldstein and Gigenrenzer (2002) recognize that the heuristic (in the original sense of a search for solutions and not the later psychological meaning of "irrationality") consists of adaptive decision-making strategies of ancient evolutionary origin. These authors make prior knowledge of familiar situations a factor in more efficient decision-making. This factor lies outside the type 2 rationality of Evans. They propose that decision-making should be:

a) ecologically rational, *i.e.*, it should exploit information from the environment

b) based on inherited evolutionary mechanisms

c) simple and fast, kicking in when computing capacities or time are limited

d) precise enough to be modeled

e) powerful enough to predict good or bad reasoning.

All of these requirements are met by the hedonic dimension of consciousness, including d) as already seen in previous chapters with thermal pleasure and the models of Ovsich (1998).

When a problem can be reasoned out, Yates *et al.* (1998) find that cultural differences emerge between Japanese subjects and Chinese or American subjects; when the solution can be guessed, all cultural differences disappear. There may be two decision-making processes at work: a rational one when all necessary information is available, including the subjects' cultural background, and a hedonic one when a problem cannot be reasoned out for one reason or another. These are the type 1 and type 2 rationalities of Evans *et al.*

Baron (1994) hypothesizes that nonconsequentialistic behavior[49] results from excessive generalization of rules that lead to desirable

---

[49] Irrational behavior that seems unaffected by adverse consequences.

outcomes only within a narrow framework. Such biases distort the decision-making process. This view is mine too, but the biases he deems parasitic seem to me more like a trace of the biological origin of the decision-making mechanism. Baron (1994) shares the same suspicion:

> "To understand where nonconsequentialist rules (norms) come from, we need to understand where any decision rules come from. I know of no deep theory about this. Some rules may result from observation of our biological behavioral tendencies ..." (p.7 para.4).

Evolution teaches us that when new properties emerge in nature—life from matter, thought from life—the laws and properties of the lower stage remain true and valid in the emergent system, a process that ultimately led to the human species. Animals make decisions, so their decision-making rules should persist in humans. What happens, then, when the animal in us has to choose between two or more motivations, between fatigue and comfort for example? The previous chapters have shown that we choose the optimal behavior and that the decision-making mechanism is based not on rationality, but on hedonicity.

But what about the paradoxical or illogical behaviors that have puzzled so many authors? Some may result from an as yet unknown search for pleasure. This hypothesis is consistent with the findings of numerous studies, if not with their authors' own views, and it would be interesting to investigate such apparently paradoxical behaviors in terms of pleasure maximization. The subject has already interested decision-making theoreticians, essentially in economics and microeconomics. Indeed, real economic behavior also strikes specialists as being irrational at times (Plott 1986). It too may enter into the framework of pleasure maximization if investigated a bit further as in the last chapter, where we investigated decisions leading to illogical behaviors like those of Baron (1994).

Imaging of the human brain has indirectly shown the involvement of pleasure in decision-making. The same centers (frontal and orbitofrontal cortex, amygdala) activate when different pleasures are being experienced and when risky decisions are being made (Morris and Dolan 2001; Ernst et al. 2002; Hamann and Mao 2002).

Although these decision-making rules were initially studied in a laboratory with behaviors that serve physiological needs, pleasure/displeasure also seems to guide decision-making processes in purely mental situations, as in Baron's experiments. If we ask with Baron (1994, p. 3, par. 6) what is the best outcome of a behavior, I would reply: the most pleasurable one. When a decision strikes an external observer as being irrational, it may simply be motivated by a pleasure he or she cannot see. For example, when Baron writes "People require more money to give up a good than they are willing to pay for the same good" (Baron 1994; Knetsch & Sinden 1984, p. 4 para. 1), this may not necessarily indicate a bias but simply the cost of change in terms of pleasure/displeasure. Larkin and McFarland (1978) show that changing an activity incurs a "cost of changing." Baron thinks likewise when he writes: "we might want to include here the benefits of emotional satisfaction ... in the process of decision making " (p. 5 para. 4). In the same vein, emotions may pave the way for efficient decision-making. This hedonicity-related process is discussed in Chapter XI and in Johnson-Laird and Oatley (1992).

Although decisions are made to maximize pleasure, this does not mean that rationality does not exist or plays no role in decision-making. It just means that the rationality of Evans *et al.* is hedonic in nature, as aptly summed up by Pascal (1670, 1972): "The heart has its reasons that reason does not know" (p. 277). Subjects apparently refuse to consume what they like because other factors, like cost, weigh in the decision (Hsee 1999). It's difficult not to consider a cost as an input into overall pleasure or displeasure. Indeed, when all information is available to subjects for decision-making, rationality and hedonicity tend to coincide (Galotti and Carmichael 2001). As the range of possible choices increases, however, the abundance of information makes decision-making difficult and people tend to choose the most rewarding behavior (Suzuki 1997). This mechanism also operates when the range of choices is limited. If someone is constrained to behave in a way contrary to personal belief, this belief will tend to fall into line with the behavior. This is true only for minor constraints (Festinger and Carlsmith 1959).

The logic of reasoning can also be rewarding. But the two

mechanisms can be separated, as seen in cases of brain damage. Manes *et al.* (2002) show that patients with prefrontal cortex lesions lose their decision-making ability, but not their rationality.

"Rather than respond in an algorithmic fashion, the brain shows an extremely high capacity to reorganize its responses according to recent history and prevalent conditions" (Dubrovsky 2002).

Of course, such a conclusion is alien to behaviorism, which disregards mental processes. Nor is it consistent with cognitivism, which is interested in algorithmic rationality. It might be named mentalism. But far from being derogatory, this name shows how far science has progressed in analyzing what seems at first sight impossible to analyze. I earlier noted that decision-making theoreticians had found a number of paradoxical human behaviors: irrational decisions, intransitive choices, and even selfsuggestion. They have described behavioral choices with such theories as Cumulative Prospect Theory and Security-Potential/Aspiration (Lopes and Oden 1999). These theories are descriptive, but largely ignore cognition and above all pleasure/displeasure. By taking these variables into account, I feel that we will simplify our understanding of human behavior and explain these apparent paradoxes.

When doing physical work, such as shoveling snow, you will pause from time to time, however urgent the task may be. You make such a decision without knowing your body temperature, your lactic acid level, or any other biological variable. You simply listen to your sensations of discomfort and compare them with your motivation to shovel snow. When two sensations are in conflict for access to the behavioral final common path, priorities are ranked solely in terms of their tendency to maximize pleasure (or minimize displeasure, essentially the same thing). You choose whichever behavior yields the highest positive algebraic sum for pleasure+displeasure. Linville and Fischer (1991) likewise suggest that affectivity[50] is additive in a way much like what I have experimentally shown for the hedonicity of different physiological and psychological motivations.

When motivations other than biological ones intervene, the process

---

[50] *i.e.*, emotion.

remains the same and works just as efficiently. The decision is still made by maximizing pleasure in the multidimensional space of consciousness, where motivations vie for attention. This is the method that has managed to produce the most efficient behaviors over eons of evolutionary time.

Executing behavior: the pleasure of action

Your typical motivational conflict: mustering the energy you need for a task. The work may be tiring but it provides rewards. If the reward minus the fatigue yields a positive balance, you'll have enough motivation to work. Let's examine each term of this equation.

Work is tiring, boring, energy-intensive, and time-consuming, but we need it to survive. There's no escaping this law of life. Although everyone likes to complain about work, perhaps out of ignorance or conformity, we often acknowledge by our behavior that work is rewarding. It provides not only a salary or income but also the joy of achievement and success. Most of us work, and often happily so. The postindustrial society, the so-called leisure society, is full of people who work willingly and untiringly. They spurn the alternative, unemployment, not simply because they fear a lower standard of living but also because they fear loss of self-respect. For them, the right to work is also the right to happiness.

Who is more self-sacrificing than a good hardworking student? Such a person will study regularly, often late into the night while others are having fun. Yes, but where is the self-sacrifice when these efforts pay off with higher marks, academic awards, and access to better jobs? The same is true for laborers, managers, politicians, and physicians who work hard and put in long hours. They may describe their behavior as selfless, but where is the selflessness if the rewards are real and many? The term "workoholic" has been coined for these apparent addicts, yet clearly work is not a curse for those who recognize its rewards.

What is more self-sacrificing than volunteer work? This sort of activity is cited as the pinnacle of selfless behavior. Without taking a sociobiological view, which sees altruism as one way to maximize

159

genetic self-interest, we should put things into perspective. Certainly, it does cost to give up your own time and potential income by doing work for a local church or a humanitarian cause. But this work brings both immediate and long-term rewards. It's often done by homemakers who wish to escape from stifling or boring household chores. There are other rewards, such as grateful beneficiaries, a feeling of making a difference and, eventually, various tokens of collective appreciation: awards, medals, public recognition, etc. Without being cynical, the balance sheet looks quite positive for such "selfless" behavior. In an article on motivations for climbing mountains and trekking to the North Pole, Loewenstein (1999) proposed desire for social recognition, self-esteem, achievement, control, and search for meaning. These sources of happiness make up for the fatigue, discomfort, pain, and sometimes mortal danger of mountaineering or polar expeditions. This point will be analyzed further in Chapter XII.

How do people maximize their balance sheet (pleasure + fatigue)? In *La Quête du plaisir*, I gave two examples: one positive, the other negative (Cabanac 1995). The first example is a humble job: pushing shopping carts in a local supermarket parking lot. These supermarket employees are mildly retarded. Shameless exploitation? I have no idea of their conditions of employment. I wish only to understand their pleasure balance. These men smile, are dedicated to their work, and visibly enjoy a job that requires all of their faculties but is nonetheless within their abilities.

The second example is an academic position. It's filled by a man who has worked his way up to the rank of professor through good marks and successive university degrees. He should be happy with his life. But he has reached his level of incompetence (Peter and Hull 1970). His position requires him to devote much of his activity to research, but he lacks the necessary creative imagination. Rightly or wrongly, academia favors research over teaching. Academics who fail to do research are deemed secondclass members of their university faculties. Our professor is profoundly unhappy despite his decent salary and high social standing off-campus.

These examples are caricatures. The balance (pleasure minus constraint) is positive in the first example and negative in the second. In each job, the sense of achievement depends on the match between the task and the worker's tastes and talents. This matching has to be finessed by each of us.

One experiment has shown how subtle a reward can be for an action. Johnson and Bickel (2002) observed no difference in response when their subjects were offered a hypothetical reward and a real financial reward of up to $150. In any experiment, therefore, the human mind must be considered in all its complexity. It may find pleasure where least expected and thus muddy the results for anyone who ignores the importance of pleasure/displeasure.

Upbringing and the morality of pleasure

For Richard Schuster, evil, when committed collectively, is also a source of pleasure.[51] He sees its origin in the evolutionary survival of small hunter-gatherer bands. The exercise of power gives some people more pleasure than anything else does through the benefits it has provided since the days of prehistory, particularly in access to mates and reproductive success. Schuster (2002) points to the paradoxical attraction of many women for men who do risky work. Similarly, wife batterers—and even serial killers— are abandoned by their wives or girlfriends only belatedly. Murder may represent the ultimate pleasure that people get from evil. According to René Girard (1978), collective murder unifies the group and Schuster (2002) says that chimpanzees forget all hierarchical quarrels when they go hunting and killing monkeys of other species. On the other hand, cooperation is pleasurable independently of its rewards.

Pleasure intervenes in social relations. In the last chapter, we showed that moderately aggressive behaviors generate pleasure in all sorts of day-to-day situations, whereas passivity is clearly disagreeable. Such minor aggressiveness is not only cathartic but also pleasurable. This finding, together with the deliberate choice by some subjects of several clearly immoral, and pleasurable, behaviors, confirms that no sphere of mental activity or decision-making can escape the irresistible

---

[51] Personal communication.

tendency to maximize pleasure.

Let's now turn to the supreme sacrifice: the decision to give up one's life for some cause. The martyr's sacrifice is deliberate. Usually there's an alternative—flight or apostasy. It is thus a free choice. Therefore, it must provide a pleasure more intense than survival itself: death for the motherland,[52] love for family and kin, or remembrance by posterity as a martyr.

In the last chapter's experiments, some subjects rated certain clearly aggressive or dishonest behaviors as pleasant, but failed to choose them when given a choice. There is thus a discrepancy between pleasure and ultimate behavior—a sign that upbringing affects the way we perceive pleasure. In general, our subjects gained more pleasure from moderately aggressive but nonviolent behaviors, preferring them to the most aggressive ones. Although the four gratuitous motivations of Loewenstein (1999)—self-esteem, achievement, control, and meaning—are probably innate, upbringing may accelerate and shape their development. Pleasure certainly plays a role in such learning and teaching, or rather upbringing. Hopefully other experiments will advance our understanding of this subject and take us beyond the stage of intuition. Until then, we're free to speculate on the moral role of pleasure.

Many of life's pleasures and joys are not innate. They're learned. Although such learning may occur spontaneously during infancy and adolescence, it is accelerated and amplified by upbringing. Upbringing bypasses trial and error, thus allowing people to accumulate key knowledge in a minimum of time. So it's important to teach reward mechanisms. It's even more important to teach that the highest rewards are moral in nature and that Loewenstein's gratuitous motivations—self-esteem, achievement, control, and meaning—are not really gratuitous. They are the most rewarding ones. It's often for them that people will sacrifice their lives (Loewenstein 1999). Since the highest rewards are learned, these motivations must be passed on through upbringing.

One such motivation is love of effort. It can and should be learned more quickly through upbringing. This means teaching children the

---

[52] *Dulce est pro patria mori* (Horace).

rewards of work and the need to weigh costs and benefits. If their intellectual abilities are great, their goals can and should be just as great. If not, their goals should be scaled down, to ensure that a positive balance remains to reward their efforts.

In the materialist societies we live in, the prevailing ideology is a frenetic pursuit of happiness, and we pursue it by consuming more and more. The time has come for a new Epicureanism—one that will teach us how to understand and apply the mechanisms of pleasure and joy. The time has come to teach "this joy of living that is so lacking in a generation caught up in material progress" (Fesquet 1962). At the risk of repeating myself, this teaching must help children understand their human nature and how it works, instead of presenting a normative morality. Many behaviors are rewarding and offer a net pleasure balance even though their outcomes are disagreeable, painful, or dangerous, witness the examples already cited. Conversely, many joys can only be gained through effort and self-denial. These realities are unknown to young children. We need to tell and show them that there's more happiness in giving than in receiving,[53] that the effort of building a stable and fruitful family provides one of the greatest joys of life, and that to reject this choice is to reject an irreplaceable human experience—the transmission of life (Chaunu 1975). Unfortunately, our words and actions don't always lead children in the right direction (Plé 1982).

Children also need to learn that reward is often anticipated. This is an essential cornerstone of upbringing. Clearly, work and self-denial aren't rewarding for children. The reward comes with the outcome of effort. It's through learning that children come to associate self-denial with reward and pain with bliss. The key role of upbringing is to teach this association, which is far from obvious to anyone who first encounters it. We should not be afraid to teach that self-sacrifice and intellectual or physical effort can be rewarding. Nor should we fear teaching that effort must be ongoing, since the emotional reward is soon gone. Upbringing is complete when this emotion is produced by anticipation itself, and hence by effort and self-denial.

---

[53] Acts 20:35. Similarly, Matthew 10:39 states: "He who finds his life will lose it, and he who loses his life for my sake will find it."

Pleasure can also flow from immoral behaviors, such as violence. We need to teach children to beware of this source of happiness, as recognized by the signatories of the Seville Statement on Violence.[54] The teaching process begins with recognition that violence can be enjoyable.

Conclusion

Of all the motivations and rewards that life offers us, moralists have always taught that moral rewards are the noblest. This teaching underlies the condemnation of Epicureanism and the triumph of Stoicism. It's time now to accept that such rewards are superior because they maximize pleasure and not because they are deemed moral. This view reconciles hormists and hedonists, Stoics and Epicureans. There is actually a dialectics of pleasure that is both a cause and an end.

If it is true that happiness is an activity consistent with virtue, it is clear that it is the one that is the most perfectly consistent with virtue, that is, the activity of the highest part of Man (Aristotle, 384-322 BC).

Whether you're a hedonist or a hormist, whether you indulge in pleasure or anticipate it, the desired outcome is always pleasure. Yes, pleasure can serve moral ends, but this is no reason for feeling less committed to morality. On the contrary, the nature of this commitment is now simply understood a bit better. This same understanding is shared by leading theologians: "For an individual, the love of action can have two sources. First of all, pleasure. Through action, he can attain a feeling of enjoyment" (Ellul 1987). This view is aptly expressed by Dietricht Bonhoeffer (1973): "If you go looking for freedom, learn above all the discipline of your senses and your soul, in order that your desires and your body do not lead you astray." By teaching us to understand pleasure, and how to channel its energies, the Epicurean way of life provides a powerful motive for action. To realize this simple truth is to take a step toward freedom.

---

[54] Seville Statement on Violence. UNESCO 1991.
http://portal.unesco.org/education/en/ev.php-
URL_ID=3247&URL_DO=DO_TOPIC&URL_SECTION=201.html

The Gospels teach us that "he who loves his life loses it, and he who hates his life in this world will keep it for eternal life"[55] and that "greater love has no man than this, that a man lay down his life for his friends."[56] These remarks are usually construed as being obligations, as a normative morality. If we look closer, however, they appear more to be observations, a descriptive teaching. "Rejoice and be glad, for your reward is great in heaven"[57] or "it is more blessed to give than to receive"[58] is perhaps not a commandment, as might seem at first glance, but rather a statement of higher wisdom. The same may hold true for all of the Beatitudes. There is thus no merit in going above and beyond the call of duty. Meritorious people are simply seeking the highest of all pleasures: self-sacrifice. By maximizing their own pleasure, they are optimizing what is good for the group, or the species. But such a choice requires a keen sense of self-understanding.

These conclusions bear out the intuitions of many philosophers, notably Bentham (1748-1832):

"Nature has placed mankind under the governance of two sovereign masters, pain and pleasure. It is for them alone to point out what we ought to do, as well as to determine what we shall do ... they govern us in all we do, in all we say, in all we think" (Bentham 1823:1).

Bentham's conclusions are now experimentally confirmed. Pleasure holds a central place in optimizing behavior and life. It facilitates survival. Does this view of morality imply or lead to a certain degree of cynicism? "I do good not for the sake of doing good but for the benefits I get out of it." Yet such a view appears in the writings of Pascal and the teachings of the Gospels[59] with no reproach being made. In reality, there's no need to condemn this view, if it exists. Rational decision-making is by nature different from hedonic decision-making.

---

[55] John 12:25.

[56] John 15:13.

[57] Matthew 5:12.

[58] Acts 20:35. It would seem more legitimate to translate this assertion by "there is more joy in giving than in receiving" (see Chapter XII).

[59] "And I say to you, make friends for yourselves by means of the mammon of unrighteousness." Luke 16:9.

The latter is conscious but not rational. If cynicism were to enter into the net balance of pleasure *vs*. displeasure, the emotional reward would disappear. You cannot cheat this mechanism. To do so would be to cheat yourself. By experiencing the highest reward for virtuous conduct, we wish to practice virtue because such behavior has become most rewarding.

Merit thus does not exist. Merit, like freedom, simply comes down to making the right choices. "The practice of virtue contains its own reward" (Seneca, see Delatte 1973). This position dovetails with that of many moralists. Stated by a Stoic, it ironically finds its place in a new effort to rehabilitate Epicureanism.

Finally, by giving pleasure such a place in thinking, anticipation, behavior, and rationality, we can make predictions about the nature of different objects in the conscious mind and the phylogenetic origin of consciousness. These predictions will be developed in the final chapters, in fulfillment of J.R. Roy's quote at the beginning of Chapter IV.[60]

---

[60] "When a research program is well developed, confirmations and verifications, and not efforts of refutation, are what assumes importance. ... Thus, a vigorous program leads to new predictions" (Roy 1998:80).

Chapter IX
Thoughts on the origin of consciousness[61]

Philosophers—and psychologists alike—have had
a difficult time trying to comprehend
consciousness. I make no pretence to solving the
problem of consciousness in this paper. My more
modest aim [is ...] to begin sketching a map that
can guide future thinking about consciousness.
Nelkin, 1989

Nelkin's aim is the same as mine in this chapter. I will examine consciousness from an evolutionary psychology standpoint while trying to reconstruct its phylogenetic origin. The implications will then be spelled out.

This effort will run into three problems that are zoological, anatomical, and semantic in nature. The first problem is phylogenetic. At what point in evolutionary time did living things begin to be conscious—and able to feel pleasure? The question is peripheral to this chapter, which deals with the utility of human consciousness, and will be addressed in the next chapter. For now, it's enough to say that consciousness emerged or "merely appeared" (Revonsuo 1994) before *Homo sapiens*.

The second problem is anatomical. I leave it to others to speculate about the physicochemical basis of consciousness (Hameroff 1987; Penrose 1994). We still don't know the nature of the anatomical link between structure and function, between brain and mind—the "binding problem" of philosophers (Lashley 1929; Delacour 1994; Baars 1995; Edelman 2000; Rees *et al.* 2002). We do know that the cerebral hemispheres are not identical and that some functions exist predominantly in one hemisphere. For instance, speech control is in the left hemisphere and spatial perception in the right. Some patients have 'separated' brains because surgery or accident has cut the commissures

---

[61] This chapter closely follows an article published in Cabanac (1996).

linking the two hemispheres. They respond verbally to a signal received in the right visual field (linked to the left hemisphere) and with gestures to the same signal in the left visual field (linked to the right hemisphere) (Dennet 1991; Mortensen *et al.* 1993; Pessin 1993). Some authors thus think that consciousness may be multiple and not single (Allport 1988; Wilkes 1988). Yet intact subjects have an intimate feeling that the self is a single entity and "identifiable not with a nonphysical soul, but rather with a set of representational capacities of the physical brain" (Churchland 2002). Although their brains use multiple parallel networks with specific functions and anatomical structures (Baars 1994; Heiligenberg 1994; Rolls 1994), their emergent consciousness is that of a single self. This is key to my argument. Consciousness is an emergent property of the infinitely complex human mind and such properties interest me.

The third problem is terminological. "The importance of clearly defining (and redefining) terms that describe behavioral processes as our knowledge of the underlying physiological mechanisms advances has repeatedly been emphasized" (White 1989). Indeed, words may be treacherous. Different disciplines don't necessarily describe the same mental objects with the same words. Conversely, the same words may be used differently by different disciplines, languages, or individuals, and thus cover somewhat dissimilar realities (Montefiore and Noble 1989). Marcel and Bisiach (1988) describe the problems of psychologists in simply defining consciousness. They show that one basic problem in studying consciousness is fuzzy semantics—at times functionalist for neuropsychology and at times phenomenological for cognitive psychology. Words like "short-term memory," "attention," "control," and "verbal expression" don't fall into the same category as "intention," "consciousness," "self-perception," "qualia," or "subjectivity." Although some uncertainty is inevitable in our attempts to discuss the invisible mind and its private data, we should still try to limit semantic fuzziness and eliminate the "intolerable vagueness" that Tulving (1995) denounces in discussions of consciousness. One way has been proposed by Ovsich (1998): use mathematical language that leaves no room for indeterminacy, or recognize the indeterminacy for what it is.

My graphic and conceptual presentation of sensation in Chapter II as a 4-dimensional model (Figure II.5) is an attempt in that direction.[62] This presentation corresponds to the equation:

$$\psi = f(x.y[t],z[t]) \qquad \text{Equation II.1}$$

Let's return to the problem of how consciousness arose. In recent years, the field of psychology has seen the development of a new perspective: evolutionary psychology (Bunge 1979; Cosmides *et al.* 1992). Darwin (1872) (Figure IX.1) and later Lashley (1949) were the first to suggest that natural selection has shaped the mind. Today, proponents of this view argue that conscious thought is the culmination of an evolutionary process and that this process must be understood before we can understand consciousness.[63] They notably maintain that 1) mental characteristics exist today because they've been retained by natural selection and are thus necessarily advantageous, from the standpoint of species survival, and that 2) the human mind evolved out of non-human predecessors (Merker 2005).

The law of natural selection implies that consciousness was advantageous to the first animals to possess it. Such animals were likelier to survive and reproduce, thus passing the trait on to subsequent generations. But what was the advantage? Or, rather, what was the disadvantage of previous modes of thinking? All conscious behaviors are possible through reflex circuits of one sort or another, much like those of Turing machines, and it's far from clear what benefits come from consciousness. Today, we're building robots that can reproduce human decision-making with increasing sophistication and the day will soon come when robots will make decisions as ably as any conscious being can (Revonsuo 1994). Just think of Sniffer (Figure VII.7). Consciousness is evidently not programmed into such robots. So how is it useful? Why was it retained by natural selection? "The more we

---

[62] This concern for semantics came up in Chapter II with sensation. It will recur again in Chapter XI with emotion and in Chapter XII with happiness.

[63] In subscribing to this viewpoint, I don't necessarily support other hypotheses of evolutionary psychology. Indeed, Bunge (2003) has rightly condemned certain theoretical meanderings by evolutionary psychologists who wish to push their theory too far.

understand mental processes in computational terms, the less need there seems for consciousness" (Oatley 1988).

Indeed, the existence of consciousness is denied by many modern thinkers in neurophysiology and ethology. A reductionist tendency prevails among those who fail to see this property in the structures and circuits they analyze (see Changeux 1983). To them, one might reply that consciousness is an emergent property of the brain's complexity and thus cannot be discerned at the neural level. An example of emergence is provided by Durkheim (1924): chemical synthesis can create new molecules whose properties cannot be foreseen in any of their constituents. This concept has been notably developed by the Montreal philosopher Mario Bunge (1979, 1989) to describe the brain's properties. Another concept that physiologists tend to forget is that of scale. The theoretical physicist Michel Gondran[64] has proposed a striking analogy with the laws of gas. No one can dispute the existence of temperature and gas pressure, yet both are emergent properties. If we were to examine a tiny gas sample containing only a few molecules, we would find neither temperature nor pressure, as both properties emerge only with huge numbers of molecules. The same is true for the nervous system: consciousness emerges only on the scale of very many neurons (Bunge 1989).

At the other end of the biological sciences, some ethologists have trouble seeing the usefulness of consciousness. Their dilemma—in reality, a paradox—is lucidly described by the ethologist Marian Dawkins (1993):

- Consciousness didn't arise through natural selection. This hypothesis would contradict the universality of natural selection and is difficult to accept for evolution-minded thinkers.
- Consciousness did arise through natural selection. Its selective advantage, however, is so difficult to pinpoint that some even claim that no difference is distinguishable between conscious and unconscious organisms.

On top of these doubts about the usefulness of consciousness, she also notes how well adapted the behavior of lower animals and robots is to

---

[64] Personal communication.

their needs. There are nonetheless good reasons for believing that consciousness preceded the advent of our species, and I will discuss them in Chapter X.

In reality, to argue that consciousness is unnecessary is to ignore certain facts.

- Presumably non-conscious lower animals have limited flexibility in their behavior. Behavioral flexibility appears only late in evolution.
- Behavior is hardwired in robots and lower animals. Decisions are made through reflex circuits that work because they have been designed by a robot maker or shaped by natural selection over many generations.
- In some living things, pleasure makes behavior fit the circumstances. Decision-making is thus more flexible. It's no longer necessary to hardwire millions of reflexes that hook up a plethora of appropriate behavioral responses to even more stimuli. Paradoxically, artificial intelligence specialists are the ones who've realized that strict rationality must be combined with a source of motivation (Cardon 2000). This is what I simply call pleasure.

The philosopher David Chalmers (1995) proposes that the problems with consciousness fall into two groups: easy problems and the hard problem.

The easy problems are:
- the ability to discriminate, to classify, and to respond to environmental stimuli;
- the integration of information;
- the possibility of reporting a mental state;
- the ability to access one's own internal state;
- the deliberate control of behavior;
- and finally the difference between being awake and sleeping.

All of these phenomena can be scientifically explained in terms of neurophysiology or cognition. On the other hand, what he calls the "hard problem" eludes scientific explanation. The real problem posed by consciousness is its very existence. Why does thought arise from the physicochemical mechanisms of our brain?

My concerns, and the experiments of the previous chapters, lie halfway between Chalmers' easy problems and his hard problem. Perhaps I can offer a solution to the hard problem. In a 3-step answer, I will address the *why* rather than the *how*.

Step 1) Mental properties arose and evolved under the pressure of natural selection. Consciousness, like any mental or psychological phenomenon, should be examined in terms of the evolution of living things, as has been done by Bunge and by Cosmides and Tooby. This leads us to Step 2).

Step 2) Postulate 1: Consciousness evolved from sensation, the first object of consciousness.

Figure IX.1   Charles Darwin, 1809-1882.
> "As many more individuals of each species are born than can possibly survive; and as, consequently, there is a frequently recurring struggle for existence, it follows that any being, if it vary however slightly in any manner profitable to itself, under the complex and sometimes varying conditions of life, will have a better chance of surviving, and thus be *naturally selected*."

Although this postulate is new, as expressed here, it harks back to the tradition of sensationalism described in Chapter II. It is less radical than Cadillac's sensationalism and makes sensation central to the phylogenetic emergence of consciousness, independently of ontogeny. Once a species has sensation, new forms of sensation are not an emergence but simply an evolution. Similarly, once a species can perform mentally, new mental performances are an evolution, the mind having already emerged. Thus, the entire mental sphere is but different variations on a basic structure of sensation. Such 'recycling' is common in evolution: each new function is cobbled together from preexisting structures (Jacob 1981). This process has been termed "increased accessibility" by Paul Rozin (1976) when speaking of social psychological evolution. Postulate 1 is just an extension of this general mechanism of living things.

Step 3) Corollary of Postulate 1: Consciousness has retained the four original dimensions of sensation. It is structurally similar to sensation and thus can be represented by the model of Figure II.5 and Equation II.1.

We've already seen that sensation can be described as a 4-dimensional mental object. Does this structure persist in all forms of consciousness? Is the above corollary justified?

It does seem borne out by simple introspection. I can analyze any thought in my mind and recognize its quality, its intensity, its hedonicity, and its duration. This corollary can also be substantiated by the following four steps:

1) The hedonic dimension of sensation—sensory pleasure or displeasure—tells us how useful a stimulus is. Pleasure/displeasure indexes this utility while motivating us to avoid the stimulus or to seek and eventually consume it.

2) Since behavior is a final common path, the brain needs a common currency to prioritize the urgency of satisfying different motivations on a time-sharing basis.

3)   Pleasure is the common currency for physiologically motivated behaviors. Physiological motivations, however, have to compete with other motivations (social, ludic, aesthetic, etc.).   Just as pleasure indexes the usefulness of a stimulus, it will also index the usefulness of any other mental object.

4)   The hedonic dimension is thus the source of motivation for consciousness, just as it is for sensation. If consciousness evolved out of sensation, it probably retains sensation's other dimensions. These four dimensions will now each be examined.

The qualitative dimension of consciousness

This dimension poses no real problem. Clearly, our consciousness has different kinds of mental objects. Sensations can differ, and so can thoughts.   Mental objects include sensations, perceptions, illusions, hallucinations, premonitions, emotions, remembrances, ruminations, dreams, reasonings, observations, gestalts, self-awareness, and so on.

These categories of mental objects differ qualitatively. They are "discrete data," in mathematical terminology. Each category may in turn be divided into subcategories.   For instance, we may divide emotion into fear, surprise, love, and so on. By representing these different mental objects on a single qualitative axis, we also resolve a major problem: the unity of consciousness. Instead of asking whether there is one or more consciousnesses, we can now see consciousness as applying to mental objects that vary in nature. Only one mental object, however, occupies consciousness at any point in time.

Dubé and LeBel (2002) asked 76 subjects to list the categories of pleasure they knew. The list varied from one subject to the next with each subject giving an average of 14. The total, 1,127 categories, could be grouped into four major divisions: intellectual/spiritual, emotional, social, and sensual/physical. To me, rather than representing different pleasures, as the authors deduce, this list seems to reflect the innumerable causes of pleasure. In other words, it encompasses the qualitative dimension of consciousness. These causes of pleasure may each have their own intensity and hedonicity, which misleadingly makes them look like different pleasures.

The qualitative dimension identifies the nature of a mental object, just as it identifies the nature of a stimulus in the special case of sensation. An idea, like a sensation, is a copy or filter of the truth. By using this dimension to designate the nature of a mental object, we're implying nothing about the nature of the structure(s) of consciousness. This point is discussed in Baars (1994) and Baars and Newman (1994).

The intensive dimension of consciousness

This dimension is easily understood in the case of sensation, but less so in the case of consciousness. Many authors have argued that consciousness may be analyzed as a structure with several levels of intensity. We've shown that this model holds true for sensory perceptions. With these authors, we'll now see how well it describes consciousness.

The principle of non-contradiction implies that one cannot be conscious and unconscious at the same time. Yet cases of "blind sight" show that the brain can adequately receive and process visual signals without any awareness by the patient, whose occipital lobe has been damaged (Weiskrantz 1991). Similarly, patients can store information received while under general anesthesia and even use it to some degree (Roorda-Hrdlicová *et al.* 1990). This would be consciousness at its lowest level of intensity. Above this threshold, different authors distinguish several levels of intensity.

For Taylor *et al.* (1998), consciousness requires neural support, *i.e.*, an integrated network of many centers with several levels. At the lowest level is unconscious processing. Above are several modules that process information consciously but without focused attention. Finally, a series of modules direct attention in a controlled manner.

Cowey (1997) proposes a list of seven kinds of consciousness (Table IX.1). On this list, entries 2 to 6 may be considered distinct categories and assigned to the qualitative (x) axis of consciousness. On the other hand, entries 1 and 7 can be assigned different places on the intensive (y) axis. Entry 1, coma and sleep, would have zero intensity and entry 7, concentrated reflection, a high level of intensity. For Jouvet (1992), one of our alert states is the deep sleep of REM (rapid eye movement) when we dream. Thus, the 4-dimensional model enables us to sort conscious states by both intensity and quality.

Tulving (1985) proposes that retrieval operations for different memory systems may be associated with levels or forms of consciousness: *anoetic* (not knowing), *noetic* (knowing), and *autonoetic* (self-knowing). These three levels would represent intensities of consciousness.

There thus seems to be consensus that intensity is a continuum for all conscious thinking in general, as with sensation. On this continuum, we can make out at least four levels of intensity: unconscious (blind vision), threshold of consciousness (daydreaming, automatic motor behavior), conscious reflection ("I'm thinking it over"), and intense consciousness exclusive of any other experience (panic, orgasm, etc.). Table IX.2 presents these four intensities for sensation and for the general case of consciousness.

This dimension of intensity doesn't imply that a single cerebral structure supports consciousness. For example, blind vision is a simple form of sensibility that connects to reflex responses below the threshold of consciousness. It seems to use a different network from that of conscious vision. When a stronger stimulus is delivered to the affected, blind side of the patient's brain, no sensation results. Yet this would happen in an intact subject, where several structures act in parallel.

For Baars and Newman, the most intense ideas or perceptions occupy the forefront of consciousness at any given moment, and hide the less intense ones. This may explain selective attention (Baars 1994). But when thoughts aren't intense, several may coexist at the same time. An experienced driver can easily drive and think about other things or listen to the radio. Does it follow, then, that we can compare the intensity of thoughts as qualitatively different as eating a banana/strawberry yogurt and reading a scientific article? Yes, according to experiments in cross-modality matching.

If consciousness is defined in terms of intensity, I suspect that some semantic and conceptual problems will disappear. As previously with the qualitative axis, this approach is more fruitful than asking whether there are one or more consciousnesses.

The hedonic dimension of consciousness

No psychologist has trouble accepting that conscious experience may evoke negative, neutral, or positive feelings, as does sensation. P.T. Young (1959) sees the hedonic process as having three attributes: sign (agreeable or disagreeable), intensity, and duration. Intensity, duration, and sign are represented by the axes y, t, and z. Duncker (1940-1941) lists four causes of pleasure:

- sensory enjoyment (or dislike), *i.e.*, the faculty of enjoying a stimulus or the consequences of a behavior;
- aesthetic enjoyment, *i.e.*, the tendency to strive for better understanding;
- desire (for a steak, a book, love, etc.), not a reaction but the fulfillment of a need;
- pleasure in achievement, dynamic joy of success or victory.

Implicitly, he has shown that very different mental objects can be classified on a single axis of the hedonic dimension.

Like the quantitative dimension, the hedonic dimension of consciousness is also a continuum. It can be marked off by several benchmarks that imperceptibly fade into each other: distress, extreme displeasure, moderate displeasure, slight displeasure, indifference, slight pleasure, moderate pleasure, delight, and rapture. Its magnitude may be zero—a mental state of indifference.

The concept of behavioral final common path is especially useful for understanding the hedonic dimension of consciousness. We've seen that the brain needs a common currency to rank different competing motivations, and to satisfy the most urgent ones. We've also seen the evidence that this common currency is sensory pleasure. Thus, the hedonic axis defines the desire to consume a stimulus or to reach a goal, and the intention to act will depend on a summation of several simultaneous positive or negative desires on that axis. This is particularly evident with feeding behavior. P.T. Young (1959) especially, but others as well (Booth 1990; Berridge 2000) have argued that pleasure is but one of several signals that encourage and stimulate feeding.

TABLE IX.1
Varieties of consciousness, after Cowey

1. Unconsciousness, coma, deep sleep
2. Unconsciousness, dreaming
3. Simple perception of (ambient) sensory stimuli: light, sounds, smells, etc.
4. Perception of symbolic representations. We identify stimuli, e.g., our homes
5. Perception of state: hunger, thirst, fatigue, etc.
6. Conscious retrieval of events or knowledge, imagery, deliberate selective attention
7. Highest level: reasoning, self-control, etc.

TABLE IX.2
Intensities of consciousness

Intensity	Phylogenetic origin (hypothetical)	Sensation	Consciousness
Level 4		Alarm	Nothing else exists
Level 3	*Homo*	Attentive sensation	"I" think it over
Level 2	Mammals and birds	Sensation	Thought
Level 1	Reptiles	Threshold of sensation	Threshold of consciousness, mood
Level 0	Amphibians	Sensibility	Blind vision

In the special case of feeding behavior, we can understand how the final decision is made if we remember that all pleasures and displeasures enter into mutual competition before they produce an

178

intention to act or to abstain. If the motivations are as different as those of Duncker's four categories, they'll need a common currency that can compare them and prioritize their access to behavior. Physiological, ludic, social, aesthetic, moral, and religious motivations must be able to speak to each other. We've seen this need for comparability in preceding chapters. We now have to find out whether the properties of sensory pleasure—contingency, transience, correlation with usefulness—are also those of consciousness. We've already shown that sensory pleasure is contingent, transient, and indicative of utility. Do these properties also apply to the general case of consciousness?

Clearly, conscious pleasure is contingent. For instance, if I think about my set of keys now, the thought will evoke a neutral feeling. In contrast, the feeling will be very negative if I come to work and discover that my keys are lost. If I retrace my steps and find them, the same mental object will be seen very positively. Pleasure varies, much as alliesthesia does.

Conscious pleasure is also transient. I'll examine the nature of happiness in greater detail in a later chapter and its transience will emerge as being fundamental. For now, just keep in mind that so many philosophers have rejected the pursuit of happiness because the word covers two entities. One is analogous to sensory comfort—stable but emotionally neutral. The other is analogous to sensory pleasure— transient, evaporating once the object is consumed and the desire satiated. Satisfaction can only be fleeting. Unknown to many, however, happiness has a more stable side. For the time being, my point will simply be that pleasure is always transient in the general case of consciousness, as in the special case of sensation.

Do all mental pleasures indicate usefulness? If sensory pleasure indexes useful stimuli, then so should consciousness, according to the corollary of Postulate 1. Indeed, positive affect is correlated positively not only with good health but also with longevity (Cohen and Pressman 2006). Because of the complexity of consciousness, however, the stimulus/mind relationship is not always one-way and some stimuli have gone beyond being passive mental objects. Drug dependence is a case in point. Clearly, some events or behaviors are pleasurable and yet have no discernable utility. This is a serious challenge to the corollary and I'll address it at some length in the following eight paragraphs:

1) From a Darwinian standpoint, pleasure or displeasure doesn't have to be useful for 100% of mental objects. To be passed on to the next generation, a trait only has to provide its possessors with *some* selective advantage, however slight. For instance, curiosity is sometimes harmful, as when it leads an animal to a predator. Yet all ethologists agree that curiosity enhances species survival because it provides reusable information and makes anticipation possible.

2) Sensory pleasure is above all proximally useful. It may be judged by its immediate survival value. But long-term survival value may also be associated with pleasure. Sexual enjoyment is a powerful recompense for reproductive behavior. It's useful not for the individual but for the species, enough for it to be preserved by natural selection. Thus, pleasure may indicate the usefulness of a behavior either in the short term for the individual or in the long term for the species. For an individual, the joy of love has no survival value (one might even suggest the opposite). Its utility lies in the outcome of reproductive behavior.

3) Kent Berridge has shown that "liking" and "wanting" are dissociated functions in the brain's neural structures. In an animal brain, one can artificially activate one without activating the other. He suggests that drug addiction may be due to the activation of wanting without liking (Berridge 1999). Of course, such dissociation is pathological and doesn't occur on its own in nature.

4) In the special case of feeding habits, the pursuit of pleasure is often maladaptive. Animals and people tend to eat what they like and may end up consuming a preferred food item to the exclusion of others, the result being a deficient diet (Galef 1991). Young (1959) shows that the acquisition of food preferences is based on an animal's nutritional needs. In nature, pleasure is divorced from usefulness only in the improbable case where a familiar food item has been made artificially deficient in a vitamin or amino acid.

5) Artificial sweeteners are a similar case. Natural selection has favored animals, including our remote ancestors, that perceive a sweet taste as pleasurable, because this is the taste of energy-rich sugars. Although chemists can now artificially separate sweetness from sugar, this taste perception remains intact, and useful, under natural conditions.

6) In an experiment, a group of monkeys was trained to delay the administration of an electric shock by responding (McKearney 1969). The conditions were then changed so that the animal's response triggered the shock, instead of delaying it. Paradoxically, in what has been named 'the McKearney effect,' the monkeys responded even faster. This situation resembles point 4) above. Pleasure indicates usefulness when new behavioral responses can be learned. The McKearney effect seems to be a pathological regression in animals that inexplicably cannot learn a new response.

7) The case of drug addiction is more complex. At first sight, pleasure seems to be improperly linked to usefulness when addicts seek and consume a neurologically active substance that provides them with pleasure but no beneficial outcome. Such a situation confirms that pleasure is a powerful motor for behavior. What remains unexplained is the apparent mismatch between pleasure and usefulness. First, we need to dissociate the first drug experience from the later stages of complete dependence. The initial contact is probably motivated by curiosity (see point 1). After more or less prolonged use, abstinence becomes so painful that the pleasure of consuming the drug may seem useful over the short term. It suppresses withdrawal symptoms. In addition, people probably turn to drugs as a way to allay the discomfort of motivational conflicts (see point 8 below).

8) The last case: something can be both useful and unpleasant:
"People often behave in ways that do not seem pleasurable as measured by other than behavioral measures. People go on diets, put themselves through unpleasant courses of study, read unpleasant books and

articles, sacrifice their own pleasure for the good of relatives, friends, compatriots, etc."[65]

All of the above examples fall into the general category of motivational conflicts, a situation already studied (chapters V and VI). In such cases, behavior is indeed motivated by pleasure maximization. What is being maximized, however, is the algebraic sum of pleasures and displeasures arising from different conflicting motivations.

The last property of sensory pleasure is its capacity to motivate behavior. We seek sensory pleasure and try to maximize it; in so doing, we're driven to act. Is this also true for the general case of consciousness? We've seen several such examples in the experiments of previous chapters, *i.e.*, pursuit of non-sensory pleasure from money and video games. The answer is likewise affirmative if we ask most philosophers. Be they hedonists or hormists, to use the classification of Duncker (1940-1941), pleasure is either the motivation or the outcome of behavior. In both cases, behavior is driven by pleasure. This particular point is discussed by Ovsich (1998) and Johnston (1999).

We can see this key role in cases where pleasure is absent, as in patients with damage to the prefrontal cortex or the basal nuclei, in particular the temporal amygdala (Bechara *et al.* 1994; Bechara *et al.* 1996; Laplane and Dubois 2001; Manes *et al.* 2002). They can reason correctly but have trouble making decisions. They also, apparently, have no sense of pleasure. Although we cannot share another person's experience of life, this anhedonia leaves many objective signs. Anhedonia is also apparent in schizophrenics (Blanchard *et al.* 1998) and depressives (Loas 1996). Among such people, however, only pleasure is absent; displeasure is stronger and even permanent. Their behavior is perturbed but they're better able to make decisions than are true anhedonics.

The hedonic dimension is therefore essential. Of all the thoughts that compete for first place on the final common path to consciousness, victory goes to the most, or least, pleasurable mental object. The

---

[65] Comment by an anonymous referee on one of my articles: Cabanac, M. (1992). The referee recommended rejection of the manuscript.

hedonic dimension focuses attention on the element with the highest value on the qualitative axis. This is what Fazio (2000) calls "attitude"—the mental disposition, the bias for or against some object, person, or situation. Attitude may be positive or negative, but it always has this hedonic dimension. Through many experiments, Fazio has shown its functional value: it usefully orients visual attention and the processes of categorization. Because decisions are faster and made more efficiently, resources are freed up for other purposes. Attitude, or rather hedonicity, is thus beneficial. Through it, consciousness can infinitely shape and reshape the decision-making process by adding new priorities and readjusting plans to reflect the unexpected (see Oatley 1988). His argument is the same as mine (Cabanac 1971, 1992). Finally, Zajonc (1994) has shown that mood, *i.e.*, the hedonic background of consciousness at any moment, is independent of cognition and may change without being cognitive. This is further evidence that the qualitative and hedonic dimensions of consciousness operate independently.

The time dimension of consciousness

All mental objects have limited duration. This property shouldn't raise any more problems for consciousness than it did for sensation, other than to raise the question of the nature of time itself. Given that time is widely believed to exist and may be measured by such instruments as stopwatches, pendulums, and clocks, I'll not challenge its existence here.

Need for consciousness

Consciousness is unnecessary for artificial intelligence and this impression of superfluity is strengthened by our inability to discern it in brain circuits and neurons. What use is consciousness if we can design robots that make decisions? Robots can detect the nature and intensity of external or internal signals, and the most advanced ones have target functions that can serve as a flexible reference for behavior, *i.e.*, they think. But this flexibility is limited to the programmed function (in the

183

mathematical sense). In the robot brain, the decision-making homunculus is the engineer who designed and built the robot. Despite their programmers' talents, robots still lack the hedonic dimension of thought. This dimension is what makes consciousness advantageous; it sets a living brain apart from a computer or robot. Pleasure eliminates the need to hardwire millions of reflexes. This is the beauty of emergence and its efficiency.

We may now return to Chalmer's difficult problem, which is also Dawkins' paradox. Although robots may be programmed so subtly that they can perfectly replicate animal behavior, and many human behaviors, their human programmers must nonetheless foresee all of the possible stimulus/environment combinations. In contrast, pleasure/displeasure frees animals from having to anticipate all possible situations in an infinitely variable environment and having to accumulate more and more hardwired stimulus-response circuits (Merker 2005). Pleasure cuts out this complexity. Its flexibility also fine-tunes adaptation to changing environments. Thus, the pursuit of pleasure for the sake of pleasure may have driven the complexification of the human mind. On this axis is located the desire to consume and achieve, thus making it a center for continual prerational calculation. Dawkins' paradox has a solution if we accept her second alternative: cognition does provide a primordial evolutionary advantage. Just as thinking marks a major qualitative leap over rules of thumb, as Dawkins has shown (her p. 97), so does cognition mark a new advance. Its advantage is essentially in the hedonic dimension. This is what distinguishes a living thing from a robot, a brain from a computer. And this will hold true as long as artificial intelligence handles what may be called 1-dimensional situations, where the system is dedicated to a single task. When many tasks have to be rapidly sorted and prioritized, the hedonic dimension outperforms rational decision-making in both living things and robots. Sensation and, likewise, general cognition are thus ranked by degree of usefulness.

Conclusions

Postulate 1 holds that sensation was the first form of consciousness and later gave rise to more advanced forms. My corollary is that all forms of consciousness retain the 4-dimensional nature of their origins.

Two dimensions—quality and intensity—should particularly be kept in mind. Some states of consciousness are often considered qualitatively different when, in reality, they probably differ only in intensity.

The hedonic dimension provides a means to resolve the difficult problem of Chalmers (1995) and the paradox raised by Dawkins (1993). The solution to this paradox is to accept its second alternative: consciousness is useful. The hedonic dimension is what makes it useful and sets conscious beings apart from robots. Before the emergence of sensory pleasure, behavior could only result from a combination of reflexes—which were becoming increasingly numerous to handle an ever more complex environment. Pleasure was the forerunner of cognition. It had the evolutionary advantage of sparing the nervous system the time and trouble of accumulating an infinite number of potentially useful stimulus-reflex circuits. It enhanced the chances of survival of those who possessed it and their descendents, including us. Concretely, it outperformed prehedonic decision-making mechanisms (in living or inanimate entities) through an easier ranking of priorities and increased flexibility in decision-making. Thus, instead of the learning instinct that William James (1890) postulated for humans, the search for pleasure may be what drove the brain's evolution, making it the information-processing unit that it is today. In the course of this evolution, it became able to talk to itself. Consciousness became self-awareness.

Our mental faculties are a product of natural selection. We inherited them from our predecessors, who inherited them from their predecessors, and so on. When did the faculty of pleasure, and hence consciousness, first emerge? We might suspect that our closest primate relatives, such as chimpanzees, or familiar house pets may conceive and feel pleasure, at least sensory pleasure. Is there more objective evidence? If we evolved from other animals, our sense of pleasure must be present among some of them. The next chapter will try to answer the question of when consciousness emerged in our distant ancestors, specifically from the standpoint of emotion and sensory pleasure.

Chapter X
The problem of animal pleasure[66]

> The senses, an animal possesses them not for being
> but for well being ... taste is because of the agreeable
> and the painful, in order that an animal perceives
> these qualities in the food, desires them, and moves
> (II,3). It does indeed appear that there is in them [in
> animals] pleasure and pain (III,11).
>
> Aristotle, 384-322 BC

Several times in the preceding chapters, Bunge (1979), Barrette (2000), and Cosmides and Tooby (Cosmides *et al.* 1992) have reminded us that over billions of years natural selection has favored those living things whose characteristics give them an edge over their rivals. These characteristics include behavior and mental capacities. If consciousness and pleasure today exist in our species, as a means to optimize behavior, they must have been preserved and perpetuated through natural selection ever since their prehuman origins. Indeed, we see signs of sophisticated behavior and mental activity in all higher animals leading up to humans. See Mcfarland's excellent and prudent chapter on that problem (McFarland, 1985). Although Morgan (1925) recommended that we "leave speculations on the process of evolution to armchair-philosophers," the question is still worth pondering. At what evolutionary stage did consciousness emerge and, with it, pleasure as a behavior optimizer (Figure X.1)?

On several occasions we've mentioned the concept of emergence. With Bunge (1979), we must now distinguish between 'emergence' and 'evolution.' We speak of 'evolution' when a life form exhibits a new sensitivity (as defined in Chapter II) that evolved out of earlier sensitivities in ancestral life forms. Sensitivity itself, and the reflex response, first emerged long ago with the appearance of simple sense organs and motile processes (flagella or cilia) in one-celled organisms. New sensitivities later appeared whenever a neuron with a sensitive ending gained the ability to detect a new variable in the external or

---

[66] This chapter borrows from and builds on Cabanac (1999).

internal environment. As for 'emergence,' we speak of this concept for the transition from sensitivity to sensation. A 'proto-sensation' has new properties that cannot be foreseen from those of its constituent elements. We likewise speak of emergence for the transition from sensation to consciousness. At what evolutionary stage did this happen?

There is much experimental data to show that neutral stimuli can acquire positive or negative properties in animals when associated with food rewards or threatening stimuli (Miller 1994; Young 1959; Berridge 2001). It's hard, though, to extrapolate from animal behavior to cognition as humans experience it. This research is probably best illustrated by electrical self-stimulation of one's own brain, a technique pioneered by Olds and Milner (Olds 1955). These authors, and many others after them, would surgically implant electrodes in a rat brain while providing the rat with a lever to deliver a weak current through the electrodes. The rat would relentlessly stimulate certain regions of its brain for hours on end (Shizgal and Murray 1989). These regions are probably not centers for orgasmic pleasure, as initially thought, because when given access to food the rat would not let itself die of hunger and would alternate between self-stimulation and feeding (Frank *et al.* 1981). The electrical stimulation may, in fact, be triggering an iterative command: "Repeat what you've just done." Such commands are required for repetitive movements we do mechanically, such as walking, without having to think. Once a rat accidentally touched the lever, it would be drawn into a never-ending feedback loop. It's still tempting to interpret this behavior as enjoyable. When the human brain is similarly hooked up to electrodes, subjects will self-stimulate the same centers and say they vaguely enjoy the feeling in a nondescript way (Sem-Jacobsen 1959).

> "In no case may we interpret an action as the outcome of the exercise of a higher psychological faculty, if it can be interpreted as the outcome of the exercise of one which stands lower in the psychological scale" (Morgan 1894, p. 24).

This obstacle may be raised if the animal experiment is done to investigate a specific aspect of consciousness, such as sensory pleasure. Do animals perceive pleasure? If so, at what point in evolution did this faculty emerge and introduce a new sphere of mental activity? I'll try to answer the second question before attempting the first.

Threshold of consciousness

Since the time of Descartes (1596-1650), who considered animal behavior to be purely reflex, the problem of consciousness has spawned innumerable theoretical and behavioral studies. It's notably addressed in a book by the ethologist Don Griffin, who discovered echolocation (Griffin 1992) and, according to his ethological observations, consciousness does exist in animals. It does seem to exist in mammals, but what about other species? (Rial *et al.,* 2008). At what point in evolution did it appear and, with it, greater flexibility in behavioral responses to external and internal stimuli? In short, when did behavior become pleasure/displeasure-motivated? Let's examine available behavioral data on the existence of consciousness in different groups. We'll begin with our closest primate relatives and then gradually descend the evolutionary line to look at less mentally advanced species.

Apes display impressive mental capacities. Chimpanzees can recognize kinship between unfamiliar chimps on facial photos, *i.e.*, by using purely cognitive information with no other signal such as smell, gestures, or vocalizations (Parr and deWaal 1999). They can identify signs of strong emotion—joy, surprise, sadness, fear, anger, and disgust—on the faces of chimpanzees, including newcomers encountered for the first time (Parr 2000). They can figure out what other chimps see and do not see (Hare *et al.* 2000). Clearly, their mental capacities are close to ours, at least qualitatively. Lower primates also show objective signs of consciousness, so much so, that some people have proposed using them in studies on the causes and treatments of human anxiety (Barros and Tomaz 2003).

Other mammals behave in ways that are contingent on and eminently adapted to the external environment. Female sheep, for instance, can recognize faces (Kendrick *et al.* 2001). Their thought processes must thus be elaborate, albeit without self-awareness. Such behavioral flexibility is not confined to mammals. Consider the apparently ludic behavior of turtles, which are probably the closest reptile to the immediate ancestors of mammals. If raised in an enriched environment with opportunities for play, they'll spend 31% of their waking hours playing with useless objects placed in their aquarium (Burghardt 1998). Pet iguanas reportedly display extensive mental capacities (Krughoff 2000).

To investigate such capacities, and the evolutionary stage that produced consciousness, we need criteria that are as objective as possible. One such criterion is response to psychological stress. Research has particularly focused on two physiological responses to stress: fever and tachycardia.

Emotional fever

The British physiologist Renbourn (1960) found that young boys before a boxing competition had higher-than-normal rectal temperatures—1°F above normal. And so did some spectators who had once been boxers. Renbourn called this an "emotional" temperature increase. The Bulgarians Gotsev and Ivanov (1962) found similarly above-normal rectal temperatures in 3,450 university students from Sofia, Plovdiv, and Budapest. A few hours before an exam, 1% of them had a temperature of 38.5°C and most were between 37.5°C and 37.7°C. Their temperatures returned to normal a few hours after the exam. This condition was a fever, there being no sensation of heat discomfort as is usually the case with hyperthermia.

This temperature rise was first studied in animals by the Venezuelan physiologists Briese and Quijada (1970). If a rat was simply picked up and handled, it would shiver and raise its body temperature by more than one degree. This was an emotional temperature rise because the readings returned to normal once the rat had discerned the handler's identity and intentions. The readings rose again whenever a new handler took over. This simple technique confirms that the body temperature rise is a fever, *i.e.*, a transient increase in the set-point of the biological thermostat. Once the rat began to shiver, its peripheral blood vessels would constrict. On reaching the new set-point, the rat would dilate the same vessels and relax its muscles. Core temperature then oscillated around the new value and peripheral vasomotricity mirrored this oscillation, a sign of both regulation and fever (Figure X.2). This experiment has produced the same findings with bats (Cabanac and Briese 1991) and chickens (*Gallus domesticus*) (Figure X.2).

Since emotional fever exists in mammals and birds and since both descend from reptilian ancestors, it may also exist in modern reptiles as well. Indeed, lizards, *Callopistes maculatus* (Figure X.2), and turtles, *Clemys insculpta* (Cabanac and Bernieri 2000), responded with fever when we picked them up and handled them to record their cloaca temperatures. Of course, reptiles are ectotherms, so the fevers were produced behaviorally. As soon as they were back in their terrariums, the reptiles went to an infrared lamp placed in one corner, thus raising and regulating their body temperatures to a higher set-point.

There was no such fever when we performed the same experiment on amphibians and fish, yet these animals can raise their body temperatures through behavior. Indeed, they did move to a warm environment after injection with a vaccine or prostaglandin (pyrogens). But no such response occurred after simple handling or injection with an inert substance (Figure X.3).

Emotional fever seems absent from pre-reptilian classes of animals. In such 'lower animals,' the fever response is hardwired to a narrow range of stimuli (e.g., microbialinfections).[67] It may have broadened with the advent of reptiles and the emergence of a more flexible system to match stimuli to appropriate responses. This seems borne out by another measure of the presence of emotion: heart rate.

Emotional tachycardia

The great physiologist W.B. Cannon (1929) first showed that heart rate provides one of the best signs of emotion in mammals. An animal will respond with tachycardia—abnormally fast heart rate—not only when handled but also when social stress occurs in the natural environment,

---

[67] The words "lower" and "higher" are used here only for convenience. We're talking about classes of animals that arose earlier or later in the course of evolution. There is no suggestion here that phylogenetically younger classes are inherently superior or better adapted than older ones. See Barrette (2000).

C. Lloyd
MORGAN
(1852-1936)

Mario
Bunge
(2002)

Leda Cosmides & John
Tooby (2002)

Figure X.1 Major figures in evolutionary psychology. Its founders and promoters include Lloyd C. Morgan, Mario Bunge, Leda Cosmides, and John Tooby. With Morgan, comparative psychology became scientific. Bunge was the initiator of evolutionary psychology and clarified the concept of emergence. More recently, Cosmides and Tooby have brought natural selection and Darwinian thinking back into psychology.

e.g., in the presence of a dominant conspecific (Sgoifo *et al.* 1994). We can discreetly monitor an animal's heart rate by relaying its electrocardiogram via a radio transmitter in its abdomen or on its back. It is thus possible to see the tachycardia that results from picking up

192

and handling a rat or simply from petting a bird's back. This response is indeed emotional because the rats are completely rested and no muscular activity could be speeding up the heart rate (Figure X.4). The same is true for iguanas and turtles. Yet handling doesn't affect the heart rate of frogs from two different species *Rana catesbeiana* and *Rana pipiens* (Cabanac and Cabanac 2000).

If amphibians lack two of the signs of emotion that are common to reptiles, birds, and mammals, it's tempting to conclude that emotion itself is absent from this class and from all phylogenetically older classes.[68] The amphibian-reptile transition may thus have seen a major qualitative shift in neural organization: complexification of the nervous system and emergence of consciousness. According to Michael Lyons,[69] the transition to life on land may have facilitated this neural rewiring to meet the challenges of a more complex environment, particularly in terms of thermal regulation. His hypothesis would explain why reptiles can make behavior fit their circumstances, why they quickly learn operant behaviors, *i.e.*, not simply stimulus-response (Holtzman *et al.* 1999), why they display play behaviors (Burghardt 1998) and, quite probably, why they feel sensory pleasure ... as we'll see further on.[70]

Learned aversion

The reptile-amphibian difference may be investigated by another method: learned aversion, as described in Chapter III. If a lizard has isotonic saline injected into its abdomen after eating a new food item, it will just as eagerly eat the same food item a second time. If, however, we inject lithium chloride (which causes digestive problems), it will no longer eat the new food item. This learned aversion, the Garcia effect,

---

[68] A similar problem is the time when consciousness emerges in ontogeny. Signs of pain perception seem to exist in the human fetus as early as the 24th and perhaps the 20th week of gestation (Mahieu-Caputo *et al.* 2000). Because pain perception is a conscious process, it's possible that consciousness emerges around that age in the human fetus.

[69] Personal communication from Michael Lyons, ATR Media Integration and Communication Research Laboratory, Kyoto.

[70] *Jurassic Park 3* may be closer to reality than spectators might think.

has been observed in another reptile, thecommon garter snake *Thamonophis radix* (Burghardt *et al.* 1973; Terrick *et al.* 1995). It does not seem to exist, however, in amphibians like toads and salamanders (Figure X.5).

These findings suggest to me that taste, as a source of pleasure or displeasure, exists in reptiles but not in amphibians. This would be another sign that consciousness emerged at some point on the evolutionary line leading from amphibians to reptiles. Therefore, all higher life forms—reptiles, mammals, and birds—should feel pleasure. Does such evidence exist?

Sensory pleasure in animals: how can we study it?

In the absence of verbal communication, we must base our conclusions on observation of an animal's behavioral responses. This method unfortunately loses in precision what it gains in objectivity. Ever since Aristotle, very many authors have assumed that animals feel pleasure. This hypothesis is most often implicitly reflected in their mentalist vocabulary. Words like "motivation," "pain," "hedonic," "hunger," and "satiation" currently appear in countless articles without the authors understanding the full implications of what they write. We need to end this ambiguity and try to spell out just what we mean with reasonable certainty. Indeed, a behavioral response isn't always stimulus-specific. Nor is it always driven by a motivation for or against the stimulus. Consider a few examples.
- Non-specificity. A food item isn't necessarily tasty because it is consumed in large quantities. It may simply have no power of satiation. Conversely, if it isn't consumed, the reason may be apraxia rather than aversion. If consumed in small quantities, it may simply have a strong power of satiation.
- Non-motivation. If an animal can choose among several food items, its choice may not indicate a perception of pleasure but rather a lesser evil among foods to be avoided. This objection can and will be answered further on. It's presented here only to stress the need for caution.

We should try other arguments before interpreting animal behavior in terms of pleasure maximization. Three techniques provide some access to the cognitive processes of animals: obstruction method; facial reflexes; and verbal expression. None of the three is perfectly satisfactory because a mental object cannot be calibrated. Taken together, however, they become persuasive.

Obstruction method

This method doesn't provide direct access to animal cognition but does enable us to compare attractive stimuli to each other in relation to an aversive benchmark. It initially involved comparing a rat's attraction to a bait with its repulsion for crossing an electric grid to reach the bait (Warden 1931). The experimenter could thus measure the reward value of stimuli (food or drink, infant of a suckling mother, sexual mate, etc.) in relation to each other and to the electric grid benchmark. The animal was driven to cross the grid by its motivation. The strength of its decision was thus estimated.

We're even closer to estimating pleasure when the animal is given everything and doesn't have to feel the discomfort of an electric grid. For instance, we can give a rat a heated home with food and water and then place a tasty bait some distance away in a freezing environment (Cabanac and Johnson 1983). Unlike the previous situation where the rat had to cross an electric grid in order to eat, it now has everything it needs in a heated home. If it leaves, it does so out of choice and at the risk of getting frostbite in a -15°C environment. Only the search for pleasure could be driving it to seek the bait.

Using a similar approach, Shizgal (1997) compared taste stimulations and intracranial electrical stimulations. He gave rats access to two levers, one providing a sweet-tasting reward, the other an electrical stimulation to the brain. Depending on the intensity of one stimulus versus the other, the rats would orient their preferences toward one of the two levers. Their choices were necessarily pleasure-driven.

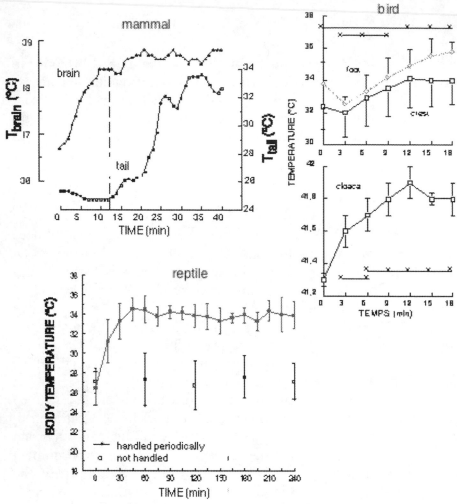

Figure X.2 Body temperatures of different animals when handled by a human. Mammal: a rat that we periodically picked up and handled while recording its brain and skin temperatures (Briese and Cabanac 1991). Bird: mean value of three roosters we handled every three minutes while taking core and skin temperatures (Cabanac and Aizawa 2000). Reptile: mean value of six identical sessions with the same lizard, during which we handled it while taking cloaca temperature every 15 min. It had a heat source in a corner of the cold terrarium (Cabanac and Gosselin 1993). In all three cases, handling produced an emotional fever in the animal with either a rise in core temperature and a constriction of peripheral vessels (rat, rooster) or a higher-than-normal set-point for thermoregulation. Temperature was being

regulated because the set-point was maintained by physiological or behavioral responses (vasomotricity in the rat and rooster; behavior in the lizard).

Facial reflexes

Grill and Norgren (1978) made a discovery that may seem minor but matters a lot in reality because it sheds light on taste pleasure in rats. They found that rats respond to taste stimuli with an array of taste-specific gestures and facial expressions (Figure X.6). A sweet taste produces mouth movements, lip-licking, paw-sucking, and head-shaking. A bitter taste produces a triangle-shaped mouth, saliva dripping on the floor, placing of chin on the floor, and hind-foot stamping. An informed observer can easily recognize the response profile after a rat has tasted a flavor that may be pleasant or unpleasant. These are reflex responses, since they even exist in rats whose brains have been largely removed. In the absence of verbal reflect pleasant and unpleasant cognitions in an intact rat. Indeed, humans have similar responses communication—they're animals after all—the gestures and expressions probably to reportedly pleasant or unpleasant stimulations (Steiner 1977). The responses also obey the same deterministic laws as does human perception of pleasant and unpleasant tastes. As we'll see further on, we can use this technique on rats with reasonable certainty to investigate how taste hedonicity is determined and to perform experiments that would be unethical with human subjects. The late 1970s also saw similar responses being described in birds. These findings weren't pursued as they were with rats (Gentle and Harkin 1979).

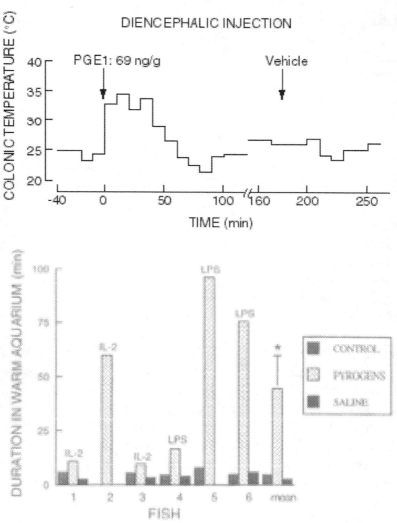

Figure X.3 **Top**: *Time course of the colonic temperature of one frog before and after injections at time zero, of 2.5 µg Prostaglandin E1, a potent pyrogen (left), and at time 180 min of the same volume of 0.9% sterile saline into the diencephalon. The frog was swimming in a 2-m long water temperature gradient in which it selected its preferred temperature. The animal was taken out of the tank and immobilized manually for the injections. It can be seen that the Prostaglandin aroused a transient fever, as seen in the frog swimming toward warmer water. The control session, however, aroused no emotional fever,*

although the animal had been manipulated, immobilized, and injected before being put back in the water tank (From Myhrre et al 1977).
Below*: Duration of stay in the warm half of a two-chamber aquarium by six red fish Carassius auratus taken each three times. Once after saline injection, once after pyrogen injection and once without treatment. It can be seen that pyrogens were folled with a behavioral fever but mere handling produced no fever (From Cabanac & Laberge 1998).*

Verbal expression

Pepperberg (1990) taught African Grey Parrots from Gabon to understand English, including abstract concepts like shape, color, hollow, full, larger, smaller, same, or different. The parrots expressed these concepts either verbally or behaviorally after oral instructions. I tried Pepperberg's method with an African Grey Parrot, named Aristote,[71] my aim being to teach a vocabulary corresponding to its thoughts and to teach it to express basic concepts like right and wrong. Aristote enjoyed being fondled and scratched on the head and neck. The bird first learned to say the French word *bon* (good) from time to time when being fondled. Next, it learned that the word *bon* could apply to yogurt, which it obviously loved. It showed an understanding of the concept 'good' when it began using the word *bon* while tasting a grape that it clearly enjoyed. I had carefully avoided associating the word with a grape stimulus, so the spontaneous transfer from an abstract concept to a different and pleasurable sensation seems to argue for the existence of pleasure in birds like Aristote (Cabanac 2001).[72] It would be interesting to see whether Aristote would use the same word without a trainer/observer and apply it to other stimuli. I had to give up this line of research, not because of its limitations, but because of the costs of caring for the parrot and the amount of work and patience needed to get results.

---

[71] After the medieval dictum: *Aristoteles dixit* (Aristotle said …)
[72] Since the French book, a longer report was publishished later in *Evolutionary Psychol.* 2009, 7:40-47 .

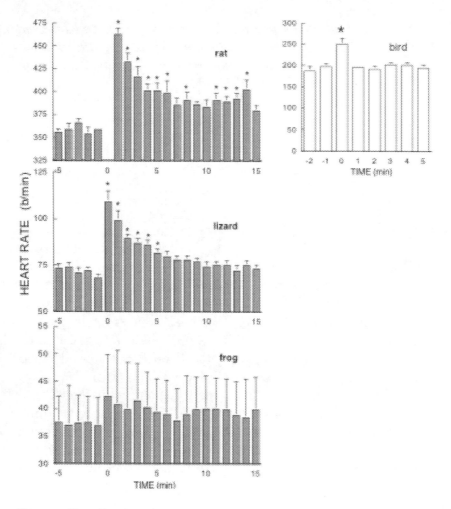

Figure X.4 Dark columns: mean heart rate obtained by telemetry in a rat, two lizards (Iguana iguana), and seven frogs (Rana catesbeiana). For each animal, the results are the mean of several sessions. At time zero, the animal was picked up by the experimenter and gently handled for a minute. It was then put back in its cage or aquarium (Cabanac and Cabanac 2000). Light columns (right): mean heart rate of three roosters (Gallus domesticus). Heart rate was likewise recorded by telemetry, but emotion was produced simply by stroking the bird's back for a minute (Cabanac and Aizawa 2000). An asterisk (*) above a column means a significant difference from control group values before

time zero (analysis of variance p<0.05). Gentle handling seems to produce emotional tachycardia in mammals, birds, and reptiles but not in amphibians.

Nonetheless, talking birds are a promising avenue for further investigation into the hedonics of animal cognition. A similar method has been used to dialogue with anthropoid apes via a computer.

Do the above methods prove that animals feel sensory pleasure? Let's examine the findings for different types of sensation.

Taste pleasure in rats

When we see animals seeking and consuming delicious food, we like to think, anthropomorphically, that they feel pleasure. Can this impression be confirmed? We can try, and animal experiments have the advantage of being free of the ethical considerations that limit the same experimentation on humans.

Rats will normally die in 11 days if deprived of their adrenal glands. The same rats, however, will live indefinitely if given access to salty water, which they'll seek and drink avidly (Richter 1936). It is tempting to conclude that the salt gives them pleasure. Indeed, this behavior does need input from the sense of taste and will disappear if the gustatory nerves are severed. The rats will thus die (Richter 1939). Furthermore, salty water is more strongly preferred when provided as drinking water than when injected directly into rat stomachs, even though the biological effect is the same (LeMagnen 1955). It is very tempting to infer that these behaviors, which resemble human behaviors (figures III.4 and III.12), are responding to the same conscious sensations. When an opening is made in the stomach to prevent ingestion of liquids, rats will drink non-stop if offered water. The sensory signal is positive (Bédard and Weingarten 1989). Dehydrated rats will gulp down any fluid from a series of vials during the first ten minutes of presentation, and will then alter their preferences according to taste (Scalera 2000). This may be gustatory alliesthesia: their pleasure from the sensation changes and their preferences change accordingly. Some rats can fine-tune their

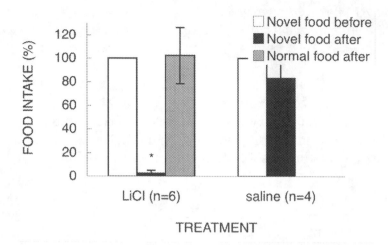

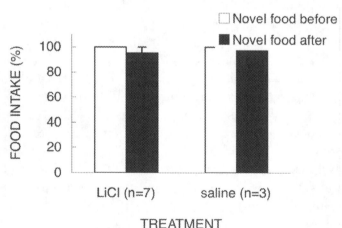

Figure X.5   Effect of injecting LiCl solution (0.15 M, 190 mg/kg) on food intake (after), as a percentage of pre-treatment food intake (before). The food items had never been given to the animals before.
***Above**, 4 lizards from 4 different species: basilisks (Basiliscus basiliscus and B. vittatus) when presented with mealworm larvae; and skinks (Eucemes schneideri and Mabuya multifasciata) when presented with caterpillars. * significant (Student's t test).*
***Below**. Four siroccoco toads (Bufo paracnemis) when presented with earthworms and mealworm larvae.*
After Paradis and Cabanac (2004)

202

preferences for sweet substances: polycose > maltose > sucrose > glucose (Sclafani and Clyne 1987). Some can turn off their innate preference for sweetened water, preferring instead pure water when dehydrated, *i.e.*, positive alliesthesia for water (Cohen and Tokieda 1972). Positive taste alliesthesia will occur if normally aversive taste stimuli are associated with intake of sugar or nutrients (Mehiel and Bolles 1988; Breslin *et al.* 1990). As in humans (Cabanac and Fantino 1977), the internal signal for smell/taste alliesthesia is intraluminal duodenal concentration (Kenney 1974; Cabanac and Lafrance 1990, 1992). The sensation thus acts similarly to its human homologue, the signal being probably mediated by the hormone cholecystokinin (Waldbillig and O'Callaghan 1980; Ettinger *et al.* 1986; Mehiel and Bolles 1988).

ACCEPTANCE

REJECTION

Figure X.6 When presented with a taste stimulus, a rat responds with gestures and facial expressions that are specific not only to the stimulus but also to its own physiological state. Above, signs of appreciation. Below, signs of aversion. After Grill and Norgren (1978).

As we've seen above, gestures and facial expressions provide interesting though indirect proof that rats feel pleasure when perceiving taste (Norgren and Grill 1982; Grill *et al*. 1996; Berridge 2000). The responses are detailed in Figure X.7. When presented with sweet solutions, rats will look initially delighted and then disgusted after concentrated glucose is injected into their stomach or duodenum (Cabanac and Lafrance 1990; Sederholm and Södersten 2001). Their facial expressions similarly resemble human taste alliesthesia for salt sensations. on a salt-free diet will look gratified when presented with salty water, which would be aversive for rats on a normal diet. Thus, these expressions are not a rigid reflex response to a given stimulus. There is also input from the rat's physiological state, *i.e.*, positive alliesthesia (Berridge *et al*. 1984).

Similar conclusions have been reached through Harvey Grill's method. Rats show positive alliesthesia for different flavors if contact with the new flavor is rewarded with a satisfying glucose injection into their stomachs (Myers and Sclafani 2001).

A rat's facial expressions are influenced by its ponderostat (weight set-point) in ways that parallel a human in the same situation. When a rat has lost weight, it will no longer respond negatively to sugar, even on a full stomach. sugar aversion reappears when the rat has regained its original weight (Cabanac and Lafrance 1991). The same aversion disappears when an opening is made in the rat's stomach to prevent the effects of ingestion (Bédard and Weingarten 1989). This is the same pattern of response we see with the human ponderostat.

The ponderostat influences rat facial expressions in two other cases:
- The estrous cycle. The facial responses of female rats to tasty stimuli change cyclically with their hormonal status (Clarke and Ossenkopp 1998). In addition, estrogen seems to adjust their ponderostat downward whereas progesterone seems to adjust it upward (Fantino and Brinnel 1986).
- The drug d-Fenfluramine (used to reduce appetite of overweight human patients). When administered to rats, it reduces positive facial responses to sugar (Gray and Cooper 1996). This drug has been shown

to lower the ponderostat, as measured by hoarding behavior (Fantino *et al.* 1986).

The rats' behavior thus closely parallels human taste sensations (Sclafani 1991; Shulkin 1991; Berridge 2000), so much so, that it has been proposed as a criterion for the moments when satiation centers activate in the brain (Sawchenko 1998). It thus becomes possible to analyze the structure of the neural paths and centers that activate whenever a pleasant or unpleasant taste is being experienced (Norgren and Grill 1982; Giza and Scott 1983; Berridge and Fentress 1985; Berridge and Cromwell 1990; Rolls *et al.* 1989; Berridge and Valenstein 1991; Shizgal and Conover 1996; Shizgal 1997). Interest has focused on the nucleus accumbens as a neural center that may motivate feeding and mediate the hedonics of taste sensation (Peciña and Berridge 2000). Shizgal (1997) provides further evidence that sensory pleasure is driving this rat behavior. Rats were given access to two levers: the first would deliver a sample of sweetened water; the second would stimulate the pleasure center in the rat's brain. The rats alternated between the two levers, but would focus on one of them if the corresponding reward for that lever increased. A similar experiment allowed rats to stimulate their brains electrically. As they lost weight through dietary restriction, the threshold for self-stimulation also fell, as if the rats were compensating for the loss of one pleasure by seeking another (Carr and Wolinsky 1993). The two rewards—feeding and electrical self-stimulation—appear to be drawing on the same underlying drive: pleasure.

Mammals seem to feel sensory pleasure. Further evidence is provided by their behavior in a cold environment.

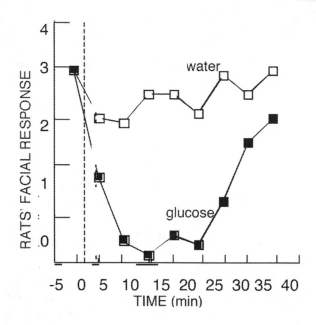

Figure X.7 Taste alliesthesia in rats. Median of results from a group of six rats. Every five minutes, we administered a small sample of sugary water directly to the rat's tongue and observed its facial expressions and gestures. The y-axis is an estimate by an onlooker (who didn't know whether water or glucose was being injected into the rat's stomach) of the positiveness or negativeness of facial expressions and gestures. If the estimate was positive, the rat looked appreciative; if negative, disgusted. Just after the first measurement, concentrated glucose (5 ml containing 1 g of glucose) was injected directly into the rat's stomach. The same volume of water (5 ml) was injected for the control session. In both cases, the injection is indicated by a vertical dashed line. After glucose injection, the sweet sensation on the rat's tongue no longer evoked a desire to consume but rather signs of disgust. Alliesthesia therefore exists in rats and the laws of pleasure are probably the same as in humans. After Cabanac and Lafrance (1990).

Thermal pleasure in rats

In humans, the sensation of heat will generate either comfort or discomfort as part of a self-regulating mechanism to maintain body core temperature (Chapter III). A signal from the body core determines the valence of the sensation's hedonic dimension. Core temperature also triggers involuntary responses, in particular shivering in response to hypothermia. Since shivering is always associated with cold temperatures, the discomfort might come from the sensation of shivering muscles rather than from the coldness of the skin. How can one sensation be dissociated from the other? The question has been answered through animal experimentation. An animal won't shiver if given the muscle relaxant curare. If it still seeks heat when exposed to cold, it will be responding in the same way that we do when our skin feels the pleasure of warmth in cold weather. This is indeed how it responds. Since a curare-treated rat cannot push a lever, we followed the technique used by Miller (1969): an electrocardiogram was hooked up to an infrared lamp, thus enabling the rat to obtain heat by altering its heart rate. The rats did, in fact, 'request' heat even though they could not shiver (Figure X.8) (Cabanac and Serres 1976). This finding leads to two conclusions: 1) shivering is unnecessary for perception of thermal discomfort, skin sensation alone being enough to motivate the rats; 2) rats do experience sensory pleasure and displeasure, in this case displeasure when exposed to the cold and pleasure when exposed to infrared heat.

Mechanical pleasure in rats

Panksepp and Burgdorf (2000) have shown that rats respond with ultrasonic vocalizations to different stimuli. Rats particularly vocalize in response to tickling, which they readily accept and seek. The authors cautiously liken the vocalizations to laughing, an indication that the stimulus is pleasurable.

Motivational conflicts in rats

When human subjects are in situations of motivational conflict, they adjust their behavior so as to respond optimally to all of their needs. As we've seen, people achieve this optimal behavioral mix by maximizing pleasure—the common currency of decision-making. Do other animals optimize behavior in the same way?

In a natural setting, pigs (Ingram and Legge 1970) or cows (Malechek and Smith 1979) will optimize behavior by alternating their search for food and the time they spend in a warm shelter, thus meeting the needs for food and warmth at the same time. When sheep are in a conflict between distance and their need for water, they'll optimize water consumption while minimizing the distance going to and fro (Squires and Wilson 1971). If rats have to work for water and are given a choice between water at 12°C and water at 36°C, they'll prefer the 12°C water. If given only a single bottle heated to different temperatures, they'll drink more as water temperature rises: 36.7°C > 26°C > 14°C. Warmer water seems to satiate less since more is needed to satisfy the rat (Ramsauer *et al.* 1974).

This conclusion is still based on indirect evidence. The following experiment directly tested the hypothesis that rats feel sensory pleasure (Cabanac and Johnson 1983; Ackroff and Sclafani 1999). A rat was placed in a climatic chamber at -15°C. It had a warm shelter, provided with its usual food and water. It had access to warmth and all the necessities of life and didn't have to leave its warm shelter to venture into the painful and hazardous cold. Yet it did, having learned during previous sessions (when the temperature of the climatic chamber was mild) that tasty baits were sometimes available at the end of a zigzagging 16-m-long pathway. The baits were pâté, shortbread, or Coca-Cola,[73] presented separately or together. The rat would venture that far despite the potentially mortal cold. If it found rat chow that was identical to that of the warm shelter, it would return home immediately and no longer go out into the cold. If, however, it found a tasty bait, it would remain, consume the bait, and go back later for more (Figure X.9). In a similar experiment, a rat could obtain tastier

---

[73] Rats seem to love Coca-Cola and will eagerly consume large quantities.

bait by pressing a lever more often (Ackroff and Sclafani 1999). Results were similar to those of the cold vs. food conflict.

As a whole, these findings suggest that the rat's decisions were influenced by the pleasure it got from eating or drinking tasty bait. It had no need to suffer the cold or exhaust itself pushing a lever. Its behavior was neither stereotyped nor inevitable. Only after discovering the nature of the bait could the rat compare the pleasure from the bait with the pain from the cold or muscular fatigue. The situation is comparable to that of humans who optimize behavior and make decisions with a view to maximizing the algebraic sum of their pleasure from many sources.

This conclusion is explicit in Spruijt *et al.* (2001), who studied anticipatory behavior in rats. The rats showed unequivocal signs of anticipating pleasure before they got a tasty reward or a sexual partner. The authors accept the idea of pleasure as a common currency that optimizes animal behavior by prioritizing motivations.

Reptiles

We've already seen that reptile behavior is flexible and that reptiles probably experience emotions. Do they also feel sensory pleasure? This conclusion is suggested by the results of an experiment identical to the one above, but done with reptiles instead of rats.

As with the rats, the principle is to place the reptiles in situations where they need not experience an unpleasant sensation because they have easy access to food and water. They're then offered a bait that they may seek at some cost. If they do, the reason will be pleasure, since need is absent. For the experiment, we kept iguanas (*Iguana iguana*) in a terrarium placed in a climatic chamber. A corner of the terrarium had an infrared lamp that kept the local temperature constant. Under the warm lamp, we placed water and food pellets (sold in specialty stores). In the opposite corner was fresh salad. From one experimental session to the next, we gradually lowered the temperature of the climatic chamber so that the salad was in an increasingly cold environment. Figure X.10 shows that the iguanas began to find the salad less tempting once the ambient temperature had fallen below 10°C and gave up eating it altogether at the lowest temperatures. This conflict, and its resolution, was probably mediated by the degree of sensory pleasure/displeasure.

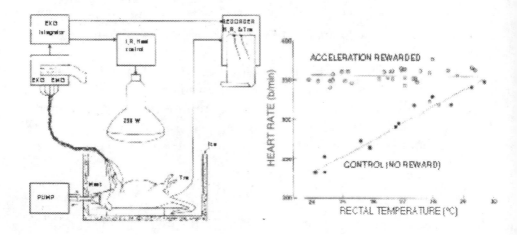

Figure X.8   Left, preparation: the curare-treated rat can turn on the infrared lamp and get a few seconds of warmth either by slowing down or by speeding up its heart rate. This may be seen in the example (right). In the control, heart rate slows down as body (rectal) temperature falls, but remains almost constant when the rat can turn the lamp on by speeding up its heart rate. Thus, even when shivering is absent, the skin's sensation of cold is experienced as unpleasurable. After Cabanac and Serres (1976).

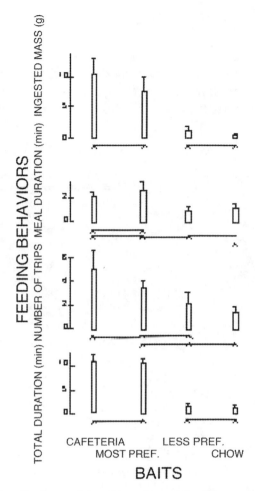

Figure X.9   Rats exchanging thermal discomfort for tastiness. The figure shows the characteristics of meals eaten by the rats at -15 °C after a long 16-m excursion away from their warm shelter. Water and food were freely available in their shelter. At the end of the pathway, they were offered various baits, either separately or together (cafeteria). The rats tended to differ in their preferences. We calculated the means for each rat's most and least frequently preferred baits. Cafeteria: several baits. Most: most frequently chosen bait. Least: least frequently chosen bait. Usual: standard rat chow for rats. The bars above the columns indicate standard error. The lines (___) join nonsignificantly different columns. Consumed food comprises what is eaten in the cold + what is eaten in the warm shelter. Mean duration of meal is the time spent eating in the cold. This information was recorded

211

indirectly. The left-hand columns are taller than the right-hand ones. This shows that the rats more often ventured out into the cold for tastier baits than for less tasty ones. After Cabanac and Johnson (1983).

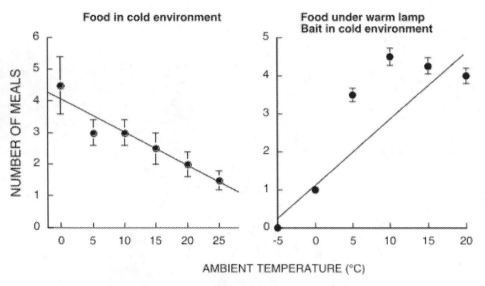

Figure X.10 Left: four Tupinambis teguixin lizards were put individually in a terrarium placed in a climatic chamber. In a corner of the terrarium, an infrared lamp provided the lizards with the means to regulate their body temperatures behaviorally. The water was in this warm area. The food, however, was further away, at the temperature of the climatic chamber (x-axis). To feed, the lizards had to go to the cold corner. The y-axis shows the mean number of trips to the food and of meals in the cold. As the ambient temperature fell, the lizards had shorter meals because they could not stay long without suffering hypothermia and dying. But they went more often, thus keeping food intake constant (not shown). After Cabanac (1985).

Right: Three iguanas were in a terrarium placed in a climatic chamber. An infrared lamp kept the temperature constant in one corner of the terrarium, with water and synthetic food available nearby. Salad was placed at the other end of the terrarium. The y-axis shows the mean number of visits to the salad (meal) as a function of climatic chamber

212

temperature, i.e., the temperature where the salad was located (x-axis). We averaged each lizard's individual results over several sessions and calculated the mean of these means for all three lizards. As the ambient temperature of the salad fell, the iguanas visited this bait less often. After Balaskó and Cabanac (1998). Thus, the second experiment differed fundamentally from the first. The reptiles could go and eat in the cold but did not have to. The bait was only a tasty pleasure. Their decision-making mechanism seems to be based on hedonicity, as in mammals.

Conclusion

With this chapter, we come to two conclusions:

1) Consciousness probably emerged among the common reptilian ancestors of contemporary amniotes, mammals, birds, and reptiles. This evolutionary innovation was so advantageous that it has been preserved, through the action of natural selection, in all descendents of these ancestral organisms. It's correspondingly absent in life forms that had branched off earlier from this evolutionary line. Such life forms are hardwired for reflex-like responses although they possess some behavioral flexibility, like that of the robot Sniffer in Figure VII.1. Indeed, their reflexes can be altered and new ones created. But this behavioral flexibility is elementary in comparison to the infinite opportunities for adjustment that consciousness makes possible.

2) Consciousness initially evolved out of sensation (postulate 1) and has retained the 4-dimensional structure of its origins. Its hedonic dimension has given reptilian and post-reptilian life forms a means to optimize their behavior.

The same conclusion has been reached, after a thorough review of the literature by the physiologist Rial (2008) and by the evolutionary psychologist Victor Johnston, who sees natural selection as the driving force for improvements in behavioral capacity. He intuitively argues that the emergence of pleasure made possible the evolution of increasing efficient and conscious life forms (Johnston 1999). Animal pleasure doesn't seem confined to sensory pleasure. Richard Schuster has convincingly shown that cooperation too is rewarding in and of itself, independently of any optimization it may produce (Schuster 2002).

It's likely, then, that all higher animals possess a mental life, with a hedonic axis that points the way to the most useful behavior. Pleasure is thus much older than our species, a sign of its effectiveness. We can now better understand the existence of anticipatory behaviors in other animals and why these behaviors are inconsistent with the rules of learning per se when feeding behavior provides no immediate reward (Cohen and Keasar 2000). Through observation of other animals, we can also better understand how human behavior is optimized through faster and more flexible decision-making. This optimizer, which goes back to the dawn of Amniotes, is pleasure maximization.

Chapter XI
What is emotion?[74]

> The heart has its reasons that reason does not
> know.
> Pascal, 1623-1662

> It is reason that makes man. It is sentiment
> that leads him.
> Rousseau, 1712-1778

In the last chapter, I used emotion, without really defining it, as a means to probe the existence of consciousness in animals, the implied assumption being of course that emotion is a mental object of our consciousness. I'll now define emotion in this chapter. Such an endeavor is appropriate in an essay on pleasure because of the preponderant role I give to the hedonic dimension of emotion. This is another application of postulate 1, which I earlier proposed to explain the origin and structure of consciousness.

Paradoxically, we have no clear definition. Yet psychologists are much interested in emotion, as seen by a large number of books and at least two academic journals (*Cognition and Emotion, Motivation and Emotion*). "Although an enormous literature exists on the psychobiology of affect, there is no singular or even preferred definition of emotion" (Chapman and Nakamura 1998). In their emotion bibliography, Kleinginna and Kleinginna (1981) list 92 definitions, including their own, and nine skeptical statements on the need for such a definition. In several pages of a book entirely about emotion, Griffiths (1997) repeatedly questions the usefulness of the very concept.[75] His pessimism may stem from the lack of an adequate definition. So we come back to the question: "What is emotion?"

---

[74] This chapter closely follows Cabanac (2002).
[75] "The general concept of emotion is unlikely to be a useful concept in psychological theory" (p. 14). "the research surveyed in this book suggests that the general concept of emotion has no role in any future psychology." "But as far as understanding ourselves is concerned the concept of emotion ... can only be a hindrance" (p. 247).

Dictionaries define emotion rather vaguely as a "strong feeling (such as fear, wonder, love, sorrow, shame) often accompanied by a physical reaction (e.g., blushing or trembling)" (*New Webster's Dictionary* 1991) or a "mental feeling or affection (e.g. pain, desire, hope, etc.) as distinct from cognitions or volitions" (*Oxford English Dictionary* 1987). *The Dictionary of Cognitive Psychology*, paradoxically, doesn't formally define emotion. From its five pages on this entry, however, we can glean an operational definition: emotion is a mental state (Oatley 1994). This definition isn't at all tautological and is less banal than may seem because emotion is often considered to be a somatic response, or the perception of a somatic response. Following William James and K.G. Lange, several recent authors have insisted on the need to consider an aroused person's autonomous responses to be intrinsic to emotion (James 1884: Lange 1885). For example:

> "Although emotions have long been categorized as purely cognitive, it is now clear that the mental representation of an emotional experience includes motor and visceral components as well as cognitive ones" (Dantzer 1989, p. 141).

In the same vein, Schachter and Singer (1962) define emotion as "a state of physiological arousal and of cognition appropriate to this state of arousal." Their definition is pretty vague. It does define emotion as a mental perception of autonomous responses, thus diverging from the definition by Cannon (1927), who deems emotion to be primarily mental and secondarily autonomous responses.

Whatever the physiological signal that triggers emotion and regardless of whether one chooses James-Lange's definition or Cannon's, the concept remains fuzzy in the literature, as we've seen. In general, the authors (Lazarus 1991; Smith and Lazarus 1993; Cosnier 1994) and the dictionaries duck the problem by just listing the different emotions: anger, disgust, fear, joy, sadness, and surprise. Defining this mental object will be the aim of the present chapter. I'll propose a descriptive definition that will logically build on the ones proposed in previous chapters for sensation and consciousness. The aim will simply be to describe emotion in the global workspace of Baars (1994), *i.e.*, the introspective experience of human subjects. We can find this approach to the mental sphere in Searle (1998).

This chapter will largely ignore:
- The cerebral neural structures that give rise to emotion. Nor will we discuss the neurotransmitters involved (for this, see Dantzer *et al.* 1996). We can agree that emotion, like other objects of consciousness, is a product of neural activity in the brain.[76] A brain scan study has shown that cognition and emotion activate the same prefrontal cortex structures (Gray *et al.* 2002). These neural structures are described in Panksepp (1991), Parrott and Shulkin (1993), Scherer (1993), Rolls (1994), Damasio (1995), LeDoux (1996), Lane *et al.* (1997, 1998), Phillips *et al.* (1998), and Watt (1998). The large number of authors underscores the abundant literature of this field despite the lack of a clear definition.
- The causes of emotions, the role of peripheral responses, and the relations between these responses and consciousness (see Zajonc 1980; Ekman *et al.* 1983; Pecchinenda and Smith 1996). Somatic responses that co-occur with emotion. Different response profiles may correspond to different emotions (Ekman *et al.* 1983).

I'll only touch on the specific roles of different emotions. Because they have run the gauntlet of natural selection over eons of evolutionary time, our existing emotions must matter in daily life (Smith and Lazarus 1990; Ekman 1992; Parrott and Shulkin 1993) and in social communication (Oatley and Johnson-Laird 1987; Kappas 1991). The origin and evolution of emotion is addressed in the preceding chapter (see also Cyrulnik 1998).

Why this interest in emotion, in a book about pleasure? If the 4-dimensional structure of sensation (Figure II.5) applies to consciousness, it should apply to all conscious manifestations. All mental objects should be 4-dimensional and use pleasure/displeasure as a common yardstick. We can test this prediction by examining emotion.

According to Figure II.5 and Equation II.1, consciousness has four dimensions: quality (x), intensity (y), hedonicity (z), and duration (t).

---

[76] Until the 16th century, the heart was deemed to be the seat of the soul and emotion (Coop-Phane 1998), probably because strong emotion makes the heart beat faster.

This model can be arrived at through introspection alone, as already seen, or through reasoning based on evolutionary psychology. A corollary is that the 4-dimensional structure of sensation should be observable in all mental objects, including emotion. is the sort of endeavor we'll embark on and one that J. Roy describes in the introductory quote for Chapter IV. We can find parallels in the thoughts of some authors who've argued, for instance, that all of cognition more or less participates in emotion (Scherer 1993) or that emotion is an "irruptive motivational complex in higher cognition" (Griffiths 1997).

Proposition: Given the above premises, we can propose that the 4-dimensional model of consciousness applies to emotion.

We'll now examine each of the four dimensions to see whether they're present in emotion.

The qualitative dimension (x-axis)

In consciousness, the x-axis identifies the nature of a mental object, just as it identifies the nature of a stimulus in a sensation.

Does this dimension apply to emotion? It can readily encompass the dictionary list: anger, disgust, joy, fear, and surprise. Other mental objects are sometimes described as emotions: hope, desire, pain, sorrow, and jealousy. Ekman and Friesen (1986) propose adding contempt. Happiness has at times been proposed as an emotion (Ekman *et al*. 1983). I'll show further on that the word joy is more suitable. The list is short, contains only words from daily life, and might be biased by the language of those who speak it and who may conceive only those words available through language. Indeed, a limited vocabulary might make us oversimplify our description of mental objects. This interdependence between word and concept is exemplified in Japanese by the word *amae*, which describes the emotion of a warm bond with one's parents or institutions. This pleasant emotion implies personal or institutional dependence and a sense of belonging (Morsbach and Tyler 1986). German expresses exactly the same concept with the adjective *heimlich*.[77] Such words are to be expected in Japanese and German, where society views the family as an institution with a history and long-established bloodline. Their absence in English and French reflects a preference for the nuclear family, individualism, and equality (Todd 1990).

All of these emotions may be characterized as responses to stimuli or events in our environment, or purely in our perception or imagination. We may, for instance, hear the howl of a wolf, smell a good meal, or see a sexual rival. Or, alternately, we might fear a crash while flying on an airplane or a failing grade while taking an exam. Regardless of whether the causation is real or imagined, the above responses differ only qualitatively and occupy the same mental reality of consciousness.

These emotions share one thing in common: a situation that triggers either a positive or negative motivation, which in turn produces a behavior to seek out or avoid the triggering stimulus. They all have a high degree of hedonicity on the z-axis, as will be seen further on. For now, I'll just describe them as mental responses to diverse stimuli from the senses, from memory, or from the imagination. They're consequently related to sensation, or more exactly to perception as defined above (Figure II.4). With this theoretical model, we can place an infinite number of emotion-generating stimuli on the x-axis. We're no longer confined to a short list. Each stimulus arouses a qualitatively different emotion. Thus, all emotions fall into a single category of discrete objects and all are simply responses to different stimuli.

The intensive dimension (y-axis)

In consciousness, the y-axis identifies the intensity of an experience, just as it identifies the intensity of a stimulus in a sensation. The intensity dimension is easy to understand for sensation but less so for consciousness. We saw in Chapter IX that this dimension runs continuously from zero to maximum. There is thus a gradation in the intensity of mental experience.

---

[77] Personal communication from the late M. Steriade.

This dimension is easily applied to emotion and is especially appropriate. Indeed, many authors consider the intensity of an experience to be a precondition for emotion (Nash 1989). For Griffiths (1997), emotion is an "irruptive motivational complex in higher cognition." Intensity is thus a key variable.

Sonnemans and Frijda (1994) describe emotion as having six factors of intensity: 1) duration of the emotion and delay of its onset and peak; 2) perceived bodily changes and strength of felt passivity; 3) recollection and re-experience of the emotion; 4) strength and drasticness of action tendency; 5) belief changes and influence on long-term behavior; and 6) overall felt intensity. Rather than being levels of intensity on the y-axis, the first factor can be easily placed on the time axis (t), as defined above, and the second and third factors on the qualitative axis (X). The fourth and fifth factors are motivation-driven and consequently better placed on the hedonic axis (Z). The sixth factor, intensity, remains as key to emotion. The authors also hypothesize that four groups of feelings determine the subjective intensity of emotion: concern, appraisal, regulation, and individual differences. But it is unlikely that any of these would arouse emotion at low intensity.

According to New (Pure) Cognitive Theory, emotion-generating thoughts are beliefs or desires that are more intense than normal (Nash 1989). Simply put, any thought can generate emotion. The intensity of the mental object is what makes emotion.

High intensity is thus a precondition for emotion, as implied by Sonnemans and Frijda and by Nash. But the reverse isn't true: an intense experience may result from a sensation or mental activity, such as problem solving, without creating any emotion. I believe there's no emotion if the thought is neither pleasant nor unpleasant. Although surprise is sometimes added to the list of emotions (Ekman *et al*. 1983), it should be considered so only when clearly pleasant or unpleasant, as I'll now discuss.

The hedonic dimension (z-axis)

In consciousness, as we've seen previously, any thought may be pleasant, unpleasant, or neutral, as is sensation. The hedonic dimension motivates and prioritizes. It is contingent and transient. It indicates the usefulness of a stimulus or response.

Do these properties exist in emotion? We've seen that several authors insist on the hedonics of emotion. Ekman *et al.* (1983) consider disgust, sadness, anger, fear, and happiness to be emotions. Each of these experiences, which easily fit on the qualitative x-axis, is well represented on the hedonic z-axis. Categories 4 (strength and drasticness of action tendency) and 5 (belief changes and influence on long-term behavior) of Sonnemans and Frijda are clearly motivational in nature, and thus fit on the z-axis. Oatley and Johnson-Laird (1992) propose the existence of five basic emotions: 1) happiness, sadness, fear, and disgust, which occur when goals of secondary importance have been accomplished; 2) loss of goal; 3) deceit by others or disappointment in a goal or project; 4) goal conflict (including conflict with self-protection); and 5) perception that something is harmful or toxic (Oatley and Johnson-Laird 1992). All of these emotions are linked to motivation. Thus, these authors implicitly see pleasure and displeasure—the motivating dimension of behavior—as key to emotion.

Damasio (1995) argues convincingly that decision-making ability declines markedly in patients when they lose their emotional process. His argument is consistent with my own that emotion has the four dimensions of consciousness and that the hedonic dimension is the one that motivates people to perform useful behaviors. When this dimension is absent or lost, emotion too should be absent and decision-making highly disturbed, or even completely lacking. Damasio's patient couldn't make decisions and is initially described by Damasio as a victim of brain injury. Was this patient also anhedonic? We saw in Chapter IX that such patients had serious trouble making decisions.

A contrario evidence is provided by alexithymia. Patients with this syndrome were once thought to be simply unable to put their emotions into words, hence the name of the illness. They're now known to suffer from a limited ability to feel emotions (Lane *et al*. 1997). They also have limited ability to feel pleasure (Prince and Berenbaum 1993). It's likely that they've lost the entire z-axis of their mental space. If so, they should also suffer from a limited ability to decide. Indeed, Lane *et al*. say that these patients are uneasy with complex or uncertain situations, a sign of emotional deficit if we follow Damasio. These observations are consistent with my argument that the hedonic axis of consciousness, and of decision-making, is especially active in emotion. Losing the hedonic dimension also means losing emotion and motivation. You no longer have the common currency of decision-making.

Let's go back to the dictionary definition of emotion as a simple list: surprise, fear, anger, love, desire, pain, contempt, sadness, disgust, joy, soreness, and *amae*. We can see that these items fall into three categories:
- desire and surprise may be pleasant or unpleasant, depending on the nature of the present or anticipated stimulus or event;
- fear, anger, pain, sadness, disgust, soreness, contempt, and jealousy are all unpleasant;
- love, joy, hope, desire, and *amae* are all highly pleasant.

Thus, all of the emotions seem to have a strong positive (pleasure) or negative (displeasure) hedonic dimension. In all of these cases, emotion may be described as a mental model of some stimulus or event in our environment or simply in our minds. All emotions are intense experiences we feel when exposed to situations directly or indirectly linked to positive or negative motivation, and all will lead us to seek or avoid the stimulus. Without this dimension, the mental experience isn't an emotion. The hedonic dimension is thus characteristic of emotion.

Several authors have come to the same conclusion, explicitly or implicitly. Kenny (1963) sees emotion as a form of intention. Zajonc (1980) believes pleasure/displeasure to be paramount in emotion. Marks (1982) writes that emotion is motivating and contains powerful desires. For Rolls (1994), "emotions can usefully be considered as states produced by reinforcing stimuli." Finally, Watson *et al*. (1999), using their experimental findings, identify two main axes in the motivational space of consciousness: arousal and pleasure. They posit two kinds of pleasure: pleasure with high arousal and pleasure with low arousal. I'm tempted to liken their arousal dimension to the y-axis of intensity and their pleasure dimension to the z-axis of hedonicity. Their findings show that hedonicity and intensity lie on different axes and may vary independently of each other.

The time dimension of emotion (t-axis)

There should be no problems with the idea that emotion, like other experiences, normally lasts for a limited time. If it lasts indefinitely, the result may be certain pathological conditions, like depression. Sonnemans and Frijda (1994) have studied the duration of emotion for different stimuli.

A definition of emotion

I can now propose a definition of emotion:

> Any mental object with high intensity and high hedonicity is an emotion.

An emotion may result from a sensation, a perception, an evocation, an appraisal, a memory, or a fantasy. According to this definition, intense pain and sexual orgasm are emotions. In fact, both are accompanied by responses that are usually thought to be signs of emotion: the skin is flushed with blood and the vessels constrict and dilate; sweat is secreted; and facial expressions become livelier. This definition is better than the dictionary lists. It is simpler and, of course, includes them.

Price (1999) states that "an emotional feeling is the felt sense of a cognitive appraisal that occurs in relation to something of personal significance, often in relation to desire and expectation." Such a definition includes the motivating aspect of emotion, but still strikes me as being too vague. In contrast, the above definition is precise. It's also consistent with the proposal that all cognition may be a source of

emotion (Scherer 1993). It has the advantage of resolving several controversies that have divided specialists:
- Is emotion primary and independent of cognition (Cannon 1927; Lazarus 1982, 1984) or secondary and always cognition-dependent (James 1980; Zajonc 1980, 1984)? It's both. What defines emotion is its hedonicity and intensity, not its origin.
- Is emotion inborn or learned? The question is raised by both Damasio (1998) and Griffiths (1997), who show that one can argue either way. The answer again is both. Any thought may be an emotion if it meets the conditions of intensity and hedonicity.

Finally, this definition reverses Watt's proposed relationship between emotion and consciousness. Instead of the central organizing mechanism leading to consciousness (Watt 1998), my new definition would have emotion being only one element among others in the global workspace of consciousness.

Discussion of the 4-dimensions hypothesis

"Research on emotion is difficult" (Lazarus 1991). This pessimism probably reflects the lack of a clear and universally accepted definition of emotion. The 4-dimensional model is useful because it provides such a definition, on top of stressing the key importance of intensity and, above all, hedonicity. Finally, it sets out the different dimensions of emotion in a single concept, as other authors have done, sometimes without specifying the nature of the variables in question (Leventhal and Scherer 1987; Parrott and Shulkin 1993). The 4-dimensional model, including the definition proposed above, should prove to be heuristically useful. Indeed, this definition is recognizable in the writings of several authors, albeit most often implicitly.

Schachter and Singer (1962) have suggested that emotion may result from an interaction between two components: a non-specific arousal due to activation of the sympathetic nervous system and a perception due to the arousal being attributed to the triggering stimulus. This view of emotion is consistent with the qualitative (X) and hedonic (Z) axes.

Plutchik (1970) proposes a 3-dimensional inverted cone model:

intensity (e.g., distinguishing fear from panic); similarity (e.g., shame and guilt); and polarity (e.g., joy versus sadness). Differences would be a matter of degree.

Russell (1980) proposes a 2-dimensional spiral model: sleepiness-arousal and distress-pleasure. This would correspond to the Y- and Z-axes of Figure II.5.

Smith and Lazarus (1993) describe emotion as 2-dimensional: knowledge and belief, corresponding to the qualitative axis, X; and appraisal of significance, corresponding to the hedonic axis, Z.

Rolls (1994) proposes a 2-dimensional description of emotion: one axis for positive reinforcement and the other for negative reinforcement. It seems to me simpler to incorporate them into a single axis (Z). Only exceptionally can an event or stimulus evoke pleasure and displeasure at the same time.

Ramos and Mormède (1998) assume that emotion is multidimensional and propose applying this concept to animals. Nash (1989) and then Griffiths (1997) have defined emotion as an "irruptive motivational complex in higher cognition." Such a definition almost matches the notion that emotion has an intensity dimension ("irruption," Y-axis) and a hedonicity dimension ("motivation," Z-axis).

Despite marked differences over the nature of the variables, there seems to be a fairly broad consensus that emotion is multidimensional and has intensity and hedonicity as dominant variables.

Emotions are therefore motivations

To say that emotions depend on pleasure/displeasure is to say that they motivate. Emotions motivate us. Bergson (1932) reasoned, through simple introspection, that emotion is a propulsive force that especially aids artistic creation. According to Plutchik (1965), emotions have always been considered adaptive responses to life events. They must be useful because they've persisted so tenaciously ever since they emerged in the reptilian ancestors of present-day reptiles, birds, and mammals. Otherwise, they would have soon been eliminated by natural selection. Yet emotions have a down side. They may paralyze, through fear or shyness, or lead to excessive anger. Can emotions do more harm than good? Isn't it better to keep your cool? Indeed, many cultures, and some psychologists, have seen emotion as contrary to reason (Frank 1988) or at best as an archaic means of decision-making unrelated to rationality (Ekman 1980). But this folk wisdom isn't shared by many authors, who lean toward Plutchik's opinion. Taylor (1984) maintains there are two kinds of emotion: appetitive and possessive. Without belaboring the point, we can see that both kinds are motivating. This line of thought has in recent years gained support in a certain number of publications. For Johnson-Laird and Oatley (1992), emotions serve to push our actions in a better direction than random choice when rationality offers no solution to a problem. For the two authors, emotions are also useful because they facilitate communication between distant cultures. The general view today is that emotions play a highly adaptive role, especially in decision-making (Damasio 1995). As we've already seen, this role is shown *a contrario* by an apparent loss of emotional experience and an inability to make coherent decisions in patients with lesions to the frontal lobes of their brains (Bechara *et al.* 1994). In sum, emotions are now held to be complimentary, and not contrary, to reason (DeSousa 1997; Cosnier 1994; Zernicki 2002).

I'm strongly tempted to discern the usefulness of emotion in its high hedonicity, whether positive or negative. Pleasure/displeasure is what drives prerational decision-making, and this axis of consciousness is what makes emotion effective. As I discussed and proposed previously, pleasure is a decision-maker that predates reason.

Rationality and emotion

Baron (1994) attributes illogical behaviors to generalization of rules of conduct that make sense only in a limited range of cases. This "bias" can distort the decision-making process. What he calls bias may have biological origins. He himself suspects as much:

> "To understand where nonconsequentialist rules (norms) come from, we need to understand where any decision rules come from. I know of no deep theory about this. Some rules may

result from observation of our biological behavioral tendencies" ... (p. 7, para. 4)

His thoughts are a good start, but we can go further. Evolution teaches that when life emerged from matter all of the laws of matter remained valid and applicable for life forms. Similarly, when thought emerged from life all of the biological laws of matter and life continued to apply to thinking life forms. We've seen that pleasure does guide behavioral choices and decisions in situations of motivational conflict and that it optimizes behavior. This decision-making and behavior-optimizing role seems to be its main function in emotion. Emotion would thus be an older, prerational mechanism for making decisions and its emergence would have freed living things from a still older and much less flexible mechanism. According to Dubrovsky (2003): "We are not prisoners of a catalogue of algorithms set in the late Pleistocene."

In purely mental decision-making situations, the inherited laws of biology still apply. Of course, rationality also guides decision-making, but the basis for the process remains hedonic and is especially operative in emergencies. This view finds support in recent studies. When subjects have to decide quickly, they rely on their emotions for quick assessment of losses versus benefits (Finucane *et al.* 2000). When brokers make snap decisions on a stock exchange floor, rapidity significantly correlates with signs of emotion (Lo and Repin 2002). As already mentioned, Price *et al.* (2001) have accepted that emotion is central to decision-making, a view that is compatible in every way with the definition proposed here. This is also the view of Mellers *et al.* (1999).

According to Todd (1990), major life choices—political decisions, freedom, marriage, childbearing, abortion, euthanasia, etc.—are determined not by logic, but by the structure of the family we've grown up in. If he's right, the tendency to maximize pleasure may be harnessed to causes that differ completely from one person to the next. What seems rational to one may be emotional to another. For instance, resistance to coercion, to use Baron's example, may be more satisfying for people raised in families that value stubbornness.

Conclusion

The introductory quote for Chapter IV states that a useful theory is one that makes accurate predictions. In this chapter, we've tried to see whether the 4-dimensional model of consciousness applies to the specific case of emotion. Indeed, it does seem to apply.

Panksepp (1986) says that a definition of emotion should be the outcome, rather than the origin, of research. This is the approach I've taken in research on pleasure. The outcome is a new definition of emotion:

Any mental object with high intensity and high hedonicity.

In addition to indirect validation of the 4-dimensional model of consciousness, this approach leads to two conclusions that are equally general:
- The hedonic axis is essential to emotion and to decision-making as it is to all of consciousness;
- because of this relationship to hedonicity, emotions are truly motivations and it's quite likely that they too optimize behavior.

This definition has one more advantage. It defines another vague word/concept: 'stress' (see Dantzer 1989). Whereas Selye's initial experiments on stress were essentially environmental (repeated shocks, severe cold, etc.), over the years the stress-producing experimental situations became purely psychological (isolation, human handling, etc.) (Selye 1974). Emotions were therefore the stress-producing cause, the stress itself being simply an autonomous and behavioral response to emotion.[78]

Finally, it's no accident that the word 'affective' covers two connotations: pleasure/displeasure and emotion. Hedonicity is the essential dimension of emotion. It's also the basis of decision-making. Rationality, of course, has been grafted onto the hedonic process to improve it, but the mechanism fundamentally remains hedonic.

---

[78] Nicolaïdis (2002) has published a stress taxonomy based on endocrine response profiles.

Chapter XII

Happiness and joy[79]

> We hold these truths to be self-evident, that all men
> are created equal, that they are endowed by their
> Creator with certain unalienable Rights, that among
> these are Life, Liberty and the pursuit of Happiness.
> Unanimous Declaration of the thirteen united States
> of America, July 4, 1776

The preceding pages have outlined how consciousness behaves like sensation, as described by the four dimensions of Figure II.5. If this model does adequately describe emotion, it's again tempting to make the same biological extrapolation with other mental objects. Let me return one last time to the evolution of mind from earlier biological substrates, as implied by the common currency concept of McFarland and Sibly and by the evolutionary psychology of Bunge, Cosmides, and Tooby. This endeavor will take us from heat sensation and sensory pleasure to a definition of comfort and then an analysis of happiness.

Sensory pleasure: negative and indifferent responses

Let's review the main properties of sensory pleasure. It is contingent, it is transient, and it motivates useful behavior. Sensory displeasure has the same properties except one: it is not necessarily transient. The difference is very important. Unlike pleasure, which is always fleeting, displeasure can last as long as the problem remains uncorrected and as long as the physiological state hasn't returned to normal. Finally, behavior will tend to maximize pleasure and minimize displeasure, both tendencies being physiologically useful. These conclusions are based on analysis of taste/smell in relation to food intake and temperature sensation in relation to thermoregulatory behavior.

When you have an energy deficit, and feel hungry, eating food will be enjoyable. As you eat more and more, the sensation will be less

---

[79] This chapter builds on M. Cabanac (1986), "Du confort au bonheur", *Psychiatrie Française*, 17:9-15.

positive and finally neutral. When you no longer need energy, the food stimuli will be perceived neutrally. All pleasure disappears with satiation; all foods will then leave you indifferent. The sensation hasn't become negative yet—you normally stop eating before that point—but it will if you continue to eat. An indifferent sensation, as with the skin's response to temperature, tells you there's no longer any need for the stimulus.

Time is necessary to study the pleasure of eating. Because satiation is reversible only after digestion, one has to wait for hours while the food is being digested and metabolized before repeating an experiment. It's easier to study the pleasure of heat or cold. A state of need can readily be created merely by raising or lowering the room temperature. Pleasure is just as easy to reverse: you simply alter the subject's internal temperature. Heat sensation thus provides a means to study sensory pleasure in general.

Figure XII.1 uses data from Figure III.2 and adds pleasure and displeasure responses from three situations: hyperthermia, hypothermia (as in Figure III.2), and normothermia (when core temperature is equal to the thermoregulatory set-point and everything is normal). Pleasure or displeasure exists when core temperature is abnormal and when the hedonic rating motivates the subject to correct the situation by seeking heat or cold. In contrast, neither pleasure nor displeasure exists during normothermia. Of course, painfully hot or cold temperatures are still unpleasant, but the cause is pain sensation rather than temperature per se.

For simplicity, Figure XII.2 presents these findings in a 3 x 3 matrix. Temperature produces pleasure in only a minority of situations—just two of the nine boxes. The most common and normal situation is a neutral response to ambient temperature. It's also the most stable one. These findings lead us to a definition of thermal comfort.

Thermal comfort

Before 1987, comfort was defined by the American Society of Heating, Refrigeration, and Air-conditioning Engineers (ASHRAE) as "the

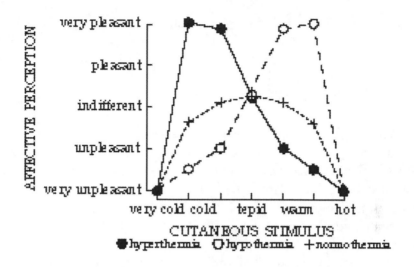

Figure XII.1 Pleasure and displeasure, expressed as positive or negative ratings by a typical subject for temperature stimuli applied to the hand. ●: hyperthermia; ○: hypothermia; +: normothermia. The hyperthermia and hypothermia responses are from Figure III.2. When internal temperature is normal (normothermia), all stimuli are neutral, i.e., between the pain thresholds for cold (15 °C) and heat (45 °C). After Cabanac (1969), Mower (1976), and Attia (1984).

subjective state of satisfaction towards the environment." The definition is imprecise, as seen in Figure XII.2. Subjective satisfaction towards the environment encompasses both pleasure and indifference—boxes P and I of the figure. The definition covers different situations and is therefore not homogeneous. Heterogeneity, though, doesn't matter as much as the stability or instability of the two situations. We've seen that the box P is transient. If hypothermic subjects are placed in a hot environment, they'll feel satisfied, *i.e.*, comfortable, using the ASHRAE definition. If they stay long enough, however, the hypothermia will correct itself and their response to the environment will become neutral and then negative. The same will happen with hyperthermic subjects in a cold environment. The ambient temperature will remain constant, yet the feeling of comfort will become less so on its own. Thus, the satisfaction isn't just towards the environment (in this case, ambient temperature). The definition is flawed.

To bring the transience of pleasure into the definition, I proposed in 1987 to redefine thermal comfort as:

A state of indifference to the environment (IUPS 1987).

That definition corresponds to a stable state. A comfortable environment can thus remain so indefinitely. Furthermore, a state of comfort is neither exciting nor elating but has the advantage of being able to last. It is by definition stable. The same reasoning holds for eating sensations, as suggested earlier in this chapter. Pleasant stimuli are those that correct an internal deficiency in energy or metabolites. In a state of comfort, these stimuli produce an indifferent sensation. Comfort is therefore a state of indifference, regardless of the sensory mode. This semantic ambiguity has been recognized by Fuller (1962), as we'll see further on.

		Stimulus		
		cold	tepid	hot
Internal state	hypothermia	U	I	P
	normothermia	U	I	U
	hyperthermia	P	I	U

Figure XII.2 Simplified chart of the results of Figure XII.1 in a 3 x 3 matrix. The hedonic dimension of the response to ambient temperature will depend on core temperature. A thermal stimulus will arouse pleasure (P), indifference (I), or displeasure (D) according to the internal state. The general case is indifference. Displeasure may persist since it is felt as long as the peripheral stimulus aggravates the internal problem. In contrast, pleasure is always transient since it is a negative feedback that corrects the internal problem. As soon as the hypothermia or hyperthermia is corrected, pleasure disappears and the sensation becomes one of indifference. After Cabanac (1979).

Let's return to the syllogism used in Chapter IX for emotion. If consciousness evolved out of sensation, its 4-dimensional structure should persist in all mental objects. All mental objects should share a comparable structure when being prioritized for access to the behavioral final common path. They should be able to speak to each other. This reasoning worked for emotion and seems applicable here. If we're physiologically driven to pursue comfort, *i.e.*, indifference, by pursuing pleasure and by consuming enjoyable stimuli that help maintain homeostasis, what about the general case of consciousness and the way we lead our lives? In Chapter VIII, we encountered good reasons for thinking that pleasure is also a signal for optimal mental functioning. If physiologically oriented behaviors lead to comfort, *i.e.*, indifference, what does the search for purely mental pleasure lead to? Is there a state of satisfaction that is a common denominator for all motivations? Could it be happiness?

What is happiness?

What is happiness? The *New Webster's Dictionary* (1991) defines it as "feelings of joy and pleasure mingled in varying degree ... the satisfaction of the deepest desire." *Le Petit Larousse* (1989) says it is "the internal state of complete satisfaction." The psychologist M. Argyle (1987) gives a similar definition: "State resulting from satisfaction with life." In reality, these definitions contain the same ambiguity as does the original ASHRAE definition of thermal comfort. The same word "satisfaction" covers both a stable state of indifference and a dynamic state of pleasure. In the case of happiness, we see this ambiguity in countless contradictory pronouncements by authors over the span of human history. Flaubert put it facetiously: "We ought never to think about happiness. It conjures up the devil, for he was the one who invented the concept to drive mankind crazy."

A few more citations:

Philo of Athens: "Neither man nor any other animal is happy."

Thomas Aquinas: "Man cannot and does not want to be happy."

Pascal: "We seek happiness and find only misery and death."

David Hume: "Neither man nor any animal is happy."

Jean Giraudoux: "God has not anticipated happiness for His creatures."

B. de Fontenelle: "The great hindrance to happiness is to expect too great a happiness."

Anton Chekhov: "We are not happy. Happiness does not exist."

René Fallet: "I learnt that happiness is the knowledge that happiness does not exist."

Herman Hesse: "No happiness can last."

Raymond Queneau: "I will never know happiness on earth."

Mario Puzo: "It is quite simply true that we cannot be happy without false illusions."

Marguerite Yourcenar: "Happiness may be only a better tolerated unhappiness."

Françoise Giroux: "I believe that happiness exists. The proof is that suddenly it no longer exists."

… and the list could go on and on.

Once again, as with the definition of comfort, a flawed word has prevented scholars from seeing what actually is going on in the mind. Their disillusionment simply flows from a semantic imperfection:

"Perhaps the most common cause of bad reasoning is the use of ambiguous terms, which mean one thing in one place and another thing elsewhere. A word with two distinct meanings is really two words" (Jevons 1890, p. 114).

The *Webster's New World Thesaurus* lists these words as approximate synonyms of happiness in the sense of inner satisfaction: exhilaration, contentment, bliss, blissfulness, joyfulness, beatitude, blessedness, enchantment, sanctity, ecstasy, rapture, transport, exultation, entrancement, peace, felicity, euphoria, peace of mind, tranquillity, inner joy, freedom from care, pleasure, elation, delirium, optimism, self-satisfaction, benignity, hopefulness, serenity, comfort, blitheness, complacency, and gratification. Clearly, the list is not homogeneous. Some words are close to indifference, others to a highly positive and enjoyable experience. By using one word, 'happiness,' for this disparate list of words, we create confusion between Proust's enthusiasm "This extension, this possible multiplication of ourselves that is happiness" and Jules Renard's thoughts of disenchantment "We are not happy; our happiness is the silence of our unhappiness." The two authors aren't necessarily mistaken, however diametrically opposed their opinions may be, but this very divergence leads to the false conclusion that happiness doesn't exist.

As with the word 'comfort,' it's clear to me that the word 'happiness' covers two entities, one stable and neutral, the other transient and highly positive. The psychologist Fuller (1962), using intuition alone, comes to a similar conclusion:

"We are accustomed to think of pleasure as a response to stimulation rather than a drive for action. A little consideration will show that, [like fear or anger] it is both a response and a drive (p. 59). Actually, there seem to be two types of pleasures, Pleasure 1 and Pleasure 2, separated both psychologically and physiologically" (p. 62).

Fuller's Pleasure 1 is what drives action. We studied it experimentally in the previous chapters. Fuller's Pleasure 2 involves a decrease in excitability and a preponderance of parasympathetic activity. For Fuller, it is the relaxation that follows a hearty meal, it is a decrease in sexual tension, or it is rest after vigorous exercise. In fact, his Pleasure 2 is my definition of comfort. Transpose it to overall consciousness and it becomes happiness.

Yet mental satisfaction does exist. If all mental objects derive their structure from sensation and if the same laws apply to all of consciousness, we should look at happiness in the same way we view comfort. Both coexist in the same word: 'pleasure.' One is patterned on sensory pleasure and is dynamic, highly positive, and transient. The other is patterned on comfort, is stable, and creates a neutral feeling of indifference. These two entities deserve separate words. I suggest 'joy' and 'happiness.'

Joy

The *New Webster's Dictionary* defines 'joy' as "intense happiness or great delight, that which gives rise to this emotion, on which the emotion centers." *Le Petit Larousse* defines it as a "feeling of intense happiness, of plenitude, limited in its duration, felt by a person whose aspiration or desire is satisfied." The *Webster's New World Thesaurus* lists these synonyms of joy in the sense of "inner contentment: ecstasy, rapture, and cheer."

Joy is to happiness what pleasure is to comfort: "The pleasure of the other species affects no portion of our body in particular, we name it pleasure of the spirit and I call it joy" (Hobbes 1651). We find the same negative-positive gradient with the hedonics of consciousness as we do with the hedonics of sensation. Sensation may follow a continuum from very unenjoyable to very enjoyable (Young 1959), and a parallel gradient runs from sadness to joy (Dumas 1900).

Joy is both galvanizing and fleeting. Like sensory pleasure, it is much sought after. Like sensory pleasure, it motivates countless behaviors. "These things I have spoken to you, that my joy may be in you, and that your joy may be full" (*John* 15:11). Schiller describes it thus:

> Joy, beautiful spark of the gods,
> Daughter of Elysium,
> We enter fire imbibed,
> Heavenly, thy sanctuary.[80]

Joy is brief. For Albert Camus, "joy is a burning sensation that is not to be savored." Like pleasure, joy vanishes once the behavior has accomplished its goal and the motivation is satisfied. Because it is so intense and fleeting, joy disappoints those naive folk who expect it to

---

[80] *Freude, schöner Götterfunken,*
Tochter aus Elysium,
Wir betreten feuertrunken,
Himmlische, dein Heiligtum.

last, for lastingness is contrary to its nature. They grasp at it, only to see it gone. To paraphrase an old Latin saying, *omnia anima post gaudium triste.*[81]

When 467 subjects were asked to name the most positive events of their lives, they replied in decreasing order of importance: falling in love, passing an exam, recovering from a severe illness, going away on holidays, making up with your spouse, getting married or engaged, becoming a parent, winning a lot of money, getting promoted, going out with friends, and finding a new job (Argyle 1987). All of these events are transitions!

> "For if a man lives many years, let him rejoice in them all; but let him remember that the days of darkness will be many. All that comes is vanity." (*Ecclesiastes* 11:8)

Joy is a sign of usefulness. Spinoza said: "Joy is the passage of man from a small to a greater perfection." On a more prosaic level, joy hastens recovery from cardiac accidents (Fredrickson and Levenson 1998). The more useful the behavior, the stronger will be your joy.

Once a motivation has been satisfied, joy will give way to happiness.

Happiness

Happiness too exists. Just as we had to dissociate pleasure from comfort, we must also dissociate joy from happiness. In the same way that thermal comfort is an unmotivated, indifferent response to ambient temperature, happiness is a state where motivation has been quenched. It is complete indifference. Such peace of mind or "ataraxia" was counseled by Greek skeptics in Antiquity[82] and persists today in the eastern religions. It is nirvana, which is Buddhist and even more so Hindu. Nirvana, is "union with the supreme spirit" or "a beatific spiritual condition attained by the extinction of desire, in which the individual is freed from karma."[83] It thus corresponds to comfort.

---

[81] *Omnia anima post coitum triste.*
[82] Pyrrhon of Athens, 365-275 BC.
[83] *New Webster's Dictionary*

Comfort exists in the absence of physiological motivation; happiness is the general case. It is the absence of all motivation. Victor Hugo said that "happiness is empty" and Aldous Huxley that "happiness is never grand."

In defining happiness as total indifference, we've deviated from the popular definition that Erich Fromm expressed after Spinoza: happiness is the opposite of depression (Fromm 1955). This, I would call joy. Like comfort, happiness may last indefinitely since it is the lack of all motivation once satisfaction has been achieved. Indeed, for Samuel Johnson, "happiness must be something solid and permanent." Like comfort, happiness is a sign that nothing is going wrong. "One cannot be wrongly happy; or be wrong for being happy" (Petit 1976).

The joy/happiness dichotomy, extrapolated from the pleasure/comfort dichotomy, calls to mind the distinction that Hess made between ergotropic and trophotropic processes for vegetative life. The former is galvanizing and transient; the latter, conservative and stable (Hess 1954). It strikes me as useful to recognize this duality and the true nature of happiness (Figure XII.3). Otherwise, we'll expect too much from happiness, in confusing it with joy, and disappointment will follow, witness the above quotes. Joy is necessarily ephemeral.

By distinguishing between happiness and joy, we can explain the paradoxes noted by authorities on happiness, without defining this word. Helson (1964) followed by Brickman and Campbell (1971) have proposed Adaptation Level Theory, *i.e.*, people judge events and present life experiences in relation to their immediate past and the intensity of their previous life experiences. Brickman *et al.* (1978) went into the field to apply this theory to happiness, but the results ran counter to expectation. Lottery winners were no happier than lottery losers whereas paraplegics were reportedly happy. The authors ended their study with the vague conclusion that happiness is relative. Their disappointment and the lack of a clear conclusion are both understandable. The subjects were asked questions, without happiness being defined, of the type "Are you happy? Were you happy previously? Do you expect to be happy?" The results reflected the ambiguity of the vocabulary being used. The definitions in this chapter should lead to more precise research on happiness and joy.

We can easily recognize the different characteristics of joy and happiness in our lives and in those of others around us. We soon forget an exam success, an athletic triumph, a promotion, or an award. After a short transition, two or three days later, things have returned to normal. We're now used to having won or being promoted. The joy of success has evaporated. Just as sensory pleasure is intense and brief, so too is joy. The victory or promotion is stunning and ephemeral. Hunters and seducers say there's more satisfaction in conquering than in consuming.[84] This is why success is delayed as long as possible in the latest video games, especially the role-playing ones, the game being an interminable quest. Finally, there's the well-known saying: "money doesn't buy happiness." Yet it does help us allay many motivating preoccupations and attain both mental and physiological satiation. Indeed it does buy happiness. But this is the happiness that corresponds to comfort, which money buys as well. Money brings an absence of inconvenience, a tepid sort of happiness. It doesn't bring lasting joy—an oxymoron if ever there were one. Freud noted this reality in wealthy countries: "Civilized man has exchanged a share of possible happiness for a share of security" (Freud 1976). Satiated humans have attained comfort and happiness. But in return they've lost joy.

The role of indifference

After looking at the role of pleasure at each stage of human behavior, I'll now turn to the key role of non-pleasure/non-pain, *i.e.*, the role of comfort and happiness, correctly defined.

There's an almost infinite number of stimuli from the environment and from the body's interior. At every passing moment, we receive countless visual, auditory, and olfactory signals. How do we manage to pick out the ones that matter? Two kinds of choices have to be made.

---

[84] Hence, troubadours preferred to sing about impossible love. Love, *la fine amor*, is forever unfulfilled (Jean Roux, lecture at Oxford, May 6, 1994). Happiness is never attained, being nothing but satisfied boredom.

	Sensation	Consciousness
Agreeable	**pleasure**	**joy**
Indifferent	**comfort**	**happiness**

Figure XII.3 Joy is to happiness as pleasure is to comfort. Pleasure and joy are transient. They last as long as the stimulus or corrective behavior is useful, and disappear as soon as their goals have been reached. Comfort and happiness are absence of all motivation and indifference to behaviors that would be unnecessary. Both are stable and thus durable.

First, we decide to eliminate or to flee the discomfort or pain. This is a kind of reverse search for pleasure that leads to a preliminary sorting. But a huge amount of information still remains unsorted. Indifference now comes into the picture. When no pleasure is to be had, indifference provides a refuge from displeasure. It tells us "there's nothing worth looking into, don't bother." This role is a fundamental one: to indicate what has no merit. It keeps us from wasting our time and thus makes way for a second level of decision-making. At this second level, we seek pleasure. We respond usefully and effectively by avoiding or disregarding countless irrelevant stimuli that leave us indifferent.

It might seem pessimistic to define happiness in the same way that we define comfort. Nothing could be further from the truth. Indifference plays a fundamental role. While discussing the acceptability of a stimulus, Ovsich contrasts the notions of comparative acceptability and absolute acceptability. He illustrates the difference with the following examples:

"If one chooses from a few good or acceptable apples, s/he also rejects the others. Does this mean that the apples which were not chosen are bad? Of course not—rejection or non-acceptance of an object as a result of choice does not mean that rejected elements of choice are unacceptable by themselves. Conversely, if someone is starving and chooses to eat one of some bad apples, only one bad apple was accepted and the others were rejected. Does this mean that the chosen bad apple is now good? Of course not, it is still the same bad apple that is just the best available one and, therefore, the chosen/accepted one. Acceptance or rejection as an outcome of choice is always a result of comparison made by a subject;..." (Ovsich, 1998)

My goal here is not to discuss Ovsich's argument, but simply to stress the importance of indifference. In the first example, once we've chosen the first apple, once we're satiated, all other apples leave us indifferent. Of the millions of signals that our brain receives from the environment and from our own body at each passing moment, only a tiny fraction are hedonically positive, *i.e.*, useful things we should seek and consume, or hedonically negative, *i.e.*, harmful or dangerous things we should avoid or flee. All other signals leave us indifferent. Comfort and happiness have a key role, defined above: ataraxia/nirvana. They indicate the irrelevance of signals from our body or our environment. They tell us that everything is going well since nothing is going wrong. "No news is good news."

Sadness and depression

If joy corresponds to sensory pleasure, discomfort and pain correspond to sorrow and unhappiness. The third component of hedonics, after pleasure/joy and indifference, is evidently a negative one: displeasure, depression, and physical and moral pain. Sadness has two characteristics. It has a role and it can last.

This role is displeasure, the reverse of joy. We can see the parallels to sensation in the case of negative hedonic experiences. A negative emotion like fear occurs when an organism's integrity is threatened. The displeasure of failure means that efforts have been made in vain. It is synonymous with waste. The preceding pages have abundantly illustrated how an unpleasant sensation or a physiological discomfort signals a threat, a danger, or a source of harm.

241

We also see this commonality between sensation and consciousness along the time dimension. Neither pain nor discomfort is transient. They indicate stimuli and situations that may harm or endanger the body's internal environment, and they last as long as their causation lasts. Thus, sadness, which corresponds to displeasure, has the same temporal properties. When pleasure and joy are transient, their brevity points to their usefulness: as soon as the internal problem is corrected, the external stimulus becomes neutral. Yet grief, displeasure, and sadness may last indefinitely. Some kinds of grief and sorrow are incurable. As long as the internal problem isn't remedied, the displeasure, discomfort, and sadness will remain. The outcome may be an equally permanent and powerful desire to escape the pain. Such negative hedonics can include decisions that profoundly alter one's existence, such as emigration. Drug use and suicide are likewise responses to desperate situations that seem to offer no better way out, especially if one believes in a hereafter or is leaving a generous death benefit for a loved one.

Such ongoing discomfort, pain, and sadness accounts for the pessimism of so many writers. Rozin and Royzman (2001) state that negative experiences are inherently given priority, probably because of their permanency.

Let us do Death justice

Let's end with some final thoughts on the nature of pleasure and joy. Pleasure and joy do serve to bring an organism back to normal, but they appear only in circumstances of *transition* to a better state, as underscored by the definition of 'joy' in *Le Petit Larousse*. In recognizing the dynamic and transient nature of pleasure, we're invited to reflect on the very nature of life. We all must die some day. Life is a transition. Perhaps this transience is the price and thereby the source of all joy. Wouldn't life be boring if it lasted forever? According to Pierre d'Ailly,[85] the mythical and immortal Hyperboreans committed suicide out of world-weariness. Why bother doing something today

---

[85] http://www.newadvent.org/cathen/01235b.htm

when we have an eternity of listlessness ahead? In contrast, when our days are numbered, we've got to get on with it while we still have time and can enjoy life. However paradoxical it may sound, life would be nothing without death. Death turns life into a transient episode, a source of joy. A future death is what makes our day in the sun joyful. It is the price of a life worth living. This point came up in a discussion between myself and Alain Cardon:[86] although models of artificial intelligence are supposed to replicate human mental mechanisms, they never take into account this sense of the ephemeral, which takes place at each moment of our consciousness. *Ecclesiastes*[87] describes this motivation, which underlies each passing second of our lives and which may even be our permanent and ultimate source of motivation. It is again mentioned in the Psalm of David.

> Lord, let me know my end,
> And what is the measure of my days;
> Let me know how fleeting my life is!
> Behold, thou hast made my days a few handbreadths,
> And my lifetime is as nothing in thy sight (Ps. 39:4-5).

---

[86] An artificial intelligence specialist and a computer science professor at the Université du Havre. The discussion was held on the premises of LIP6, Paris, September 2002.
[87] See: *Eccl.* III; XII:1-7.

Postface

When a scientist publishes new findings in a peer-
reviewed journal, everyone believes them, except
the scientist, who still has some doubts. When a
scientist publishes a new hypothesis or theory, no
one believes it, except the scientist, who has no
doubts.   Anonymous

Pleasure is an outcome of behavior for hedonist philosophers and a cause for hormists. Both groups believe it motivates behavior, either as a cause or as an anticipated result. Both feel it optimizes behavior, whether a posteriori or a priori. Thus, pleasure may be what drives the human mind—this third infinity of the universe.

In the preface, I made an implicit promise. I would show that we're universally and continually motivated by the pursuit of pleasure and that this pursuit optimizes our behavior. Pleasure is thus the fifth influence of the universe. Have I kept my bargain? Clearly, as Teilhard de Chardin argued, the human brain is the third infinity of nature. Its complexity, as shown by many indexes, should be cause for both pride and humility. Pride, because each of us is such a marvel of coherent complexity. Humility, because each of us, however modest we may be in others' eyes, is also the seat of this third infinity. Is our brain driven by pleasure? I think so. The experiments described in this book may not cover all human motivations, but they do cover a broad enough spectrum to support this conclusion.

Pleasure is rooted in biology. Its proximal usefulness is shown by physiological data and by its apparent adaptive value, as seen in the persistence of sensory pleasure from its origin in ancestral reptiles to present-day mammals and birds. This persistence over evolutionary time all but proves its usefulness. Pleasure maximization seems to be the driving force behind all behaviors, from the most humble to the most complex, from simple stimulus-response to abstract thought and social relations. The global workspace of Bernard Baars (1994) is hedonically organized. Without necessarily saying so, each of us knows and experiences this reality. But to bring common knowledge

245

into the realm of science, one sometimes has to start at square one and prove it all point by point, however obvious the demonstration may be. Nonetheless, the scientific community is now taking an interest in this common knowledge that each of us has stored away (Kahneman *et al.* 1997; Ovsich 1998; Sher 1998; Johnston 1999; Ovsich, book in preparation).

Pleasure has proven its efficiency over a broad range of daily, ongoing mental tasks ever since its reptilian origins. This evolutionary perspective brings to light four striking parallels:

In Chapter III, pleasure was shown to be contingent. We see this in alliesthesia: the same stimulus can produce more pleasurable or less pleasurable sensations depending on the subject's state. Alliesthesia closely resembles what Adam Smith, the founder of economics, called the diminishing value of consumer goods (Smith 1776). If we go to the market to buy a cart, we'll be ready to pay the full price because we need this good. If the merchant offers a second cart, we may buy it too, as a spare, but at a lower price. The parallel with alliesthesia is striking: the same object can lose its attractiveness and thus depreciate in 'pleasure value.' It is no longer worth its initial price.

A second parallel exists between pleasure as a common currency and the biochemical mechanisms for energy transfer. In living cells, free energy circulates from glucose to ATP in several stages that combine endothermic and exothermic reactions (Lehninger 1965). At each stage, synthesis of energy-rich molecules is made possible by a concurrent destruction of molecules that are a little less energy-rich. At each stage of energy transfer, the energy stored by the endogenous reaction is a little less than the energy lost by the exogenous reaction. And so are constructed molecules whose existence would otherwise be improbable. This accumulation of free energy at the expense of total energy loss is quite similar to what we saw on Figure IV.2: an improbable behavior A, which produces displeasure, may nonetheless be carried out if twinned with behavior B, which produces more pleasure than behavior A produces displeasure. These two exchanges, one intracellular, the other mental, at the extremes of the continuum of living processes, present a parallel that evokes a profound unity in the mechanisms of life.

A third parallel concerns a law of physics. In these pages, I judged optimization with my physiologist's eye: maximum performance, constant power, minimization of duration, proportionality of thermogenesis to ambient temperature, and so on. Physicists too know the concept of optimization. For them, since Maupertuis (1698-1759), Euler (1707-1783) and Lagrange (1736-1813), a fundamental law of nature is the minimization of action, defined as:

$$Action = Work \times Duration.$$

By maximizing sensory pleasure, subjects will behave in such a way as to produce work in proportion to the ambient temperature. Action is thus minimized. They will also minimize action when producing work at a constant power output to climb a 300-m rise in elevation. The shortest possible time is taken for a constant amount of work. Thus, pleasure maximization obeys the principle of least effort. By seeking and maximizing pleasure, we maximize our work within the time window for a job. Because time is limited, we continually need to optimize effort, and this ongoing concern is present, at least in the background, at each moment of consciousness.

Finally, another parallel came up several times in the preceding chapters: the one between mechanisms of sensory pleasure and those of joy. This parallel may be drawn from the common currency function of the hedonic dimension of consciousness. It leads to a conclusion I only touched on lightly, for it hasn't been tested by any experiment and remains mere speculation. Although most sensory pleasures are innate and linked to the nature of the stimulus, be it hot, cold, mechanical, or chemical, many pleasures are learned, especially food-related ones. If the laws of sensory pleasure and joy share the same structure, this similarity points to a new conclusion: joy too may be learned. Teaching can and ought to hasten and optimize this fundamental property.

The last chapter relies as much on intuition as it does on science. But it is based on experimental evidence that others can replicate. Throughout the pages of this essay, I've tried to maintain a scientific level of discourse, *i.e.*, I've backed my line of argument with evidence that any educated reader may access and understand, including evidence that pertains to the mind and its workings. I've referred the reader to many examples and figures, sometimes redundantly so—but proving a point necessarily requires some rehashing—all this to show the central influence of pleasure-seeking and displeasure-avoidance in our lives. My approach has thus been one of scientific reasoning. But the ultimate stage of all reasoning is to advance a hypothesis and, at that point, a researcher cannot avoid some subjectivity. "I know" gives way to "I believe." In making this transition, I hope I've clearly indicated what belongs to science and what doesn't. Let me return to the model of consciousness as multidimensional. In the consciousness of each of us there's a spiritual (artistic, religious) dimension that is independent of the rational dimension. This spiritual dimension is inherent to human thought, religious or otherwise. Its origin probably lies in human nature itself. Anthropologists distinguish the human species from others by its spiritual manifestations and its concern for existence due to its knowledge of death (Hobbes 1651; Frank 1988; Johnson-Laird and Oatley 1992; Evans *et al.* 1993; Baron 1994; Cabanac 1996; DeSousa 1997; Goldstein and Gigerenzer 2002; Shafir and LeBoeuf 2002). In my arguments, I've accepted the existence of this dimension in myself. And this dimension too is hedonically driven. I feel that those experiences that moralists deem the highest, such as a sense of accountability or a feeling of unhindered decision-making, are also driven by maximization of pleasure/joy. But such a response is learned through proper upbringing. Knowing this drive is learned, however, doesn't lessen its effectiveness or the joy of obeying it.

Joy isn't the same thing as happiness, and this distinction may help us better understand the Sermon on the Mount. Christianity owes its joy to the impossibility of its commandments. An unattainable morality characterizes the entire Sermon on the Mount. For instance:

"You have heard that it was said to the men of old, 'You shall not kill' ... But I say to you that every one who is angry with his brother shall be liable to judgment" (Matthew V:21-22).

"You have heard that it was said, 'You shall not commit adultery.' But I say to you that every one who looks at a woman lustfully has already committed adultery with her in his heart" (Matthew V:27-

248

28).
"Again, you have heard that it was said to the men of old, 'You shall not swear falsely ...' Let what you say be simply 'Yes' or 'No'; anything more than this comes from evil" (Matthew V:33-37).

These teachings are impossible to practice. Happiness, as defined in Chapter XII, is impossible under that law. The preconditions cannot be attained. Yet "[t]hese things I have spoken to you, that my joy may be in you, and that your joy may be full" (John 15:11). How can we explain the contradiction? Of course, there's no pleasure in feeling guilty, but a believer can gain joy. The pain of imperfection is alleviated by the certainty of forgiveness, which generates a much stronger joy in the Jew/Christian:

"Blessed is he whose transgression is forgiven, whose sin is covered. Blessed is the man to whom the Lord imputes no iniquity, and in whose spirit there is no deceit." (*Psalms* 32:1-2).

"Thou hast multiplied the nation, thou hast increased its joy (Isaiah 9:3). And the ransomed of the Lord shall return, and come to Zion with singing; everlasting joy shall be upon their heads; they shall obtain joy and gladness, and sorrow and sighing shall flee away" (Isaiah 35:10).

"And the prayer of faith will save the sick man, and the Lord will raise him up; and if he has committed sins, he will be forgiven" (James 5:15).

"If we confess our sins, he is faithful and just, and will forgive our sins and cleanse us from all unrighteousness" (1 John 1:9).

REFERENCES

Aagmo, A. (1999). Sexual motivation - an inquiry into events determining the occurence of sexual behavior. *Behavioural Brain Research,* 105, 129-150.

Aagmo, A., & Marroquin, E. (1997). Role of gustatory and postingestive actions of sweeteners in the generation of positive affect as evaluated by place preference conditioning. *Appetite,* 29, 269-289.

Aalto, S., Naatanen, P., Wallius, E., Metsahonkala, L., Stenman, H., Niemi, P. M., et al. (2002). Neuroanatomical substrata of amusement and sadness: a PET activation study using film stimuli. *Neuroreport,* 13, 67-73.

Ackroff, K., & Sclafani, A. (1999). Palatability and foraging cost interact to control caloric intake. *Journal of Experimental Psychology: Animal Behavior Processes,* 25, 28-36.

Adrian, E. D. (1928). *The Basis of Sensation.* London: Christophers.

Aharon, I., Etcoff, N., Ariely, D., Chabris, C. F., O'Connor, E., & Breiter, H. C. (2001). Beautiful faces have variable reward value: fMRI and behavioral evidence. *Neuron,* 32, 537-551.

Ainslie, G. (1975). Specious Reward: A behavioral theory of impulsiveness and impulse control. Psychological Bulletin, 82, 463-496.

Allport, A. (1988). What concept of consciousness? In A. J. Marcel & E. Bisiach (Eds.), *Consciousness in Contemporary Science* (pp. 159-182). Oxford: Oxford University Press.

Aquinas, T. (1984-1986). *Summa Theologie* (Traduction française). Paris: Cerf.

Argyle, M. (1987). *The Psychology of Happiness.* London: Methuen and Co.

Aristote. (322-284 Av. J.C.). *De l'ame* (J. Tricot, Trans.). Paris: Librairie philosophique J. Vrin.

Aristote. (322-284, Av. J.C.). *Éthique de Nicomaque* 10 (J.Voilquin, Trans.). Paris: Flammarion.

Arnold, M. B. (1970). Perenial problems in the field of emotion. In M. B. Arnold (Ed.), *Feelings and Emotions* (pp. 169-183). New York: Academic Press.

Attia, M. (1984). Thermal pleasantness and temperature regulation in man. *Neuroscience and Biobehavioral Reviews,* 8, 335-343.

Attia, M., & Engel, P. (1980). A field study of thermal stress and recovery using thermoregulatory behavioral and physiological indicators. *International Archives for Occupational and Environmental Health,* 47, 21-33.

Attia, M., & Engel, P. (1981). Thermal alliesthesial response in Man is independent of skin location stimulated. *Physiology and Behavior,* 27, 439-444.

Attia, M., & Engel, P. (1982). Thermal pleasantness sensation: an indicator of thermal stress. *European Journal of Applied Physiology,* 50, 55-70.

Baars, B. J. (1983). Conscious contents provide the nervous system with coherent global information. In R. J. D. e. al. (Ed.), Consciousness and Self-Regulation (Vol. 3): Plenum Press.

Baars, B. J. (1994). A global workspace theory of conscious experience. In A. Revonsuo & M. Kamppinen (Eds.), *Consciousness in Philosophy and Cognitive Neuroscience* (pp. 149-171). Hillsdale, New Jersey: Laurence Erlbaum Associates.

Baars, B. J. (1995). Can physics provide a theory of consciousness? *Psyche*, 2(8).

Baars, B. J. (1997). *In the Theater of Consciousness: The Workspace of the Mind*. Oxford: Oxford University Press.

Baars, B. J., & Newman, J. (1994). A neurobiological interpretation of global workspace theory. In A. Revonsuo & M. Kamppinen (Eds.), *Consciousness in Philosophy and Cognitive Neuroscience* (pp. 211-226). Hillsdale, New Jersey: Laurence Erlbaum Associates.

Baerends, G. P. (1956). Aufbau des tierischen Verhaltens. In W. Kükenthal & T. Krumbach (Eds.), *Handbuch der Zoologie* (Vol. VIII Mammalia, pp. Teil 10 (Lfg 17)). Berlin: De Gruyter & Co.

Baker, R. B., & Bellis, M. A. (1993). Human sperm competition: ejaculate manipulation by females and a function for the female orgasm. *Animal Behaviour*, 46, 887-909.

Balaskó, M., & Cabanac, M. (1998a). Behavior of juvenile lizards (Iguana iguana) in a conflict between temperature regulation and palatable food. *Brain Behavior and Evolution*, 52, 257-262.

Balaskó, M., & Cabanac, M. (1998b). Grammatical choice and affective experience in a second-language test. Neuropsychobiology, 37, 205-210.

Banks, W. P. (1991). Perception. *Annual Review of Psychology*, 42, 305-331.

Baron, J. (1994). Nonconsequentialist decisions. *Behavioral Brain Sciences*, 17, 1-42.

Barrette, C. (2000). *Le miroir du monde*. Sainte Foy (Québec): Éditions Multimondes.

Barros, M., & Tomaz, C. (2002). Non-human primate models for investigating fear and anxiety. *Neuroscience and Biobehavioral Reviews*, 26, 187-201.

Barrow, J. D., & Tipler, F. T. (1986). *The Anthropic Cosmological Principle*. Oxford: Oxford University Press.

Bartlett, R. G. (1955). Physiologic responses during coitus. *Journal of Applied Physiology*, 9, 469-472.

Bartoshuk, L. M. (1988). Taste. In *Stevens' handbook of experimental psychology* (2th ed., Vol. 1 Perception and Motivation, pp. 461-499). New York: John Wiley & Sons.

Bartoshuk, L. M. (1991). Taste, Smell, and Pleasure. In R. C. Bolles (Ed.), *The Hedonics of Taste* (pp. 15-28). Hillsdale, New Jersey: Lawrence Erlbaum Ass.

Beauchamp, G. K., & Cowart, B. J. (1985). Congenital and experiential factors in the development of human flavor preferences. *Appetite*, 6, 357-372.

Beauchamp, G. K., & Mason, J. R. (1991). Comparative hedonics of taste. In R. C. Bolles (Ed.), *The Hedonics of Taste* (pp. 159-183). Hillsdale, New Jersey: Lawrence Earlbaum Ass.

Bechara, A., Damasio, A. R., Damasio, H., & Anderson, S. W. (1994). Insensitivity to future consequences following damage to human prefrontal cortex. *Cognition*, 50, 7-15.

Bechara, A., Tranel, D., Damasio, H., & Damasio, A. R. (1996). Failure to respond autonomically to anticipated future outcomes following damage to prefrontal cortex. *Cerebral Cortex*, 6, 215-225.

Bédard, M., & Weingarten, H. P. (1989). Postabsorptive glucose decreases excitatory effects of taste on ingestion. *American Journal of Physiology*, 256, R1142-R1147.

Beebe-Center, J. G. (1932). *The Psychology of Pleasantness and Unpleasantness*. Princeton, New Jersey: Van Nostrand.

Bellisle, F. (1992). Rôle et mécanismes de l'apprentissage dans les goûts et conduites alimentaires. In I. Giachetti (Ed.), *Plaisir et préférence alimentaires* (pp. 1-30). Paris: Polytechnica.

Bentham, J. (1823 (1748-1832)). *An Introduction to the Principles of Morals and Legislation* (reedited,1948). New York,: Hafner Pub. Co.

Bergson, H. (1932). *Les deux sources de la morale et de la religion*. Paris: Presses Universitaires de France.

Berlyne, D. E. (1950-1951). Novelty and curiosity as determinants of exploratory behavior. *British Journal of Psychology*, 41, 68-80.

Bermudez-Rattoni, F., Forthman, D. L., Sanchez, M. A., Perz, J. L., & Garcia, J. (1988). Odor and taste aversion conditioned in anesthetized rats. *Behavioral Neuroscience*, 102, 726-732.

Bernouilli, D. (1738). Specimen theiriae nervae de mensura sertis. *Commentarii Academiae Scientiarum Imperialis Petropolitanae*, 5, 175-192.

Berridge, K. C. (1991). Modulation of taste affect by hunger, caloric satiety, and sensory-specific satiety in the rat. *Appetite*, 16, 103-120.

Berridge, K. C. (1999). Pleasure, pain, desire, and dread: hidden core processes of emotion. In N. Kahneman, E. Diener & N. Schwartz (Eds.), *Well-Being: The Foundations of Hedonic Psychology* (pp. 525-557). New York: Russel Sage Foundation.

Berridge, K. C. (2000). Measuring hedonic impact in animals and infants microstructure of affective taste reactivity patterns. *Neuroscience and Biobehavioral Reviews*, 24, 173-198.

Berridge, K. C. (2001). Reward learning: reinforcement, incentives, and expectations. In D. L. Medlin (Ed.), *The Psychology of Learning and Motivation* (Vol. 40, pp. 223-278). New York: Academic Press.

Berridge, K. C., & Cromwell, H. C. (1990). Motivational-sensorimotor interaction controls aphagia and exaggerated treading after striatopallidal lesions. *Behavioral Neuroscience*, 104, 778-785.

Berridge, K. C., & Fentress, J. C. (1985). Trigeminal-taste interaction in palatability processing. *Science*, 228, 747-750.

Berridge, K. C., Flynn, F. W., Schulkin, J., & Grill, H. J. (1984). Sodium depletion enhances salt palatability in rats. *Behavioral Neuroscience*, 98, 652-661.

Berridge, K. C., & Valenstein, E. S. (1991). What psychological process mediates feeding evoked by electrical stimulation of the lateral hypothalamus? *Behavioral Neuroscience*, 105, 3-14.

253

Berthoud, H. R. (2002). Multiple neural systems controlling food intake and body weight. *Neuroscience and Biobehavioral Reviews*, 26, 393-428.

Bertola, F., & Curi, U. (1993). *The Anthropic Principle: Proceedings of the Second Venice Conference on Cosmology and Philosophy.* Cambridge: Cambridge University Press.

Blanchard, J. J., Mueser, K. T., & Bellack, A. S. (1998). Anhedonia, positive and negative affect, acid social functioning in schizophrenia. *Schizophrenia Bulletin*, 24, 413-424.

Bleichert, A., Behling, K., Scarperi, M., & Scarperi, S. (1973). Thermoregulatory behavior of man during rest and exercise. *Pflügers Archiv*, 338, 303-312.

Bloch, O. R. (1971). *La philosophie de Gassendi.* La Haye: Martinus Nijhoff.

Bocker, K. B. E., Baas, J. M. P., Kenemans, J. L., & Verbaten, M. N. (2001). Stimulus-preceding negativity induced by fear: a manifestation of affective anticipation. *International Journal of Psychophysiology*, 43, 77-90.

Boggio, V. (1992). Les choix alimentaires chez les jeunes enfants. In I. Giachetti (Ed.), *Plaisir et préférence alimentaires.* Paris: Polytechnica.

Booth, D. A. (1991). Learned ingestive motivation and the pleasures of the palate. In R. C. Bolles (Ed.), *The Hedonics of Taste.* Hillsdale, New Jersey: Lawrence Erlbaum Associates.

Boring, E. G. (1942). *Sensation and Perception in the History of Experimental Psychology.* New York: Appleton Century Crofts inc.

Bowring, J. (1962). *The works of Jeremy Bentham published under the superintendance of his executor John Bowring 1833-1844* (Vol. I). New York: Russell & Russell inc.

Breslin, P. A. S., Davidson, T. L., & Grill, H. J. (1990). Conditioned reversal of reactions to normally avoided tastes. *Physiology and Behavior*, 47, 533-538.

Breuer, R. (1991). *The Anthropic Principle. Man as the Focal Point of Nature.* Boston: Birkhäuser.

Brickman, P., & Campbell, D. T. (1971). Hedonic relativism and planning the good society. In M. H. Appley (Ed.), *Adaptation Level Theory: A Symposium* (pp. 287-302). New York: Academic Press.

Brickman, P., Coates, D., & Janoff-Bulman, R. (1978). Lottery winners and accident victims: Is happiness relative? *Journal of Personality and Social Psychology*, 36, 917-927.

Briese, E., & Cabanac, M. (1991). Stress hyperthermia: Physiological arguments that it is a fever. *Physiology and Behavior*, 49, 1153-1157.

Briese, E., & deQuijada, M. G. (1970). Colonic temperature of rats during handling. *Acta Physiologica Latinoamericana*, 20, 97-102.

Briese, E., & Quijada, M. (1979). Positive alliesthesia after insulin. *Experientia*, 35, 1058.

Brillat-Savarin, A. (1828). *Physiologie du goût, ou Méditations de gastronomie transcendante; ouvrage théorique, historique et à l'ordre du jour* (2th ed.). Paris: A. Sutelet et Cie, Libraires.

Brondel, L., & Cabanac, M. (2007). Alliesthesia in visual and auditory sensations from environmental signals. *Physiology and Behavior*, 91, 196-201.

Bunge, M. (1979). The mind-body problem in an evolutionary perspective. In C. F. Symp (Ed.), *Brain and Mind* (Vol. 69, pp. 53-77). Amsterdam: Excerpta Medica.

Bunge, M. (1980). *The Mind-Body Problem*. Oxford: Pergamon Press.

Bunge, M. (1989). From neuron to mind. *News in Physiological Science*, 4, 206-209.

Bunge, M. (2003). *Emergence and Convergence*. Toronto: University of Toronto Press.

Burghardt, G. M. (1998). The evolutionary origins of play revisited: lessons from turtles. In M. Bekoff & J. A. Byers (Eds.), *Animal Play: Evolutionary, Comparative, and Ecological Perspectives* (pp. 1-26). Cambridge: Cambridge University Press.

Burghardt, G. M., Wilcoxon, H. C., & Czaplicki, J. A. (1973). Conditioning in garter snakes: aversion to palatable prey induced by delayed illness. *Animal Learning and Behavior*, 1(4), 317-320.

Byrne, C. C., & Kurland, J. A. (2001). Self-deception in an evolutionary game. *Journal of Theoretical Biology*, 212, 457-480.

Cabanac, A., & Briese, E. (1991). Handling elevates the colonic temperature of mice. *Physiology and Behavior*, 51, 95-98.

Cabanac, A., & Cabanac, M. (2000). Heart rate response to gentle handling of Frog and Lizard. *Behavioural Processes*, 52, 89-95.

Cabanac, M. (1969). Plaisir ou déplaisir de la sensation thermique et homéothermie. *Physiology and Behavior*, 4, 359-364.

Cabanac, M. (1971). Physiological role of pleasure. *Science*, 173, 1103-1107.

Cabanac, M. (1979a). Gustatory pleasure and body needs. In J. H. A. Kroese (Ed.), *Preference Behaviour and Chemoreception* (pp. 275-288). London: IRL.

Cabanac, M. (1979b). Les signaux physiologiques du confort thermique. In J. Durand & J. Reynaud (Eds.), *Confort thermique: Aspects physiologiques et psychologiques*. Paris: Editions de l'INSERM.

Cabanac, M. (1979c). Sensory Pleasure. *Quarterly Review of Biology*, 54, 1-29.

Cabanac, M. (1985a). Optimisation du comportement par la minimisation du déplaisir dans un espace sensoriel à deux dimensions. *Comptes Rendus de l'Académie des Sciences* (Paris), 300 III, 607-610.

Cabanac, M. (1985b). Strategies adopted by juvenile lizards foraging in a cold environment. *Physiological Zoology*, 58, 262-271.

Cabanac, M. (1986a). Du confort au bonheur. *Psychiatrie Française*, 17, 9-15.

Cabanac, M. (1986b). Money versus pain: experimental study of a conflict in humans. *Journal of the Experimental Analysis of Behavior*, 46, 37-44.

Cabanac, M. (1987). Alliesthesia. In G. Adelman (Ed.), *Encyclopedia of Neurosciences* (pp. 27). Boston: Birkhäuser.

Cabanac, M. (1989). La maximisation du plaisir, réponse à un conflit de motivations. *Comptes Rendus de l' Académie des Sciences* (Paris), 309 III, 397-402.

Cabanac, M. (1992). Pleasure: the common currency. *Journal of Theoretical Biology*, 155, 173-200.

Cabanac, M. (1995a). *La quête du plaisir*. Montréal: Liber.

Cabanac, M. (1995b). Palatability vs. money: experimental study of a conflict of motivations. *Appetite*, 25, 43-49.

Cabanac, M. (1995c). What is sensation? In R. Wong (Ed.), *Biological Perspectives on Motivated Activities*. (pp. 409-428). Norwood, New Jersey: Ablex.

Cabanac, M. (1996a). On the origin of consciousness, a postulate and its corrollary. *Neuroscience and Biobehavioral Reviews*, 20, 33-40.

Cabanac, M. (1996b). The evolutionary point of view: rationality is elsewhere. Commentary on J. Baron's Nonconsequentialist Decisions. *Behavioral and Brain Sciences*, 19, 322.

Cabanac, M. (1999). Emotion and phylogeny. *Japanese Journal of Physiology*, 49, 1-10.

Cabanac, M. (2001). Do birds experience sensory pleasure? *Abstracts of the Psychonomic Society*, 6, 25 (173).

Cabanac, M. (2002). What is emotion? *Behavioural Processes*, 60, 69-84.

Cabanac, M., & Aizawa, S. (2000). Fever and tachycardia in a bird (Gallus domesticus) after simple handling. *Physiology and Behavior*, 69, 541-545.

Cabanac, M., & Bernieri, C. (2000). Behavioral rise in body temperature and tachycardia by handling of a turtle (*Clemys insculpta*). *Behavioural Processes*, 49, 61-68.

Cabanac, M., Bonniot-Cabanac, M.-C., Ramirez, M. J., & Coello-Garcia, M.-T. (2008). Pleasure from agressivity as a function of age sex and impulsivity. *Open Criminality Journal*, 1, 19-26.

Cabanac, M., Cabanac, R., & Hammel, H. T. (1999). The fifth influence. Paper presented at the *43rd Annual Conference of the International Society for the Systems Sciences* (CD),.

Cabanac, M., & Chatonnet, J. (1964). Influence de la temperature interne sur le caractere affectif d'une sensation thermique cutanee. *Journal de Physiologie*, 56, 540-541.

Cabanac, M., & Duclaux, R. (1973). Alliesthésie olfacto-gustative et prise alimentaire chez l'homme (revue) . *Journal de Physiologie*, 66, 113-135.

Cabanac, M., Duclaux, R., & Spector, N. H. (1971). Sensory feedbacks in regulation of body weight: is there a ponderostat? *Nature*, 229, 125-127.

Cabanac, M., & Fantino, M. (1977). Origin of olfacto-gustatory alliesthesia: intestinal sensitivity to carbohydrate concentration? *Physiology and Behavior*, 18, 1039-1045.

Cabanac, M., & Ferber, C. (1987). Pleasure and preference in a two-dimensional sensory space. *Appetite*, 8, 15-28.

Cabanac, M., & Frankham, P. (2002). Evidence that transient nicotine lowers the body-weight set-point. *Physiology and Behavior*, 76, 539-542.

Cabanac, M., & Gosselin, F. (1993). Emotional fever in the lizard Callopistes maculatus. *Animal Behaviour*, 46, 200-202.

Cabanac, M., Guillaume, J., MBalaskó, & Fleury, A. (2002). Pleasure in decision

256

making situations. *Biomed. Central.*, http://www.biomedcentral.com/1471-244X/2/7/.

Cabanac, M., & Johnson, K. G. (1983). Analysis of a conflict between palatability and cold exposure in rats. *Physiology and Behavior*, 31, 249-253.

Cabanac, M., & Laberge, F. (1998). Fever in goldfish is induced by pyrogens but not by handling. *Physiology and Behavior*, 63, 377-379.

Cabanac, M., & Lafrance, L. (1990). Postingestive alliesthesia: The rat tells the same story. *Physiology and Behavior*, 47, 539-543.

Cabanac, M., & Lafrance, L. (1991). Facial consummatory responses in rats support the ponderostat hypothesis. *Physiology and Behavior*, 50, 179-183.

Cabanac, M., & Lafrance, L. (1992). Duodenal preabsorptive origin of gustatory alliesthesia in rats. *American Journal of Physiology*, 263, R1013-R1017.

Cabanac, M., & LeBlanc, J. (1983). Physiological conflict in humans: fatigue *vs* cold discomfort. *American Journal of Physiology*, 244, R621-R628.

Cabanac, M., Massonnet, B., & Belaiche, R. (1972). Preferred hand temperature as a function of internal and mean skin temperatures. *Journal of Applied Physiology*, 33, 699-703.

Cabanac, M., & Minaire, Y. (1966). The influence of alimentary ingestion on the affective character of a constant gustative sensation. Paper presented at the *Abstracts of the International Congress of Nutrition*, Hambourg.

Cabanac, M., Minaire, Y., & Adair, E. R. (1968). Influence of internal factors on t he pleasantness of a gustative sweet sensation. *Communications in Behavioral Biology* Part A, 1, 77-82.

Cabanac, M., Pouliot, C., & Everett, J. (1997). Pleasure as a sign of efficacy of mental activity. *European Psychologist*, 2, 226-234.

Cabanac, M., & Rabe, E. F. (1976). Influence of a monotonous food on body weight regulation in humans. *Physiology and Behavior*, 17, 675-678.

Cabanac, M., Ramel, P., Duclaux, R., & Joli, M. (1969). Indifférence à la douleur et confort thermique. Étude expérimentale de deux cas. *Presse Médicale*, 77, 2053-2054.

Cabanac, M., & Russek, M. (1982). *Régulation et contrôle en biologie.* Québec: Presses de l'Université Laval.

Cabanac, M., & Serres, P. (1976). Peripheral heat as a reward for heart rate response in the curarized rat. *Journal of Comparative and Physiological Psychology*, 90, 435-441.

Cain, W. S. (1988). Olfaction. In *Stevens' handbook of experimental psychology* (2th ed., Vol. 1 Perception and Motivation, pp. 409-459). New York: John Wiley & Sons.

Cannon, W. B. (1927). The James-Lange theory of emotions: a critical examination and an alternation. *American Journal of Psychology*, 39, 106-124.

Cannon, W. B. (1929). *Bodily Changes in Pain, Hunger, Fear, and Rage* (2nd ed.). New York: Appleton.

Cantin, I., & Dubé, L. (1999). Attitudinal moderation of correlation between food liking and consumption. *Appetite*, 32, 367-381.

Cardon, A. (2000). *Conscience artificielle et systèmes adaptatifs*. Paris: Éditions Eyrolles.

Carr, K. D., & Wolinsky, T. D. (1993). Chronic food restriction and weight loss produce opioid facilitation of perifornical hypothalamic self-stimulation. *Brain Research*, 607, 141-148.

Carrel, A. (1935). *L'homme cet inconnu*. Paris: Plon.

Carretie, L., MartinLoeches, M., Hinojosa, J. A., & Mercado, F. (2001). Emotion and attention interaction studied through event-related potentials. *Journal of Cognitive Neuroscience*, 13, 1109-1128.

Carver, C. S., & Scheier, M. F. (1990). Origins and functions of positive and negative affect. *Psychological Review*, 97, 19-35.

Chalmers, D. J. (1995a). Facing up to the problem of consciousness. *Journal of Consciousness Studies*, 2(3), 200-219.

Chalmers, D. J. (1995b). Minds, machines, and mathematics. Psyche, 2, 11-20.

Changeux, J.-P. (1983). *L'homme neuronal*. Paris: Fayard.

Changizi, M. A., & Hall, W. G. (2001). Thirst modulates a perception. *Perception*, 30, 1489-1497.

Chapman, C. R., & Nakamura, Y. (1998). A bottom up view of emotion. *ASSC Seminar*, http://server.phil.vt.edu/assc/watt/chapman1.html.

Chaunu, P. (1975). *Le refus de la vie : analyse historique du présent*. Paris: Calmann Lévy.

Chen, B. Y., Jones, N. L., & Killian, K. J. (1999). Is there a conflict between minimizing effort and energy expenditure with increasing velocities of muscle. *Journal of Physiology*, 518, 933-940.

Churchland, P. S. (1986). *Neurophilosophy. Towards a Unified Science of Mind/Brain*. Cambridge, MA: M.I.T. Press.

Churchland, P. S. (2002). Self-representation in nervous system. *Science*, 296, 308-310.

Cicero, M. T. (44 Av. JC). *De senectute*. Paris: Garnier-Flammarion 1967.

Cicero, M. T. (45 Av. JC). *Disputationes Tusculanae*. I-II.

Cines, B. M., & Rozin, P. (1982). Some aspects of the liking for hot coffee and coffee flavor. *Appetite*, 3, 23-34.

Cisek, P. (1999). Beyond the computer metaphor. *Journal of Consciousness Studies*, 6, 125-142.

Clarke, S. N. D. A., & Ossenkopp, K. P. (1998). Taste reactivity responses in rats: influence of sex and the estrous cycle. *American Journal of Physiology*, 43, R718-R724.

Cohen, D., & Keasar, T. (2000). Anticipation and prediction of the future profitability of unfamiliar food sources after learning: a necessary component of sampling and learning in foraging. Paper presented at the *International Society for Behavioral Ecology*, Zürich.

Cohen, P. S., & Tokieda, F. K. (1972). Sucrose water preference reversal in the water deprived rat. *Journal of Comparative and Physiological Psychology*,

79, 254-258.

Cohen, S., & Pressman, S. D. (2006). Positive affect and health. *Current Directions in Psychological Science*, 15, 122-125.

Conche, M. (1977). *Epicure: lettres et maximes*. Villers sur Mer: Editions de Mégare.

Condillac, E. B. d. (1754). *Traité des sensations* (1984 ed.). Paris: Arthème Fayard.

Coop-Phane, C. (1998). L'âme au coeur. *médecine/science*, 14, 1089-1096.

Cooper, M. (1957). Pica. In A. P. Association (Ed.), *Diagnostic and Statistical Manual of Mental Disorders*. Springfield, IL.: Charles C. Thomas.

Corso, J. F. (1967). *The Experimental Psychology of Sensory Behavior*. New York: Holt, Rinehart & Winston inc.

Cosmides, L., & Tooby, J. (1995). From evolution to adaptations of behavior. In R. Wong (Ed.), *Biological Perspectives on Motivated Activities* (pp. 11-74). Northwood, New Jersey: Ablex Publ. Co.

Cosmides, L., Tooby, J., & Barkow, J. H. (1992). Introduction: evolutionary psychology and conceptual integration. In J. H. Barkow, L. Cosmides & J.

Tooby (Eds.), *The Adapted Mind* (pp. 3-15). New York: Oxford University Press.

Cosnier, J. (1994). *Psychologie des émotions et des sentiments*. Paris: Retz.

Cosnier, J. (1998). *Le retour de Psychée. Critique des nouveaux fondements de la psychologie*. Paris: Desclée de Brouwer.

Cowey, A. (1997). Current awareness: Spotlight on consciousness - The 1996 Ronnie Mac Keith Lecture. *Developmental Medicine and Child Neurology*, 39, 54-62.

Croiset, A., & Bodin, L. (1955). *Protagoras* (5ème ed.). Paris: Les Belles Lettres.

Csikszentmihalyi, M. (1990). *Flow: The Psychology of Optimal Experience*. New York: Harper and Row.

Cunningham, D. J., & Cabanac, M. (1971). Evidence from behavioral thermoregulatory responses of a shift in set point temperature related to the menstrual cycle. *Journal de Physiologie*, 63, 236-238.

Cyrulnik, B. (1998). Ethology of anxiety in phylogeny and ontogeny. *Acta Psychiatrica Scandinavica*, 98 Suppl. 393, 44-49.

Damasio, A. R. (1995). *L'erreur de Descartes* (M. Blanc, Trans.). Paris: Éditions Odile Jacob.

Damasio, A. R. (1998). Emotion and consciousness. *ASSC Seminar*, http://www.phil.vt.edu/assc/esem.html.

Dantzer, R. (1989). *L'illusion psychosomatique*. Paris: Odile Jacob.

Dantzer, R., Bluthé, R. M., Aubert, A., Goodall, G., Bret-Dibat, J. L., Kent, S., et al. (1996). Cytokine actions on behavior. In N. J. Rothwell (Ed.), *Cytokines in the Nervous System* (pp. 117-144). Austin, Texas: R. G. Landes Co.

Darwin, C. (1858). *The origin of species by means of natural selection, or, The preservation of favoured races in the struggle for life*. New York: New American Library, 1958.

Darwin, C. (1872). *The Expression of Emotion in Man and Animals*. London:

Murray.

Davidson, R. J., & Irwin, W. (1999). The functional neuroanatomy of emotion and affective style. *Trends in Cognitive Sciences*, 3, 11-21.

Dawkins, M. S. (1993). *Through our eyes only?* (1 ed.). Oxford: W. H. Freeman & Co.

Delacour, J. (1994). *Biologie de la conscience*. Paris: Presses Universitaires de France.

deLaRochefoucault, F. (1613-1680). *Maximes et réflexions diverses*. Paris: J. Truchet Garnier-Flammarion, 1977.

Delatte, L. (1973). *Sénèque le philosophe. Lettres morales à Luci*lius (Vol. 81). La Haye: Mouton.

Dennet, D. C. (1991). *Consciousness Explained*. Boston: Little, Brown.

Descartes, R. (1637). *Discours de la méthode*. Paris: Vrin 1947.

Deschaux, P. (1988). Neuroimmunologie: le système immunitaire est-il un organe sensoriel? *Archives Internationales de Physiologie et Biochimie*, 96, A78-A89.

DeSousa, R. (1997). *The Rationality of Emotion*. Cambridge, Massachussetts: MIT Press.

Doassans-Wilhem, M. (1978). *Régulation pondérale et obésité. Étude de l'alliesthésie gustative chez 91 sujets obèses*. Unpublished Doctorat en médecine, Paris-VI.

Dostoïevski, F. M. (1950). *Le Joueur*. Montréal: Institut Litéraire du Québec.

Doty, R. L., Ford, M., Preti, G., & Huggins, G. R. (1975). Changes in the intensity and pleasantness of human vaginal odors during the menstrual cycle. *Science*, 190, 1316-1318.

Dubé, L., & Cantin, I. (2000). Promoting health or promoting pleasure? A contingency approach to the effect of informational and emotional appeals on food liking and consumption. *Appetite*, 35, 251-262.

Dubé, L., & LeBel, J. L. (2002). The categorical structure of pleasure. *Cognition and Emotion*, 17, 263-297.

Dubrovsky, B. (1990). A comment on three topics in volume 7 of the Treatise: teleology, the mind-body problem, and health and disease. In P. Weingartner & G. J. W. Dorn (Eds.), *Studies on Mario Bunge's Treatise: Rodopi*.

Dubrovsky, B. (2000). The specificity of stress responses to different nocuous stimuli: Neurosteroids and depression. *Brain Research Bulletin*, 51, 443-455.

Dubrovsky, B. (2002). Evolutionary psychiatry. Adaptationist and nonadaptationist conceptualizations. *Progress in Neuro-Psychopharmacology and Biological Psychiatry*, 26, 1-19.

Dubrovsky, B. (2003). Concerning fundamental neuroscience and psychiatry. *Paper presented at the Evolutionary Psychiatry*, Apeiron-Roma.

Duclaux, R., & Cabanac, M. (1970). Effets d'une ingestion de glucose sur la sensation et la perception d'un stimulus olfactif alimentaire. *Comptes Rendus de l' Académie des Sciences*, 270 D, 1006-1009.

Duclaux, R., Feisthauer, J., & Cabanac, M. (1973). Effets du repas sur l'agrément d'odeurs alimentaires et non alimentaires chez l'homme. *Physiology and Behavior*, 10, 1029-1033.

Dumas, G. (1900). La tristesse et la joie. Paris: Félix Alcan Éditeur.

Duncker, K. (1940-1941). On pleasure, emotion, and striving. *Philosophy and Phenomenological Research*, 1, 391-430.

Durkheim, E. (1924). *Sociologie et philosophie*. Paris: Librairie Félix Alcan.

Eckblad, G. (1972). The attractiveness of uncertainty III. Attractivity of patterns in a guessing game. *Scandinavian Journal of Psychology*, 13, 292-305.

Eckblad, G. (1978). Stimulus seeking and curiosity: A review and re-interpretation of studies in the Berlyne tradition. *Reports of the Institute of Psychology University of Bergen* (1), 1-81.

Edelman, G. (2000). *Biologie de la conscience*. Paris: Livre de Poche.

Einhorn, H. J., & Hogarth, R. M. (1981). Behavioral decision theory: process of judgement and choice. *Annual Review of Psychology*, 32, 53-88.

Ekkekakis, P. (2003). Pleasure and displeasure from the body: Perspectives from exercise. *Cognition and Emotion*, 17, 312-239.

Ekkekakis, P., & Hall, E. E. (2005). Variation and universality in affective responses to physical activity of varying intensities: An alternative perspective on dose-response based on evolutionary considerations. *Journal of Sport Sciences*, 23, 477-500.

Ekkekakis, P., Hall, E. E., & Petruzzello, S. J. (2004). Practical markers of the transition from aerobic to anaerobic metabolism during exercise: rationale and a case for affect-based exercise prescription. *Preventive Medicine*, 38, 149-159.

Ekman, P. (1980). *The Face of Man*. New York: Garland.

Ekman, P. (1992). An argument for basic emotions. *Cognition and Emotion*, 6, 169-200.

Ekman, P., & Friesen, W. V. (1986). A new pan-cultural facial expression of emotion. *Motivation and Emotion*, 10, 159-168.

Ekman, P., Levenson, R. W., & Friesen, W. V. (1983). Autonomic nervous system activity distinguishes among emotions. *Science*, 221, 1208-1210.

Ellul, J. (1987). *Ce que je crois*. Paris: Bernard Grasset.

Ennis, D. M., & Mullen, K. (1986). Theoretical aspects of sensory discrimination. *Chemical Senses*, 11, 513-522.

Erev, I., & Roth, A. E. (1998). Predicting how people play games: reinforcement learning in games with unique strategy equilibrium. The *American Economic Review*, 88(848-881).

Ernst, M., Bolla, K., Mouratidis, M., Contoreggi, C., Matochik, J. A., Kurian, V., et al. (2002). Decision-making in a risk-taking task: A PET study. *Neuropsychopharmacology*, 26, 682-691.

Ettinger, R. H., Thompson, S., & Staddon, J. E. R. (1986). Cholecystokinin, diet palatability, and feeding regulation in rats. *Physiology and Behavior*, 36, 801-809.

Evans, J. S. B. T., Over, D. E., & Manktelow, K. I. (1993). Reasoning, decision making, and rationality. *Cognition*, 49, 165-187.

Fantino, E. (1998). Behavior analysis and decision making. *Journal of the Experimental Analysis of Behavior*, 69, 355-364.

Fantino, M. (1984). Role of sensory input in the control of food intake. *Journal of the Autonomic Nervous System*, 10, 326-347.

Fantino, M. (1992). État nutritionnel et perception affective de l'aliment. In I. Giachetti (Ed.), *Plaisir et préférence alimentaires* (pp. 31-48). Paris: Polytechnica.

Fantino, M. (1995). Nutriments et alliesthésie alimentaire. *Cahiers de Nutrition et de Diététique*, 30, 14-18.

Fantino, M., Baigts, F., Cabanac, M., & Apfelbaum, M. (1983). Effects of an overfeed regime on the affective component of the sweet sensation. *Appetite*, 4, 155-164.

Fantino, M., & Brinnel, H. (1986). Body weight set-point changes during the ovarian cycle: experimental study of rats during hoarding behavior. *Physiology and Behavior*, 36, 991-996.

Fantino, M., Faion, F., & Rolland, Y. (1986). Effect of dexfenfluramine on body weight set-point: study in the rat with hoarding behaviour. *Appetite*, 7 Suppl., 115-126.

Faurion, A. (1993). Why 4 semantic taste descriptors and why only 4? Paper presented at the *11th International Conference on the Physiology of Food and Fluid Intake*, Oxford.

Fazio, R. H. (2000). Accessible attitudes as tools for object appraisal: their costs and benefits. In G. R. Maiof & J. M. Olson (Eds.), *Why We Evaluate: Functions of Attitudes* (pp. 1-36). Mahwah, New Jersey: Lawrence Erlbaum Associates.

Fechner, G. T. (1860). *Elemente der Psychophysik* (H. E. A. 1966, Trans.). New York: Holt, Rinehart & Winston.

Fesquet, H. (1962). *Le catholicisme religion de demain?* Paris: Grasset.

Festinger, L., & Carlsmith, J. M. (1959). Cognitive consequences of forced compliance. *Journal of Abnormal Sociology and Psychology*, 58, 203-210.

Finucane, M. L., Alhakami, A., & Slovic, P. (2000). The affect heuristic in judgements of risks and benefits. *Journal of Behavioral Decision Making*, 13, 1-17.

Finucane, M. L., Peters, E., & Slovic, P. (2003). Judgment and decision making: the dance of affect and reason. In S. L. Schneider & J. Shanteau (Eds.), *Emerging perspectives on Decision Research* (pp. 327-364). Cambridge: Cambridge University Press.

Folkins, C. H. (1976). Effects of physical training on mood. *Journal of Clinical Psychology*, 32, 385-388.

Fox, C. A., & Fox, B. (1969). Blood pressure and respiratory patterns during human coitus. *Journal of Reproduction and Fertility*, 19, 405-415.

Frank, M. E. (1985). Sensory physiology of taste and smell discriminations using conditioned food aversion methodology. *Annals of the New York Academy of*

Sciences, 443, 89-99.

Frank, R. A., Pritchard, W. S., & Stutz, R. M. (1981). Food versus inracranial self-stimulation: failure of limited access self depriving rats to self-deprive in a continuous access paradigm. *Behavioral and Neural Biology, 33,* 503-508.

Frank, R. H. (1988). *Passions within Reason: The Strategic Role of the Emotions.* New York: Norton.

Fredrickson, B. L. (2000). Cultivating positive emotions to optimize health and well being. *Prevention and Treatment, 3,* 1-19.

Fredrickson, B. L., & Levenson, R. W. (1998). Positive emotions speed recovery from the cardiovascular sequelae of negative emotions. *Cognition and Emotion,* 12, 191-220.

Freud, S. (1920). *Au-delà du principe de plaisir.* http://www.uqac.uquebec.ca/zone30/Classiques_des_sciences_sociales/li vres/freud_sigmund/essais_de_psychanalyse/Essai_1_au_dela/Au_dela_principe_plaisir.pdf.

Freud, S. (1976). Malaise dans la civilisation. Paris: Presses Universitaires de France.

Fromm, E. (1955). The Sane Society. New York: Routledge.

Fuller, J. L. (1962). *Motivation A Biological Perspective.* New York: Random House.

Galef, B. J. J. (1991). A contrarian view of the wisdom of the body as it relates to dietary selection. *Psychological Review,* 98, 218-223.

Galotti, K. M., & Carmichael, K. E. (2001). Decision-making styles and real-life decision making. 659. *Abstracts of the Psychonomic Society,* 6, 96.

Gandevia, S. C., & McCloskey, D. I. (1977). Sensation of heaviness. *Brain,* 100, 345-354.

Garcia, J., Hankins, W. G., & Rusiniak, K. W. (1974). Behavioral regulation of the milieu interne in man and rat. *Science,* 184, 824-831.

Garcia, J., Kimerdorf, D. J., & Koelling, R. A. (1955). Conditionned Aversion to Saccharin Resulting from Exposure to Gamma Radiation. *Science,* 122, 157-158.

Garcia, J., Lasiter, P. S., Bermudez-Rattoni, F., & Deems, D. A. (1985). A general theory of aversion learning. *Annals of the New York Academy of Sciences,* 443, 8-21.

Gehring, W. J., & Willoughby, A. R. (2002). The medial frontal cortex and the rapid processing of monetary gains and losses. *Science,* 295, 2279-2282.

Geldard, F. A. (1972). *The Human Senses* (2nd ed.). New York: John Wiley & Sons.

Gell-Mann, M. (1994). *The Quark and the Jaguar.* New York: W. H. Freeman & Co.

Gentle, M. J., & Harkin, C. (1979). The effect of sweet stimuli on oral behaviour in the chicken. *Chemical Senses and Flavor,* 4, 183-190.

Giachetti, I. (1992). *Plaisir et préférence alimentaires.* Paris: Polytechnica.

Gilbert, D. G., & Hagen, R. L. (1980). Taste in underweight, overweight and normal-weight subjects before,during and after sucrose ingestion. *Journal of Affective Disorders*, 5, 137-142.

Girard, R. (1978). *Des choses cachées depuis la fondation du monde*. Paris: Grasset.

Giza, B. K., & Scott, T. R. (1983). Blood glucose selectively affects taste-evoked activity in rat Nucleus tractus solitarius. Physiology and Behavior, 31, 643-650.

Glossary. (1987). IUPS Commission for thermal physiology Glossary of terms for thermal physiology. *Pflügers Archiv*, 410, 567-587.

Goldstein, D. G., & Gigerenzer, G. (2002). Models of ecological rationality: The recognition heuristic. *Psychological Review*, 109, 75-90.

Gotsev, T., & Ivanov, A. (1962). Psychogenic elevation of body temperature. *Proceedings of the International Union of Physiological Societies*, 2, 501.

Gray, J. R., Braver, T. S., & Raichle, M. E. (2002). Integration of emotion and cognition in the lateral prefrontal cortex. *Proceedings of the National Academy of Sciences of the United States of America*, 99, 4115-4120.

Gray, R. W., & Cooper, S. J. (1996). d-Fenfluramine's effects on normal ingestion assessed with taste reactivity measures. *Physiology and Behavior*, 59, 1129-1135.

Green, D. M. (1988). Psychophysics and perception. In *Stevens' handbook of experimental psychology* (2th ed., Vol. 1 Perception and Motivation, pp. 327-376). New York: John Wiley & Sons.

Griffin, D. R. (1992). *Animal Minds*. Chicago: University of Chicago Press.

Griffiths, P. E. (1997). *What Emotions Really Are*. Chicago: The University of Chicago Press.

Grill, H. J., & Norgren, R. (1978). Chronically decerebrate rats demonstrate satiation but not bait shyness. *Science*, 201, 267-269.

Grill, H. J., Roitman, M. F., & Kaplan, J. M. (1996). A new taste reactivity analysis of the integration of taste and physiological state information. *American Journal of Physiology*, 40, R677-R687.

Guy-Grand, B., & Sitt, Y. (1974). Alliesthésie gustative dans l'obésité humaine. *Nouvelle Presse Médicale*, 3, 92-93.

Hall, E. E., Ekkekakis, P., & Petruzzello, S. J. (2002). The affective beneficence of vigorous exercise. *British Journal of Health Psychology*, 7, 47-66.

Hamann, S., & Mao, H. (2002). Positive and negative emotional verbal stimuli elicit activity in the left amygdala. *Neuroreport*, 13, 15-19.

Hameroff, S. R. (1987). *Ultimate Computing: Biomolecular Consciousness and Nano-Technology*. Amsterdam: North Holland.

Hare, B., Call, J., Agnetta, B., & Tomasello, M. (2000). Chimpanzees know what conspecifics do and do not see. *Animal Behaviour*, 59, 771-785.

Hashim, S. S., & VanItalie, T. B. (1965). Studies in normal and obese subjects with a monitored food dispensing device. *Annals of the New York Academy of Sciences*, 131, 654-661.

Hatzfeld, H. (1993). Les racines de la religion. Paris: Éditions du Seuil.

Hayes, S. C., Kapust, J., Leonard, S. R., & Rosenfarb, I. (1981). Escape from freedom: choosing not to choose in pigeons. *Journal of the Experimental Analysis of Behavior, 36*, 1-8.

Heiligenberg, W. (1994). Distributed systems in sensory information processing. *Paper presented at the Emergence of prerational Intelligence in Biology: from Sensorimotor Intelligence to Collective Behavior*, Bielefeld.

Helmoltz, H. L. F. V. (1866). *Physiological Optics* (J. P. C. S. 1962, Trans.). New York: Dover.

Helson, H. (1964). *Adaptation-Level Theory*. New York: Harper & Row.

Henry, M. (1987). *La barbarie*. Paris: Bernard Grasset.

Hertwig, R., & Ortmann, A. (2001). Experimental practices in economics: a methodological challenge for Psychologists? *Behavioral and Brain Sciences, 24*, 383-403.

Hess, W. R. (1954). *Das Zwischenhirn Syndrome, Lokalisationen, Funktionen*. Basel: Benno Schwab & Co.

Hobbes, T. (1651). *Human Nature, or the Fundamental Elements of Policy* (Baron d'Holbach, Trans.). Paris: Librairie Philosophique J. Vrln, 1971.

Hofbauer, R. K., Rainville, P., Duncan, G. H., & Bushnell, M. C. (2001). Cortical representation of the sensory dimension of pain. *Journal of Neurophysiology, 86*, 402-411.

Holt, B., & Schleidt, M. (1977). The importance of human odour in non-verbal communication. *Zeitschrift für Tierpsychologie, 43*, 225-238.

Holtzman, D. A., Harris, T. W., Aranguren, G., & Bostock, E. (1999). Spatial learning of an escape task by young corn snakes, *Elaphe guttata guttata*. *Animal Behaviour, 57*, 51-60.

Hoyle, F. (1994). *Home is Where the Wind Blows*. Mill Valley, California: University Science Books.

Hsee, C. K. (1999). Value seeking and prediction-decision inconsistency: why don't people take what they predict they'll like the most? *Psychonomic Bulletin and Review, 6*, 555-561.

Hsee, C. K., & Abelson, R. P. (1991). Velocity relation: satisfaction as a function of the first derivative of outcome over time. *Journal of Personality and Social Psychology, 60*, 341-347.

Huffman, E. K., Gulick, T., Chabris, C., Ariely, D., Aharon, I., H C Breiter, et al. (2000). Reward value of visual representations of food depends on a satiety deficit state. *Obesity Research, 8*(Suppl. 1), PB56.

Huxley, A. (1954). *Les portes de la perception*. Paris: Éditions Pygmalion.

Ikeda, K. (1909). On a new seasoner. *Journal of the Tokyo Chemical Society, 30*, 820-836.

Ingram, D. L., & Legge, K. F. (1970). The thermoregulatory behavior of young pigs in a natural environment. *Physiology and Behavior, 5*, 981-987.

Izard, C. E. (1977). *Human Emotions*. London: Plenum.

Jacob, F. (1981). *Le jeu des possibles*. Paris: Fayard.

265

Jacobs, H. L. (1958). Studies on sugar preference: I. The preference for glucose solutions and its modifications by injections of insulin. *Journal of Comparative and Physiological Psychology*, 51, 304-310.

James, W. (1884). What is an emotion? *Mind*, 9, 188-205.

James, W. (1890). *The Principles of Psychology* . Dover Publications Inc.

Jeannière, A. (1959). *La pensée d'Héraclite d'Éphèse et la vision*. Paris: Aubier Montaigne.

Jenkins, T. N., Warner, L. H., & Warden, C. J. (1926). Standard apparatus for the study of animal motivation. *Journal of Comparative Psychology*, 6, 361-382.

Jevons, W. S. (1871). *The theory of political economy*. London: MacMillan.

Jevons, W. S. (1890). *Logic*. New York: American Book Company.

Johnson, K. G., & Cabanac, M. (1982). Homeostatic competition between food intake and temperature in rats. *Physiology and Behavior*, 28, 675-679.

Johnson, K. G., & Cabanac, M. (1983). Human thermoregulatory behavior during a conflict between cold discomfort and money. *Physiology and Behavior*, 30, 145-150.

Johnson, M. W., & Bickel, W. K. (2002). Within-subject comparison of real and hypothetical money rewards in delay discounting. *Journal of the Experimental Analysis of Behavior*, 77, 129-146.

Johnson-Laird, P. N., & Oatley, K. (1992). Basic emotions, rationality, and folk theory. *Cognition and Emotion*, 6, 201-223.

Johnston, V. S. (1999). *Why We Feel: The Science of Human Emotions*. Reading, Massachussetts: Perseus Books.

Jollien, A. (2003). *Éloge de la faiblesse*. Paris: Éditions du Cerf.

Jouvet, M. (1992). *Le sommeil et le rêve*. Paris: Odile Jacob.

Kahneman, D., Wakker, P. P., & Sarin, R. (1997). Back to Bentham? Explorations of experienced utility. *Quarterly Journal of Economics*, 112, 375-405.

Kandel, E. R., & Schwartz, J. H. (1985). *Principles of Neural Science* (2nd ed.). Amsterdam: Elsevier Science Publ. Co.

Kant, I. (1788). *Kritik der praktischen Vernunft* (Trad. Fr. F. Picavet, 1983) (F. Picavet, Trans. Vol. 1). Paris: Presses Universitaires de France.

Kappas, A. (1991). The illusion of the neutral observer: on the communication of emotion. *Cahiers de Linguistique Française*, 12, 153-168.

Katz-Salamon, M. (1986). Increased CO_2 drive for ventilation in healthy human subjects may interfere with their ability to control lung volumes voluntarily. *Acta Physiologica Scandinavica*, 127, 343-347.

Kendrick, K. M., daCosta, A. P., Leigh, A. E., Hinton, M. R., & Peirce, J. W. (2001). Sheep don't forget a face. *Nature*, 414, 165-166.

Kenney, N. J. (1974). Postingestive factors in the control of glucose intake by satiated rats. *Physiological Psychology*, 2, 433-434.

Kenny, A. (1963). *Action, Emotion, and Will*. London: Routledge and Kegan Paul.

Khrennikov, A. (1998). Human subconscious as a p-adic dynamical system. *Journal of Theoretical Biology*, 193, 179-196.

Killeen, P. R. (1962). Incentive theory. In D. J. Bernstein (Ed.), Nebraska

Symposium on Motivation 1981. *Response Structure and Organisation* (pp. 169-216). Lincoln: University of Nebraska Press.

Kim, S. H., & Tokura, H. (1998). Visual alliesthesia - Cloth color preference in the evening under the influence of different light intensities during the daytime. *Physiology and Behavior*, 65, 367-370.

Kiss, G., & Reichgelt, H. (1991). Towards a semantics of desires. Paper presented at the *Modelling Autonomous Agents, in Multi-Agent*. World Conference, Kayserslautern.

Kleifield, E. I., & Lowe, M. R. (1991). Weight loss and sweetness preferences: the effects of recent versus past weight loss. *Physiology and Behavior*, 49, 1037-1042.

Kleinginna, P. R., & Kleinginna, A. M. (1981). A categorized list of emotion definitions, with suggestions for a consensual definition. *Motivation and Emotion*, 5, 345-379.

Knetsch, J. L., & Sinden, J. A. (1984). Willingness to pay and compensation: Experimental evidence of an unexpected disparity in measures of value. *Quarterly Journal of Economics*, 99, 508-522.

Koepp, M. J., Gunn, R. N., Lawrence, A. D., Cunningham, V. J., Dagher, A., Jones, T., et al. (1998). Evidence for striatal dopamine release during a video game. *Nature*, 393, 266-268.

Kofka, K. (1935). *Principles of Gestalt Psychology*. New York: Harcourt, Brace & Co.

Kotani, Y., Hiraku, S., Suda, K., & Aihara, Y. (2001). Effect of positive and negative emotion on stimulus-preceding negativity prior to feedback stimuli. *Psychophysiology*, 38, 873-878.

Kraepelin, E. (1968). *Lectures on Clinical Psychiatry*. Darien, CT: Hafner Publishing.

Krughoff, D. (2000). Anna my green friend. Hoyleton, IL: *myiguana.com*.

Kubovy, M. (1999). On the pleasures of the mind. In N. Kahneman, E. Diener & N. Schwartz (Eds.), *Well-Being: The Foundations of Hedonic Psychology* (pp. 134-154). New York: Russel Sage Foundation.

Kuhn, T. S. (1970). *The Structure of Scientific Revolutions* (2nd ed.). Chicago: University of Chicago Press.

Külpe, O. (1893). *Grundriss der Psychologie*. Leipzig: W. Engelmann.

Lamarre, j. M. (1986). *Traduction française de Saint Augustin: De trinitate*. Paris: Magnard.

Lane, R. D., Ahern, G. L., Schwartz, G. E., & Kaszniak, A. W. (1997). Is alexithymia the emotional equivalent of blindsight? *Biological Psychiatry*, 42, 834-844.

Lane, R. D., Reiman, E. M., Axelrod, B., Yun, L. S., Holmes, A., & Schwartz, G. E. (1998). Neural correlates of levels of emotional awareness: Evidence of an interaction between emotion and attention in the anterior cingulate cortex. *Journal of Cognitive Neuroscience*, 10, 525-535.

Lange, K. G. (1885). *Om Sindsbevægelser*. København. *Om Sindsbevaegelser et Psyko-Fysiologisk Studie*.

Laplane, D., & Dubois, B. (2001). Auto-activation deficit: a basal ganglia related syndrome. *Movement Disorders*, 16, 810-814.

Larkin, S., & McFarland, D. J. (1978). The cost of changing from one activity to another. *Animal Behaviour*, 26, 1237-1246.

LaRochefoucauld, F. d. (1827). *Réflexions ou sentences et maximes morales*. Paris: Lefèvre.

Lashley, K. S. (1929). *Brain Mechanisms and Intelligence*. Chicago: University of Chicago Press.

Lashley, K. S. (1949). Persistent problems in the evolution of mind. *Quarterly Review of Biology*, 24, 28-42.

Lazarus, R. S. (1982). Thoughts on the relations between emotion and cognition. *American Psychologist*, 37, 1019-1024.

Lazarus, R. S. (1984). On the primacy of cognition. *American Psychologist*, 39, 124-129.

Lazarus, R. S. (1991). *Emotion and Adaptation*. Oxford: Oxford University Press.

Lea, S. E. G., Tarpy, R. M., & Webley, P. (1987). *The Individual in the Economy*. Cambridge: Cambridge University Press.

LeBel, J. L., & Dubé, L. (1998). Understanding pleasures: source, experience, and remembrances. *Advances in Consumers Research*, 25, 176-180.

LeDoux, J. (1996). *The Emotional Brain. The mysterious underpinnings of emotional life*. New York: Simon and Schuster.

Lehninger, A. L. (1965). *Bioenergetics. The molecular basis of biological energy transformations*. New York: W. A. Benjamin Inc.

LeMagnen, J. (1952). Les phénomènes olfacto-sexuels chez l'homme. *Archives des Sciences Physiologiques*, 6, 125-160.

LeMagnen, J. (1953). Activité de l'insuline sur la consommation spontanee des solutions rapides. *Comptes Rendus des Séances de la Société de Biologie*, 147, 1753-.

LeMagnen, J. (1955). Le role de la réceptivité gustative au chlorure de sodium dans le mécanisme de régulation de la prise d'eau chez le rat blanc. *Journal de Physiologie*, 47, 405-418.

LeMagnen, J. (1956). Le role des stimulations olfacto-gustatives dans les mécanismes de régulations de la prise alimentaire. *Annales de la Nutrition et de l'Alimentation*, 10, 153-188.

LeMagnen, J. (1960). Effets d'une pluralité de stimuli alimentaires sur le déterminisme quantitatif de l'ingestion chez le rat blanc. *Archives des Sciences Physiologiques*, 15, 411-419.

Leshem, M., Abutbul, A., & Eilon, R. (1999). Exercise increases the preferencer for salt in humans. *Appetite*, 32, 251-260.

Leshem, M., & Rudoy, J. (1997). Hemodialysis increases the preference for salt in soup. *Physiology and Behavior*, 61, 65-69.

Letarte, A., Dube, L., & Troche, V. (1997). Similarities and differences in affective and cognitive origins of food likings and dislikes. *Appetite*, 28, 115-129.

Leventhal, H., & Scherer, K. (1987). The relationship of emotion to cognition: a functional approach to a semantic controversy. *Cognition and Emotion*, 1, 3-28.

Levine, M. W., & Shefner, J. M. (1981). *Fundamentals of Sensation and Perception*. Reading, Massachussetts: Addison-Wesley Publ. Co.

Lévy, T. (1984). *Le crime en toute humanité*. Paris: B. Grasset.

Levy-Valensi, J. (1933). Sensibilité et motricité. In *Traité de physiologie normale et pathologique* (Vol. XI, pp. 235-262). Paris: Masson.

Linville, P. W., & Fisher, G. W. (1991). Preferences for separating or combining events. *Journal of Personality and Social Psychology*, 59, 5-21.

Lipsey, R. G., Steiner, P. O., & Purvis, D. D. (1984). Economics (7ième ed.). New York: Harper & Row.

Lo, A. W., & Repin, D. V. (2002). The psychophysiology of real-time financial risk processing. *Journal of Cognitive Neuroscience*, 14, 323-339.

Loas, G. (1996). Vulnerability to depression: a model centered on anhedonia. Journal of Affective Disorders, 41, 39-53.

Loewenstein, G. (1996). Out of control: visceral influences on behavior. *Organizational Behavior and Human Decision Processes*, 65, 272-292.

Loewenstein, G. (1999). Because it is there: the challenge of mountaineering... for utility theory. *Kyklos*, 52, 315-344.

Loewenstein, J., Thompson, L., & Gentner, D. (1999). Analogical encoding facilitates knowledge transfer in negociation. *Psychonomic Bulletin and Review*, 6, 586-597.

Lopes, L., & Oden, G. C. (1999). The role of aspiration level in risky choice: A comparison of cumulative prospect theory and SP/A theory. *Journal of Mathematical Psychology*, 43, 286-313.

Ludel, J. (1978). *Introduction to Sensory Processes*. San Francisco: W.H. Freeman & Co.

MacLean, P. (1993). On the evolution of three mentalities. In J. Ashbrook (Ed.), *Brain Culture and the Human Spirit* (pp. 15-44). Lantham, N.Y.: University Press of America.

MacLeod, P. (1992). Circuits nerveux de la préférence et du plaisir. In I. Giachetti (Ed.), *Plaisir et préférences alimentaires* (pp. 89-96). Paris: Polytechnica.

Magnussen, S., Sunde, B., & Dymes, S. (1994). Patterns of perceptual asymmetry in processing facial expression. *Cortex*, 30, 214-229.

Mahieu-Caputo, D., Dommergues, M., Muller, F., & Dumez, Y. (2000). La douleur chez le fœtus. *Presse Médicale*, 29, 663-669.

Malechek, J. C., & Smith, B. S. (1979). Behavior of range cows in response to winter weather. *Journal of Range Management*, 29, 9-12.

Manes, F., Sahakian, B., Clark, L., Rogers, R., Antoun, N., Aitken, M., et al. (2002). Decision-making processes following damage to the prefrontal cortex. *Brain*, 125, 624-639.

Marcel, A. J., & Bisiach, E. (1988). A cautious wellcome: an introduction and guide to the book. In A. J. Marcel & E. Bisiach (Eds.), *Consciousness in Contemporary Science* (pp. 1-15). Oxford: Oxford University Press.

Marcus, P., & Belyavin, A. (1978). Thermal sensation during experimental hypothermia. *Physiology and Behavior*, 21, 909-914.

Marks, J. (1982). A theory of emotions. *Philosophical Studies*, 42, 227-242.

Marks, L. E. (1974). *Sensory Processes, the New Psychophysics*. New York: Academic Press.

Marks, L. E., & Gonzalez, R. R. (1977). Thermal sensation: perceived intensity and pleasantness related to skin temperature. *Proceedings of the International Union of Physiological Societies*, 13, 1418.

Maule, W. F., Baer, P. E., & Fuhrer, M. J. (1975). A device for studying the psychophysiologic effects of thermal stimulation of the human esophagus. *Psychophysiology*, 12, 212-216.

McDougall, W. (1923). *Outline of Psychology*. New York: Scribner's.

McFarland, D. J. (1985). *Animal Behaviour*. London: Pitman.

McFarland, D. J., & Sibly, R. M. (1975). The behavioural final common path. *Philosophical Transactions of the Royal Society*, 270, 265-293.

McKearney, J. W. (1969). Fixed-interval schedules of electric shock presentation: extinction and recovery of performance under different shock intensities and fixed interval durations. *Journal of the Experimental Analysis of Behavior*, 12, 301-313.

McKemy, D. D., Neuhausser, W. M., & Julius, D. (2002). Identification of a cold receptor reveals a general role for TRP channels in thermosensation. *Nature*, 416, 52-58.

McKenna, F. (1996). Understanding risky choices. In D. M. Warburton & N. Sherwood (Eds.), *Pleasure and Quality of Life* (pp. 157-170). Chichester: John Wiley & Sons Ltd.

McNamara, J. M., & Houston, A. I. (1986). The common currency for behavioural decisions. *American Naturalist*, 127, 358-378.

Mehiel, R. (1991). Hedonic-shift conditioning with calories. In R. C. Bolles (Ed.), *The Hedonics of Taste* (pp. 15-28.). Hillsdale, New Jersey: Lawrence Earlbaum Ass.

Mehiel, R., & Bolles, R. C. (1988). Hedonic shift learning based on calories. *Bulletin of the Psychonomic Society*, 26, 459-462.

Melchior, J. C., Rigaud, D., Colas-Linhart, N., Rozen, R., Fantino, M., & Apfelbaum, M. (1990). Negative alliesthesia and decreased endogenous opiate system activity in anorexia nervosa. *Pharmacology Biochemistry and Behavior*, 35, 885-888.

Mellers, B. A. (2000). Choice and relative pleasure consequences. *Psychological Bulletin*, 126, 910-924.

Mellers, B. A., Schwartz, A., & Cooke, A. D. J. (1998). Judgment and decision making. *Annual Review of Psychology*, 49, 447-477.

Mellers, B. A., Schwartz, A., Ho, K., & Ritov, I. (1997). Decision affect theory:

270

Emotional reactions to the outcome of risky options. *Psychological Science,* 8, 423-429.

Mellers, B. A., Schwartz, A., & Ritov, I. (1999). Predicting choices from emotions. *Journal of Experimental Psychology,* G: 128, 332-345.

Melzack, R., & Casey, K. L. (1968). Sensory, motivational, and central control determinants of pain. In D. R. Kenshalo (Ed.), *The Skin Senses* (pp. 423-439). Springfield, Illinois: Charles C. Thomas.

Merker, B. (2005). The liabilities of mobility: A selection pressure for the transition to consciousness in animal evolution. *Consciouness and Cognition,* 14, 89-114.

Merleau-Ponty, M. (1945). *Phénoménologie de la perception.* Paris: Gallimard.

Milinski, M., Semmann, D., & Krambeck, H. J. (2002). Donors to charity gain in both indirect reciprocity and political reputation. *Proceedings of the Royal Society of London Series B - Biological Sciences,* 269, 881-883.

Mill, J. (1869). *Analysis of the Phenomena of the Human Mind. Edited with additional notes of J. S. Mill* (1967 ed.). New York: Kelley.

Miller, J. F., Mekalanos, J. J., & Falkow, S. (1989). Coordinate regulation and sensory transduction in the control of bacterial virulence. *Science,* 243, 916-922.

Miller, N. E. (1944). Experimental studies of conflict. In J. M. Hunt (Ed.), *Personality and the Behavior Disorders* (pp. 431-465). New York: Ronald Press.

Miller, N. E. (1969). Learning of visceral and glandular responses. *Science,* 163, 434-445.

Montaigne, M. de (1533-1592). *Essais* (P. Michel (1965) ed.). Paris: Livre de poche.

Montefiore, A., & Noble, D. (1989). General introduction. In A. Montefiore & D. Noble (Eds.), *Goals, No-Goals and Own Goals* (pp. 3-13). London: UnWin Hyman Ltd.

Mook, D. G. (1974). Sacharin preference in the rat: some unpalatable findings. *Psychological Review,* 81, 475-490.

Morgan, C. L. (1894). *An Introduction to Comparative Psychology.* London: Walter Scott.

Morgan, C. L. (1925). *Life, Mind, and Spirit.* New York: Henry Holt & Co.

Morris, J. S., & Dolan, R. J. (2001). Involvement of human amygdala and orbitofrontal cortex in hunger-enhanced memory for food stimuli. *Journal of Neuroscience*(21), 5304-5310.

Morsbach, H., & Tyler, W. J. (1986). A Japanese emotion: amae. In R. Harré (Ed.), *The Social Construction of the Emotions.* London: Oxford University Press.

Mortensen, C., O'Brien, G., & Paterson, B. (1993). Distinctions: subpersonal and subconscious. Commentary on Puccetti on Split-Brain. *Psycholoquy,* 93.4.62.

Mower, G. D. (1976). Perceived intensity of peripheral thermal stimuli is

271

independant of internal body temperature. *Journal of Comparative and Physiological Psychology*, 90, 1152-1155.

Mrosovsky, N. (1990). *Rheostasis, the Physiology of Change*. New York: Oxford University Press.

Myers, K. P., & Sclafani, A. (2001). Conditioned enhancement of flavor evaluation reinforced by intragastric glucose II. Taste reactivity analysis. *Physiology and Behavior*, 74, 495-505.

Myhre, K., Cabanac, M., & Myhre, G. (1977). Fever and behavioural temperature regulation in the frog Rana esculenta. *Acta Physiologica Scandinavica*, 101, 219-229.

Nadel, E. R., Horvath, S. M., Dawson, C. A., & Tucker, A. (1970). Sensitivity to central and peripheral thermal stimulation in man. *Journal of Applied Physiology*, 29, 603-609.

Nafe, J. P. (1924). An experimental study of the affective qualities. *American Journal of Psychology*, 35, 507-544.

Nash, R. A. (1989). Cognitive theories of emotion. *NOUS*, 23, 481-504.

Navarick, D. J. (1985). Choice in humans: functional properties of reinforcers established by instruction. *Behavioural Processes*, 11, 269-277.

Nelkin, N. (1986). Pains and pain sensations. *Journal of Philosophy*, 83, 129-148.

Nelkin, N. (1989). Unconscious sensations. *Philosophical Psychology*, 2, 129-141.

Newton, I. (1730). *Opticks* (3th ed.). New York: Dover Publications, 1952.

Nicolaïdis, S. (1977). Physiologie du comportement alimentaire. In P. Meyer (Ed.), *Physiologie humaine* (pp. 908-922). Paris: Flammarion.

Nicolaïdis, S. (1992). Quelques mécanismes de préférences alimentaires. In I. Giachetti (Ed.), *Plaisir et préférence alimentaires* (pp. 77-96). Paris: Polytechnica.

Nicolaïdis, S. (2002). A hormone-based characterization and taxonomy of stress: possible usefulness in management. *Metabolism*, 51((Suppl. 1)), 31-36.

Nisbett, R. E., Hanson, L. R., Harris, A., & Stair, A. (1973). Taste responsiveness, weight loss and the ponderostat. *Physiology and Behavior*, 11, 641-645.

Norgren, R., & Grill, H. J. (1982). Brain-stem control of ingestive behavior. In D. W. Pfaff (Ed.), *The Physiological Mechanisms of Motivation* (pp. 99-131). New York: Springer-Verlag.

Nutin, J. (1975). La motivation. In J. Piaget (Ed.), *Traité de psychologie expérimentale* V (3ième ed., pp. 5-96). Paris: Presses Universitaires de France.

Nybo, L., & Nielsen, B. (2001). Perceived exertion is associated with an altered brain activity during exercise with progressive hyperthermia. *Journal of Applied Physiology*, 91, 2017-2023.

Oatley, K. (1988). On changing one's mind: a possible function of consciousness. In A. J. Marcel & E. Bisiach (Eds.), *Consciousness in Contemporary Science* (pp. 369-389). Oxford: Oxford University Press.

Oatley, K. (1994). Emotion. In M. W. Eysenck (Ed.), *The Blackwell Dictionary of Cognitive Psychology* (pp. 129-134). Oxford: Blackwell.

Oatley, K., & Johnson-Laird, P. N. (1987). Towards a cognitive theory of emotions. *Cognition and Emotion*, 1, 29-50.

Olds, J. (1955). Physiological mechanism of reward. In M. R. Jones (Ed.), *Nebraska Symposium on Motivation*. Lincoln: University of Nebraska Press.

Oppenheimer, J. R. (1972). *La science et le bon sens*. Paris: Gallimard.

Overskeid, G. (2000). The slave of the passions: experiencing problems and selecting solutions. *Review of General Psychology*, 4, 284-309.

Ovsich, A. J. (1998). Outlines of the theory of choice: attitude, desire, attention, will. http://www.bu.edu/wcp/Papers/Acti/ActiOvsi.htm [internet].

Ovsich, A. J. (Book in preparation). *Homo Hedonicus*.

Panksepp, J. (1986). The anatomy of emotions. In R. Plutchik & H. Kellerman (Eds.), *Emotion: Theory, Research, and Experience* (Vol. 3, pp. 91-124). Orlando: Academic Press.

Panksepp, J. (1991). Affective Neuroscience: A conceptual framework for the neurobiological study of emotions. In K. Strongman (Ed.), *International Reviews of Emotion Research* (pp. 59-99). Chichester, U.K.: Wiley.

Panksepp, J., & Burgdorf, J. (2000). 50-kHz chirping (laughter?) in response to conditioned and unconditioned tickle-induced reward in rats: effects of social housing and genetic variables. *Behavioural Brain Research*, 115, 25-38.

Papez, J. A. (1937). A prposed mechanism of emotion. *Archives of Neurology and Psychiatry*, 38, 725-744.

Paradis, S., & Cabanac, M. (2004). Flavor aversion learning induced by lithium chloride in reptiles but not in amphibians. *Behavioural Processes*, 67, 11-18.

Parr, L. A. (2000). *Understanding Emotion in Chimpanzees*. Unpublished *Ph.D.* Doctoral Thesis, Emory University.

Parr, L. A., & deWaal, B. M. (1999). Visual kin recognitionin chimpanzees. *Nature*, 399, 647-648.

Parrott, W. G., & Schulkin, J. (1993). Neuropsychology and the cognitive nature of the emotions. *Cognition and Emotion*, 7, 43-59.

Pascal, B. (1623-1662a). *Discours sur les passions de l'amour*. Paris: Delmas 1950.

Pascal, B. (1623-1662b). *Pensées*. Paris: Livre de poche 1969.

Pasquet, P., & Apfelbaum, M. (1994). Recovery of initial body weight and composition after long-term massive overfeeding in men. *American Journal of Clinical Nutrition*, 60, 861-863.

Pecchinenda, A., & Smith, C. A. (1996). The affective significance of skin conductance activity during a difficult problem-solving task. *Cognition and Emotion*, 10, 481-503.

Peciña, S., & Berridge, K. C. (2000). Opioid site in nucleus accumbens shell mediates eating and hedonic 'liking' for food: map based on microinjection Fos plumes. *Brain Research*, 863, 71-86.

Pelchat, M. C., Grill, H. J., Rozin, P., & Jacobs, J. (1983). Quality of acquired responses to tastes by Rattus norvegicus depends on type of associated discomfort. *Journal of Comparative Psychology*, 97, 140-153.

Pelchat, M. L., & Rozin, P. (1982). The special role of nausea in the acquisition of food dislikes by humans. *Appetite*, 3, 341-351.

Penrose, R. (1994). *Shadows of the Mind*. Oxford: Oxford University Press.

Penrose, R. (1996). Beyond the doubting of a shadow. *Psyche*, 2(23).

Pepperberg, I. M. (1990). An investigation into the cognitive capacities of an African Grey Parrot (Psittacus erithacus). In P. J. B. Slater, J. S. Rosenblatt & C. Beer (Eds.), *Advances in Study of Behavior*. New York: Academic Press.

Perkins, K. A., Epstein, L. H., Fonte, C., Mitchell, S. L., & Grobe, J. E. (1995). Gender, dietary restraint, and smoking's influence on hunger and the reinforcing value of food. *Physiology and Behavior*, 57, 675-680.

Pessin, A. (1993). One mind too many? Commentary on Puccetti on Split-brain. *Psycholoquy*, 29Dec.

Peter, L. J., & Hull, R. (1970). *Le principe de Peter* (Transl.). Paris: Stock.

Petit, H. (1976). *Carnets*. R 700 033.

Pfaffmann, C. (1960). The pleasures of sensation. *Psychological Review*, 67, 253-268.

Phillips, M. L., Young, A. W., Scott, S. K., Calder, A. J., Andrew, C., Giampietro, V., et al. (1998). Neural responses to facial and vocal expressions of fear and disgust. *Proceedings of the Royal Society of London* Series B - Biological Sciences, 265, 1809-1817.

Platon. (427-347 av. J.C.). *Phédon* (Traduction par Léon Robin). Paris: Les Belles Lettres.

Platon. (1968). *La république*. Paris: Gonthier.

Plé, A. (1982). *Par devoir ou par plaisir*. Paris: Éditions du Cerf.

Plott, C. R. (1986). Rational choice in experimental markets. *Journal of Business*, 59, S301-S327.

Plutchik, R. (1965). What is an emotion? *Journal of Psychology*, 61, 295-303.

Plutchik, R. (1970). Emotions, evolution, and adaptive process. In M. B. Arnold (Ed.), *Feelings and Emotions* (pp. 3-24). New York: Academic Press.

Plutchik, R., & Ax, A. F. (1967). A critique of "Determinants of Emotional State" by Schachter and Singer. *Psychophysiology*, 4, 79-82.

Pompidou, G. (1964). *Anthologie de la poésie française*. Paris: Hachette.

Popper, K. R. (1972). *Objective Knowledge: An Evolutionary Approach*. Oxford: Clarendon Press.

Pradines, M. (1928-1934). *Philosophie de la sensation*. Paris: Les Belles Lettres.

Price, D. D. (1999). *Psychological Mechanisms of Pain and Analgesia*. Seattle: IASP Press.

Price, D. D., Riley, J., & Barrell, J. J. (2001). Are lived choices based on emotional processes? *Cognition and Emotion*, 15, 365-379.

Prince, A., & Smolensky, P. (1997). Optimality: from neural networks to universal grammar. *Science*, 275, 1604-1610.

Prince, J. D., & Berenbaum, H. (1993). Alexithymia and hedonic capacity. *Journal of Research in Personality*, 27, 15-22.

Rainville, P. (2002). Brain mechanisms of pain affect and pain modulation. *Current Opinion in Neurobiology*, 12, 195-204.

Rainville, P., Carrier, B., Hofbauer, R. K., Bushnell, M. C., & Duncan, G. H. (1999). Dissociation of sensory and affective dimensions of pain using hypnotic modulation. *Pain*, 82, 159-171.

Rainville, P., Duncan, G. H., & Bushnell, M. C. (2000). Représentation cérébrale de l'expérience subjective de la douleur chez l'homme. *médecine/science*, 16, 519-527.

Rainville, P., Duncan, G. H., Price, D. D., Carrier, B., & Bushnell, M. C. (1997). Pain affect encoded in human anterior cingulate but not somatosensory cortex. *Science*, 277, 968-971.

Ramírez, J. M., Bonniot-Cabanac, M.-C., & Cabanac, M. (2005). Can aggression provide pleasure? *European Psychologist*, 10, 136-145.

Ramos, A., & Mormède, P. (1998). Stress and emotionality: a multidimensional and genetic approach. *Neuroscience and Biobehavioral Reviews*, 22, 33-57.

Ramsauer, S., Mendelson, J., & Freed, W. J. (1974). Effects of water temperature on the reward value and satieting capacity of water in water-deprived rats. *Behavioral Biology*, 11, 381-393.

Rees, G., & Frith, C. D. (1998). How do we select perceptions and actions? Human brain imaging studies. *Philosophical Transactions of the Royal Society*, 353 B, 1283-1293.

Rees, G., Kreiman, G., & Koch, C. (2002). Neural correlates of consciousness in humans. *Nature Reviews Neuroscience*, 3, 261-270.

Reid, T. (1785). *Essays on the Intellectual Powers of Man.* Cambridge, Massachussetts: M.I.T Press.

Renbourn, E. T. (1960). Body temperature and the emotions. *Lancet*, 2, 475-476.

Revel, J. F. (1997). *Mémoires. Le voleur dans la maison vide.* Paris: Plon.

Revonsuo, A. (1994). In search of the science of consciousness. In A. Revonsuo & M. Kamppinen (Eds.), *Consciousness in Philosophy and Cognitive Neuroscience* (pp. 249-285). Hillsdale, New Jersey: Laurence Erlbaum Associates.

Revusky, S. H., & Bedarf, E. W. (1967). Association of illness with prior ingestion of novel foods. *Science*, 155, 219-220.

Rial, R. V., Nicolau, M. C., Gamundí, A., Akaârir, M., Garau, C., & Esteban, S. (2008). The evolution of consciouness in animals. In P. Århem & H. Liljenström (Eds.), *Consciousness Transitions - Phylogenetic, Ontogenetic, and Physiological Aspects* (pp. 45-76). Amsterdam: Elsevier.

Richter, C. P. (1936). Increased salt appetite in adrenalectomized rats. *American Journal of Physiology*, 115, 155-161.

Richter, C. P. (1939). Transmission of taste sensation in animals. *Transactions of the American Neurological Association*, 65, 49-50.

Richter, C. P. (1942-1943). Total self regulatory functions in animals and human beings. *Harvey Lecture Series*, 38, 63-103.

Ritov, I. (1996). Probability of regret: Anticipation of uncertainty resolution in choice. *Organizational Behavior and Human Decision Processes*, 66, 228-236.

Ritov, I., & Baron, J. (1994). Judgements of compensation for misfortune: the role of expectation. *European Journal of Social Psychology*, 24, 525-539.

Ritov, I., & Baron, J. (1995). Outcome knowledge, regret, and omission bias. *Organizational Behavior and Human Decision Processes*, 64(2), 119-127.

Rodin, J., Moskowitz, H. R., & Bray, G. (1976). Relationship between obesity, weight loss, and taste responsiveness. *Physiology and Behavior*, 17, 591-597.

Rodin, J., Wack, J., Ferrannini, E., & DeFronzo, R. A. (1985). Effect of insulin and glucose on feeding behavior. *Metabolism*, 34, 826-831.

Roland, P. E. (1975). Do muscular receptors in man evoke sensations of tension and kinesthesia? *Brain Research*, 100, 162-165.

Rolls, B. J., Rolls, E. T., & Rowe, A. (1981). Sensory specific satiety in man. *Physiology and Behavior*, 27, 137-142.

Rolls, B. J., Rowe, E. A., & Turner, R. C. (1980). Persistent obesity in rats following a period of consumption of a mixed high energy diet. *Journal of Physiology*, 298, 415-427.

Rolls, E. T. (1994). A theory of emotion and consciousness, and its application to understanding the neural basis of emotion. In M. S. Gazzaniga (Ed.), *The Cognitive Neurosciences* (pp. 1091-1105). Boston: M.I.T. Press.

Rolls, E. T., Sienkiewick, Z. J., & Yaxley, S. (1989). Hunger modulates the responses to gustatory stimuli of single neurons in the caudolateral orbitofrontal cortex of the macaque monkey. *European Journal of Neuroscience*, 1, 53-60.

Roorda-Hrdlicová, V., Wolters, G., Bonke, B., & Phaf, R. H. (1990). Unconscious perception during general anesthesia, demonstrated by an implicit memory task. In B. Bonke, W. Fitch & K. Millar (Eds.), *Memory Awareness in Anaesthesia* (pp. 151-155). Amsterdam: Swets and Zeitlinger.

Rossetti, Y., Meckler, C., & Prablanc, C. (1994). Is there an optimal arm posture? Deterioration of finger localization precision and comfort sensation in extreme arm-joint postures. *Experimental Brain Research*, 99, 131-136.

Rossetti, Y., Tadary, B., & Prablanc, C. (1994). Optimal contributions of head and eye positions to spatial accuracy in man tested by visually directed pointing. *Experimental Brain Research*, 97, 487-496.

Roth, A. E., & Erev, I. (1995). Learning in extensive-form games: experimental data and simple dynamic models in the intermediate term. *Games and Economic Behavior*, 8(Special issue), 164-212.

Rousseau, J.-J. (1712-1778). *La nouvelle Héloïse*. Paris: Librairie de Firmin Didot Frères, Fils et Cie, 1866.

Roy, J. R. (1998). *Les héritiers de Prométhée*. Québec: Presses de l'université Laval.

Rozin, P. (1976). The evolution of intelligence and access to the cognitive unconscious. In J. A. Sprague & A. N. Epsyein (Eds.), *Progress in Psychobiology and Physiological Psychology* (Vol. 6, pp. 245-280). New

York: Academic Press.

Rozin, P. (1999a). Food is fundamental, fun, frightening, and far-reaching. *Social Research*, 66(Food & Culture), 9-30.

Rozin, P. (1999b). Preadaptation and the puzzles and properties of pleasure. In D. Kahneman, E. Diener & N. Schwarz (Eds.), *Weel-Being: The Foundation of Hedonic Psychology* (pp. 109-133). New York: Russell Sage Foundation.

Rozin, P., Ebert, L., & Schull, J. (1982). Some like it hot: a temporal analysis of hedonic responses to chili pepper. *Appetite*, 3, 13-22.

Rozin, P., & Royzman, E. B. (2001). Negativity bias, negativity dominance, and contagion. *Personality and Social Psychology Review*, 5, 296-320.

Rozin, P., & Schiller, D. (1980). The nature and acquisition of a preference for chili pepper by humans. *Motivation and Emotion*, 4, 77-101.

Rubin, D. C., & Friendly, M. (1986). Predicting which words get recalled: measures of free recall, availability, goodness, and pronounceability for 925 nouns. *Memory and Cognition*, 14, 79-94.

Russel, M. J. (1976). Human olfactory communication. *Nature*, 260, 520-522.

Russell, J. A. (1980). A circumplex model of affect. *Journal of Personality and Social Psychology*, 39, 1161-1178.

Russell, J. A. (1987). Reading emotions from and into faces: Resurecting a dimensional-contextual perspective. In J. A. Russell & J. M. Fernández-Dol (Eds.), *The Psychology of Facial Expression* (pp. 295-320). Paris: Éditions de la Maison des Sciences de l'Homme.

Russell, J. A., & Fehr, B. (1987). Relativity in the perception of emotion in facial xpressions. *Journal of Experimental Psychology (General)*, 116, 223-237.

Saint-Augustin. *Le livre de la vie heureuse* (A. d'Andilly, Transl. Vol. XXXIV).

Saulnier, V. L. (1988). *Essais, I. Édition conforme au texte de l'exemplaire de Bordeaux par Pierre Valley* (Montaigne, M. de). Paris: Presses Universitaires de France.

Sawchenko, P. E. (1998). Toward a new neurobiology of energy balance, appetite, and obesity: the anatomists weigh in. *Journal of Comparative Neurology*, 402, 435-441.

Scalera, G. (2000). Taste preference and acceptance in thirsty and dehydrated rats. *Physiology and Behavior*, 71, 457-468.

Schachter, S., & Singer, J. E. (1962). Cognitive, social, and physiological determinants of emotional state. *Psychological Review*, 69, 379-399.

Scherer, K. R. (1993). Neuroscience projections to current debates in emotion psychology. *Cognition and Emotion*, 7, 1-41.

Schiffman, H. R. (1982). *Sensation and Perception an Integrated Approach*. New York: John Wiley &Sons.

Schleidt, M., Neumann, P., & Morishita, H. (1988). Pleasure and disgust: memories and associations of pleasant and unpleasant odours in Germany and Japan. *Chemical Senses*, 13, 279-293.

Scholander, P. F., Anderson, N., Krog, J., Lorentzen, F. V., & Steen, J. (1957). Critical temperature in Lapps. *Journal of Applied Physiology*, 10, 231-234.

277

Schuster, R. (2002). Cooperative coordination as a social behavior: Experiments with an animal model. *Human Nature*, 13(1), 47-83.

Schwartz, M. D., Jacobsen, P. B., & Bovbjerg, D. H. (1996). Role of nausea in the development of aversions to a beverage paired with chemotherapy treatment in cancer patients. *Physiology and Behavior*, 59, 659-663.

Sclafani, A. (1978). Dietary obesity. In G. A. Bray (Ed.), *Recent Advances in Obesity Research II* (pp. 123-132): Newman Publ.

Sclafani, A. (1991). The hedonics of sugar and starch. In R. C. Bolles (Ed.), *The Hedonics of Taste* (pp. 59-87). Hillsdale, NJ: Lawrence Earlbaum Associates.

Sclafani, A., & Clyne, A. E. (1987). Hedonic response of rats to polysaccharide and sugar solutions. *Neuroscience and Biobehavioral Reviews*, 11, 173-180.

Sclafani, A., & Springer, D. (1976). Dietary obesity in adult rats: similarities to hypothalamic and human obesity syndromes. *Physiology and Behavior*, 17, 461-471.

Scott, T. R. (1992). Taste, feeding, and pleasure. *Progress in Psychobiology and Physiological Psychology*, 15, 231-291.

Searle, J. R. (1998). How to study consciousness scientifically. *Brain Research Reviews*, 26, 379-387.

Sederholm, F., & Södersten, P. (2001). Aversive behavior during intraoral intake in male rats. *Physiology and Behavior*, 74, 153-168.

Selye, H. (1974). *Stress sans détresse*. Montréal: La Presse.

Sem-Jacobsen, C. W. (1959). Effects of electrical stimulation of the human brain. *EEG and Clinical Neurophysiology*, 11, 379.

Sénèque. *Lettres morales* (ou, Lettres à Lucilius). 81, 19.

Sforzo, G. A. (1989). Opioids and exercise. An update. *Sports Medicine*, 7, 109-124.

Sgoifo, A., Stilli, D., Aimi, B., Parmigiani, S., Manghi, M., & Musso, E. (1994). Behavioral and electrocardiographic responses to social stress in male rats. *Physiology and Behavior*, 55, 209-216.

Shafir, E., & LeBoeuf, R. A. (2002). Rationality. *Annual Review of Psychology*, 53, 491-517.

Shephard, R. N. (1964). On subjectivity optimum selections among multi-attribute alternatives. In M. W. Shelly & G. L. Bryan (Eds.), *Human Judgements and Optimality* (pp. 257-281). New York: Wiley.

Sher, L. (1998). The endogenous euphoric reward system that reinforces physical training: a mechanism for mankind survival. *Medical Hypotheses*, 51, 449-450.

Sherrington, C. S. (1906). *The Integrative Action of the Nervous System*. New Haven, Connecticut: Yale University Press.

Shin, L. M., Whalen, P. J., Pitman, R. K., Bush, G., Macklin, M. L., Lasko, N. B., et al. (2001). An fMRI study of anterior cingulate function in posttraumatic stress disorder. *Biological Psychiatry*, 50, 932-942.

Shizgal, P. (1997). Neural basis of utility estimation. *Current Opinion in*

Neurobiology, 7, 198-208.

Shizgal, P. (1999). Motivation. In *Encyclopedia of the Cognitive Sciences* (pp. 566-568). Cambridge, Massachussetts: MIT Press.

Shizgal, P., & Conover, K. (1996). On the neural computation of utility. *Current Directions in Psychological Science, 5,* 37-43.

Shizgal, P., & Murray, B. (1989). Neuronal basis of intracranial self-stimulation. In J. M. Liebman & S. J. Cooper (Eds.), *The Neuropharmacological Basis of Reward* (pp. 106-163). Oxford: Oxford University Press.

Shulkin, J. (1991). Hedonic consequences of salt hunger. In R. C. Bolles (Ed.), *The Hedonics of Taste* (pp. 89-105). Hillsdale, NJ: Lawrence Earlbaum Associates.

Small, D. M. (2002). Toward an understanding of the brain substrates of reward in humans. *Neuron, 33,* 668-671.

Small, D. M., Zatorre, R. J., Dagher, A., Evans, A. C., & JonesGotman, M. (2001). Changes in brain activity related to eating chocolate - From pleasure to aversion. *Brain,* 124, Part 9, 1720-1733.

Smith, A. (1776). *An Inquiry into the Nature and Causes of the Wealth of Nations* (Vol. I). London: W. Strachan & T. Cadell.

Smith, C. A., & Lazarus, R. S. (1990). Emotion and adaptation. In L. A. Pervin (Ed.), *Handbook of Personality: Theory and Research* (pp. 609-637). New York: Guilford.

Smith, C. A., & Lazarus, R. S. (1993). Appraisal components, core relational themes, and the emotions. *Cognition and Emotion, 7,* 233-269.

Smith, G. P., & Young, R. C. (1974). Cholecystokinin and intestinal satiety in the rat. *Federation Proceedings, 33,* 1246-1250.

Söderpalm, A. H. V., & Hansen, S. (1999). Alcohol alliesthesia: Food restriction increases the palatability of alcohol through a corticosterone-dependent mechanism. *Physiology and Behavior, 67,* 409-415.

Sonnemans, J., & Frijda, N. H. (1994). The structure of subjective emotional intensity. *Cognition and Emotion, 8,* 329-350.

Sonnemans, J., & Frijda, N. H. (1995). The determinants of subjective emotional intensity. *Cognition and Emotion, 9,* 483-506.

Sontag, C., Kettaneh, A., Fain, O., Eclache, V., & Thomas, M. (2001). Pagophagie prolongée régressant rapidement sous traitement martial d'une anémie. *Presse Médicale,* 30(7), 321.

Soussignan, R., Schaal, B., & Marlier, L. (1999). Olfactory alliesthesia in human neonates: Prandial state and stimulus familiarity modulate facial and autonomic responses to milk odors. *Developmental Psychobiology, 35,* 3-14.

Spence, K. W. (1948). The postulates and methods of behaviorism. *Psychological Review, 55,* 67-78.

Spencer, H. (1855). *The Principles of Psychology.* London: Longman, Brown, Green & Longmans.

Spinoza, B. (1632-1677). *L'Éthique* (1961 ed.). Paris: : Presses universitaires de France.

279

Spruijt, B. M. (1998). Reward centres in the brain: the animal's own welfare centre. Paper presented at the *32nd Congress of the International Society for Applied Ethology*, Clermont-Ferrand.

Spruijt, B. M., vandenBos, R., & Pijlman, F. T. A. (2001). A concept of welfare based on reward evaluating mechanisms in the brain: anticipatory behaviour as an indicator for the state of reward systems. *Applied Animal Behaviour Science*, 72, 145-171.

Squires, V. R., & Wilson, A. D. (1971). Distance between food and water supply and its effects on drinking frequency, and food and water intake of Merino and Border Leicester sheep. *Australian Journal of Agricultural Research*, 22, 283-290.

Steffens, A. B., Strubbe, J. H., Balkan, B., & Scheurink, A. J. W. (1990). Neuroendocrine mechanisms involved in regulation of body weight, food intake and metabolism. *Neuroscience and Biobehavioral Reviews*, 14, 305-313.

Steiner, J. E. (1977). Facial expressions of the neonate infant indicating the hedonics of food related chemical stimuli. In J. E. Weiffenbach (Ed.), *Taste and Development.* (pp. 173-189). Bethesda, MD: U.S. Dept. Health Educ. Welfare.

Stevens, S. S. (1959). Measurements, psychophysics, and utility. In C. C. W & P. Ratoosh (Eds.), *Measurement: Definitions and Theories* (pp. 18-63). New York: Wiley.

Stolwijk, J. A. J., Saltin, B., & Gagge, A. P. (1968). Physiological factors associated with sweating during exercise. *Aerospace Medicine*, 39, 1101-1105.

Straus, E. (1963). *The Primary World of Senses* (J. Needleman, Trans.). London: The Free Press of Glencoe.

Strigo, I. A., Carli, F., & Bushnell, M. C. (2000). Effect of ambient temperature on human pain and temperature perception. *Anesthesiology*, 92, 699-707.

Sulzer, M. (1751). Recherches sur l'origine des sentimens agréables et désagréables. *Mémoires de L'Académie Royales des Sciences et Belles Letttres*, Berlin, 7, 57-100.

Suzuki, S. (1997). Effects of number of alternatives on choice in humans. *Behavioural Processes*, 39, 205-214.

Talbot, G. L. (1990). Personality correlates and personal investment of college students who persist and achieve. *Journal of Research and Development in Education*, 20, 131-140.

Taylor, C. C. W. (1984). Emotions and wants. In J. Marks (Ed.), *Ways of Desire.* Chicago: Precedent Publishing.

Taylor, J. G., Jancke, L., Shah, N. J., Nosselt, T., Schmitz, N., Himmelback, M., et al. (1998). A three stage model of awareness: formulation and initial experimental support. *Neuroreport*, 9, 1787-1792.

Teilhard de Chardin, P. (1955). *Le phénomène humain.* Paris: Éditions du Seuil.

Teilhard de Chardin, P. (1965). La place de l'homme dans la nature. Paris:

Éditions du Seuil.

Teitelbaum, P. (1964). Appetite. *Proceedings of the American Philosophical Society*, 108, 464-472.

Terrick, T. D., Mumme, R. L., & Burghardt, G. M. (1995). Aposematic coloration enhances chemosensory recognition of noxious prey in the garter snake *Thamnophis radix*. *Animal Behaviour*, 49, 857-866.

Thaler, R. H., & Johnson, E. J. (1990). Gambling with the house money and trying to break even: the effects of prior outcomes on risky choice. *Management Science*, 36, 643-660.

Thompson, D. A., & Campbell, R. G. (1977). Hunger in humans induced by 2 deoxy-d-glucose: glucoprivic control of taste preference and food intake. *Science*, 198, 1065-1068.

Tinbergen, N. (1950). The hierarchical organization of mechanisms underlying instinctive behaviour. Experimental Biology, 4, 305-312.

Titchener, E. B. (1908). *Lectures on the Elementary Psychology of Feeling and Attention*. New York: MacMillan.

Titchener, E. B. (1909). *Lectures on the Experimental Psychology of the Thought-Process*. New York: MacMillan.

Toates, F. (1986). *Motivational Systems*. Cambridge: Cambridge University Press.

Todd, E. (1990). *L'invention de l'Europe*. Paris: Éditions du Seuil.

Tolman, E. C. (1918). Nerve process and cognition. Psychological Review, 25, 423-442.

Tomljenovic-Borer, K. (1974). Absence of weight regulation in exercising hamsters. *Physiology and Behavior*, 12, 589-597.

Tremblay, A. (2001). Clinical implications of the ponderostat concept: view from the chair. *International Journal of Obesity*, 25, S4-S6.

Tulving, E. (1983). *Elements of Episodic Memory*. Oxford: Oxford University Press.

Tulving, E. (1985). Memory and consciousness. *Canadian Psychology*, 26, 1-26.

Tulving, E. (1995). Varieties of consciousness and level of awareness in memory (pp.283-300). In A. Baddely & L. Weiskrantz (Eds.), *Attention: Selection, Awareness and Control. A Tribute to Donald Broadbent*. Oxford: Oxford University Press.

Tulving, E., & Kroll, N. (1995). Novelty assessment in the brain and long-term memory encoding. *Psychonomic Bulletin and Review*, 2, 387-390.

Tversky, A., & Kahneman, D. (1981). The framing of decisions and the psychology of choice. *Science*, 211, 453-458.

Tversky, A., & Kahneman, D. (1986). Rational choice and the framing of decisions. *Journal of Business*, 59, S251-S278.

Vance, E. B., & Wagner, N. N. (1976). Written descriptions of orgasm. A study of sex differences. *Archives of Sexual Behavior*, 5, 87-98.

Varey, C. A., & Kahneman, D. (1992). Experiences extended accross time: evaluation of moments and episodes. *Journal of Behavioral Decision Making*, 5, 169-185.

Waldbillig, R. J., & O'Callaghan, M. (1980). Hormones and hedonics cholecystokinin and taste: A possible behavioral mechanism of action. *Physiology and Behavior*, 25, 25-30.

Warburton, D. M. (1996). The functions of pleasure. In D. M. Warburton & N. Sherwood (Eds.), *Pleasure and Quality of Life* (pp. 1-10). Chichester: John Wiley and Sons.

Warden, C. S. (1931). *Animal Motivation, Experimental Studies on the Albino Rat*. New York: Columbia University Press.

Watson, D., Wiese, D., Vaidya, J., & Tellegen, A. (1999). The two general activation system of affect, structural finding, evolutionnary considerations, and psychobiological evidence. *Journal of Personality and Social Psychology*, 76, 820-838.

Watt, D. F. (1998). Emotion and consciousness: Implications of affective neuroscience for extended reticular thalamic activating system theories of consciousness. *Association for the Scientific Study of Consciouness* September/October, http://server.phil.vt.edu/assc/watt/default.html.

Wehrhahn, C. (2000). Evidence for perceptual learning in vision. In H. Ritter, H. Cruse & J. Dean (Eds.), *Prerational Intelligence: Adaptive Behavior and Intelligent Systems Without Symbols and Logic* (Vol. 2). Dordrecht: Kluwer Academic Publishers.

Weiskrantz, L. (1991). Disconnected awareness for detecting, processing, and remembering in neurological patients. *Journal of the Royal Society of Medicine*, 84, 466-470.

White, N. M. (1989). Reward or reinforcement: what's the difference? *Neuroscience and Biobehavioral Reviews*, 13, 181-186.

Wiepkema, P. R. (1985). Abnormal behaviours in farm animals: ethological implications. *Netherland Journal of Zoology*, 35, 279-299.

Wilkes, K. V. (1988). ____, yishi, duh, um, and consciousness. In A. J. Marcel & E. Bisiach (Eds.), *Consciousness in Contemporary Science* (pp. 16-41). Oxford: Oxford University Press.

Williams, B. (1979). Conflict of Values. In The Idea of Freedom. *Essays in Honour of Isaiah Berlin* (pp. 221-232). Oxford: Oxford University Press.

Wolf, J. C. (1996). Hédonisme. In M. Canto-Sperber (Ed.), *Dictionnaire d'éthique et de philosophie morale* (pp. 632-637). Paris: Presses Universitaires de France.

Wolfe, J. M. (1988a). Foreword. In *Readings from the Encyclopedia of Neurosciences* (Vol. Sensory systems II). Boston: Birkhäuser.

Wolfe, J. M. (1988b). *Readings from the Encyclopedia of Neurosciences: Sensory systems* II. Boston, Massachussetts: Birkhäuser.

Wundt, W. (1874). *Grundzüge der Physiologischen Psychologie*. Leipzig: Englemann.

Wundt, W. (1902). *Grunzüge des Physiologischen Psychologie*. Leipzig: Engelmann.

Yates, J. F., Lee, J. W., Shinotsuka, H., & Siek, W. R. (1998). Oppositional deliberation: toward explaining overconfidence and its cross-cultural variations. *Abstracts of the Psychonomic Society*, 3, 4.

Yokoyama, M. (1921). The nature of the affective judgement in the method of paired comparison. *American Journal of Psychology*, 32, 357-369.

Young, P. T. (1959). The role of affective processes in learning and motivation. *Psychological Review*, 66, 104-123.

Young, P. T., & Christensen, K. R. (1962). Algebraic summation of hedonic process. *Journal of Comparative and Physiological Psychology*, 55, 332-3336.

Zajonc, R. B. (1980). Feeling and thinking: preferences need no inferences. *American Psychologist*, 35, 151-175.

Zajonc, R. B. (1984). On the primacy of affect. *American Psychologist*, 39, 117-123.

Zajonc, R. B. (1994). Emotional expression and temperature modulation. In S. H. M. VanGoozen, N. E. VanDePoll & J. A. Sergeant (Eds.), *Emotions: Essays on Emotion Theory* (pp. 3-27). Hillsdale New Jersey: Laurence Erlbaum Ass.

Zernicki, B. (2002). Affective percept and voluntary action: A hypothesis. *Acta Neurobiologiae Experimentalis*, 62, 99-110.

Ziehen, T. (1924). *Leitfaden der physiologischen Psychologie* (12 ed.). Iena: G. Fischer.